THE GRAPEVINE GUIDE TO

Rhode Island's
Best Restaurants

RECIPES, MENUS AND REVIEWS FROM OVER 100 RESTAURANTS

BY LINDA BEAULIEU AND DEBORAH MOXHAM

Linda Beaulieu and Deborah Moxham
GRAPEVINE: THE FOOD CONSULTANTS
One Richmond Square
Providence, RI 02906
(401) 831-7500

GRAPHIC DESIGNER
Alex Delany

PHOTOGRAPHY
Linda Beaulieu, Jill Brody, Constance Brown,
Ron Manville, Deborah Moxham, Marshall Rose
and the Providence Tourism Council

RECIPE TESTING
Mary Ann Almeida, Linda Beaulieu, Jane Kay,
Deborah Moxham, Holly Smith and Richard Wood

OFFICE INTERNS
Nathalie Jordi, Alexis Chase Simmering,
Sydney Simmering and Elizabeth Trafton

Printed in the United States of America
First edition

Introduction

BACK IN 2000, Linda Beaulieu wrote *Divine Providence: An Insider's Guide to the City's Best Restaurants*, and it was a great success. Everyone seemed to love the reviews and recipes. When it came time to update the book, Linda joined forces with Deborah Moxham to create a guide that went beyond Providence. And here it is – *The Grapevine Guide to Rhode Island's Best Restaurants*, with more than 100 dining establishments listed.

Linda and Deborah are partners in Grapevine: The Food Consultants. This is the first in a series of Grapevine Guides which they have planned. With this book, their aim was to come up with the 100 best restaurants in the state, no easy task considering Rhode Island's wonderful dining scene.

One person's taste in food is totally subjective. Linda and Deborah hope that by combining their tastes, they have succeeded in determining what are the best restaurants in the state overall – small and large, casual and formal, inexpensive and pricey. All the restaurants chosen to be in this guide were given a full page at no cost to them; however, some of the restaurants saw this as a wonderful opportunity and chose to pay a fee to have a second page in this book, which helped cover our many expenses.

If you don't see your favorite restaurant listed in this guide, it might be simply because the restaurant failed to respond to the authors' request for information, or it could be a dining establishment that Linda and Deborah need to investigate. They would love to hear your comments and recommendations for future publications.

You'll find all kinds of restaurants in this book, from tiny diners to big and bold steakhouses. Hopefully, *The Grapevine Guide to Rhode Island's Best Restaurants* has something for everybody, just the right restaurant to suit your mood and occasion.

Linda and Deborah hope that you enjoy this book as much as they enjoyed researching and writing it.

Dedication

To Deborah's daughters, Michaele, Chase and Sydney,
and to Ted, who add the richness and flavor to her life.

To Brian, Linda's faithful dining companion.

And to Fanny and Pepper, who always enjoyed their doggie bags.

Many thanks to VENDA RAVIOLI on Federal Hill in Providence,
where so many of the ingredients for recipes in this book can be found.

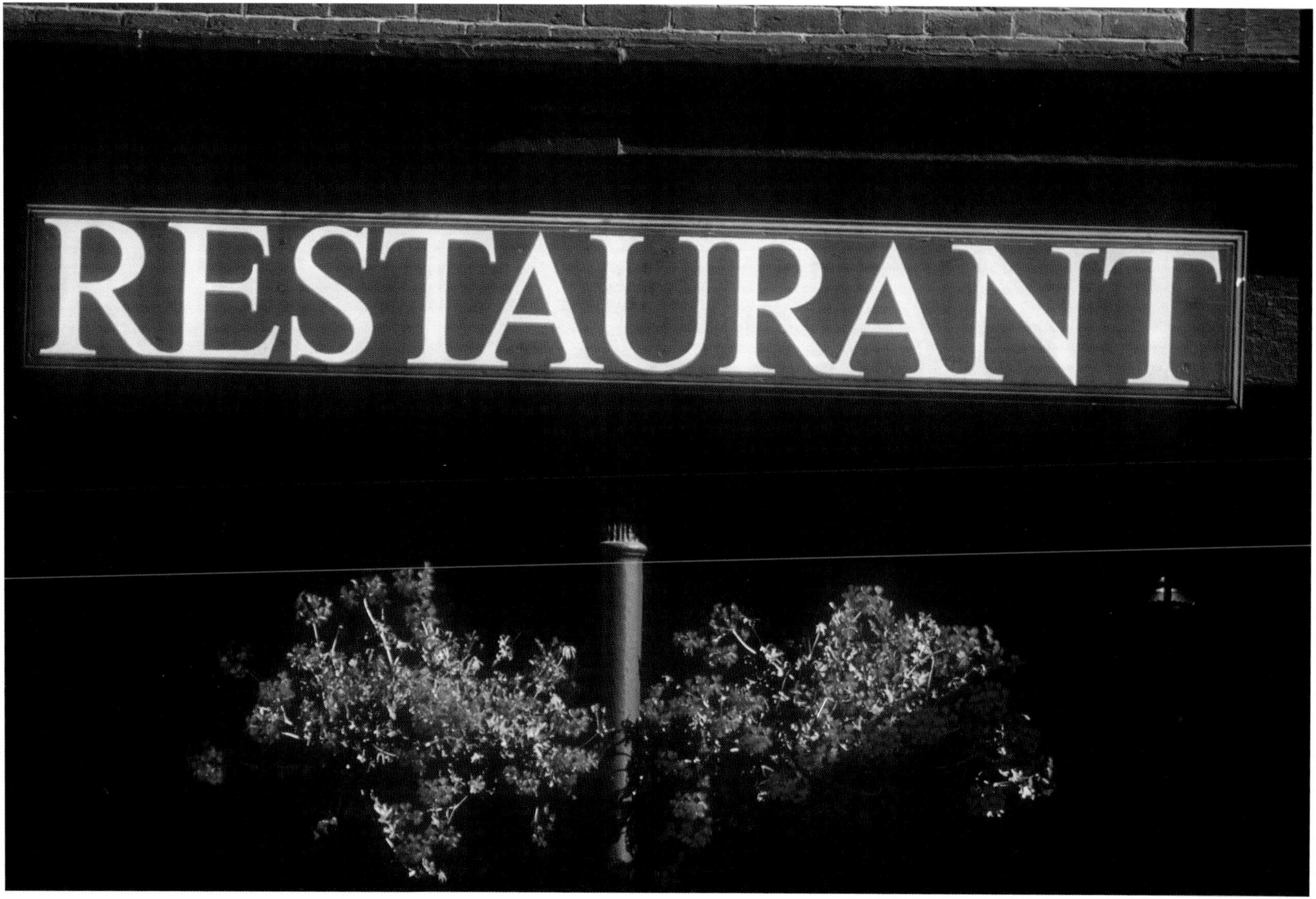
RESTAURANT

Contents

Foreword

It is with great pleasure that I write the Foreword to *The Grapevine Guide to Rhode Island's Best Restaurants*.

The city of Providence has become a culinary wellspring, home to dozens of award-winning restaurants and the world's largest culinary institution, Johnson & Wales University. Author Dione Lucas once wrote, "The preparation of good food is merely another expression of art, one of the joys of civilized living." As Mayor of Providence, I am particularly proud to know that many of the very best restaurants in Rhode Island are located in the city.

Providence is a city rich in cultural diversity and creative energy. This unique combination has placed our city on the cutting edge of culinary excellence. Thousands of men and women from all over Europe, Latin America and, most recently, Southeast Asia, have left an indelible culinary mark on Providence and the state of Rhode Island.

Two of New England's most respected culinary experts, Deborah Moxham and Linda Beaulieu, have successfully captured that essence in *The Grapevine Guide to Rhode Island's Best Restaurants*. This book offers readers a veritable culinary guide to Rhode Island and a fresh perspective on the multicultural influences that make our state, and our capital city, so unique and attractive.

David N. Cicilline

Mayor
City of Providence

Adesso

STILL CRAZY AFTER ALL THESE YEARS

Adesso was quite impressive when it opened in 1987, and this popular cafe continues to delight its many fans with creative chef Chow Malakorn manning the open kitchen and wood grill. The cuisine is Cal/Ital, a blend of California and Italy – the best of both worlds, most would say, especially when it comes to Adesso's grilled pizza. One of the signature dishes is a legendary Caesar salad with sliced rare grilled tuna and a tomato/thyme salsa over romaine, a favorite among East Siders and the college crowd (Brown University and Rhode Island School of Design) that frequent Adesso.

GRAPEVINE GEM: When it was open for lunch, Deborah ordered the mushroom crostini at least 300 times.

INSIDE SCOOP

CHEF	CHOW MALAKORN	LIQUOR	FULL LIQUOR
OWNER	BLAZE MARFEO	SMOKING	PERMITTED
OPEN SINCE	1987	SERVICES	BANQUET FACILITIES
CUISINE	CALIFORNIAN/ITALIAN		HEALTHY/LOW-FAT MENU ITEMS
SPECIALTY	GRILLED PIZZA		VEGETARIAN MENU ITEMS
PRICE RANGE	APPETIZERS $8 TO $14		HANDICAPPED ACCESSIBLE
	ENTREES $13 TO $30		TAKE-OUT ORDERS AVAILABLE
CREDIT CARDS	MAJOR CREDIT CARDS ACCEPTED		CATERING
RESERVATIONS	RECOMMENDED		PRIVATE DINING ROOM
HOURS	OPEN SEVEN DAYS A WEEK	DRESS CODE	TASTEFUL, SMART, CASUAL
	FOR LUNCH AND DINNER	PARKING	THE ADESSO PARKING LOT,
	MONDAY THROUGH THURSDAY,		NEARBY STREETS AND THROUGH
	5 TO 10:30 P.M.		THE VALET SERVICE
	FRIDAY AND SATURDAY, 5 TO 11:30 P.M.		
	SUNDAY, 4:30 TO 10:30 P.M.		

APPETIZERS

BELGIAN ENDIVE SALAD WITH SLICED APPLE, BLUE CHEESE, WALNUTS AND
WATERCRESS

WILD AND DOMESTIC MUSHROOMS IN A GARLIC AND WHITE WINE SAUCE
OVER CROSTINI

OVEN-ROASTED MUSSELS WITH A SPICY ORIENTAL BLACK BEAN SAUCE

PASTA

BLACK PEPPER LINGUINE WITH SHRIMP, ASPARAGUS, SHALLOTS AND SUN-
DRIED TOMATOES, VODKA AND TOMATO CREAM SAUCE

CRESTO DI GALLO WITH GRILLED CHICKEN, ITALIAN SAUSAGE, FIRE-ROASTED
RED AND YELLOW PEPPERS, FRESH AND SUN-DRIED TOMATOES IN
ESPAGNOLE SAUCE WITH BALSAMIC VINEGAR, ALE AND ROSEMARY

ENTREES

FRESH ASIAN LACQUERED ROASTED LONG ISLAND DUCK, SEMI-BONELESS, WITH
RED WINE AND SZECHUAN PEPPERCORN SAUCE SERVED WITH BABY BOK
CHOY AND PICKLED GINGER

ROASTED DOUBLE PORK CHOP WITH A PANCETTA, GARLIC AND ROSEMARY
STUFFING AND CHIANTI BUTTER SAUCE, SERVED WITH ROASTED GARLIC
MASHED POTATOES

GRILLED SESAME-CRUSTED TUNA WITH FETTUCCINE AND CHEF'S VEGETABLES
SAUTÉED IN GARLIC, GINGER, SOY AND SESAME OIL, GARNISHED WITH
WASABI AND PICKLED GINGER

PRIME SIRLOIN WITH A SHALLOT AND BALSAMIC VINEGAR REDUCTION AND
HAND-CUT STEAK FRITES

CHICKEN BREAST SALAD
WITH FRESH ARTICHOKE AND CHAMPAGNE VINAIGRETTE DRESSING
Serves 4

2 artichokes	1/8 teaspoon salt
Water, lemon juice and salt, as needed	1/2 teaspoon freshly ground black pepper
2 whole chicken breasts, boneless	24 Belgian endive spears
2 tablespoons extra-strong Dijon mustard	1 small head radicchio
4 egg yolks	6 cups assorted baby field greens
3/4 cup champagne vinegar	1 cup poached haricots verts
1 tablespoon minced garlic	2 tablespoons thinly sliced sun-dried tomatoes
1 tablespoon minced fresh rosemary	1/4 cup fresh corn kernels
1/2 cup grated Parmigiano-Reggiano cheese	1/8 cup shaved Parmigiano-Reggiano cheese
1 cup virgin olive oil	

Trim artichokes and cut out whole bottoms. Poach bottoms until tender in simmering water with a little lemon juice and salt to retain color. Cool and slice.

Grill chicken. Cool completely and slice thinly.

Whisk the mustard and egg yolks together until well blended and lightened. Blend in vinegar, garlic, rosemary and grated cheese. Slowly add oil in a thin steady stream while whisking vigorously. When totally infused, whisk in salt and pepper.

For each salad, arrange a ring of 6 Belgian endive spears, then an outer ring of radicchio leaves. Place field greens in the middle. Set haricots verts on outer ring of endive spears.

Toss grilled chicken slices and sliced artichoke bottoms with a small portion of the dressing. Arrange on top of the field greens. Garnish with sun-dried tomatoes, fresh corn kernels and shaved cheese.

Al Forno

577 South Main Street, Providence | 401-273-9760 | www.alforno.com

IN THE BEGINNING

If one restaurant can be credited with bringing national attention to Providence, it would have to be Al Forno, owned by husband-and-wife chefs and artists George Germon and Johanne Killeen. Since 1980, Al Forno has been winning accolades for its original modern Italian cuisine, especially for its positively addictive wood-grilled Pizza Margarita, spicy Clams Al Forno, Dirty Steak, and Baked Pasta in the Pink. Not to be missed are the desserts, especially the rustic fruit tarts. Delightful any time of the year, Al Forno is at its best in warm weather when guests can spend time in the beautiful outdoor courtyard, so reminiscent of a Tuscan villa.

INSIDE SCOOP

CHEF-OWNERS	JOHANNE KILLEEN	SMOKING	NO
	GEORGE GERMON	SERVICES	HEALTHY/LOW-FAT MENU ITEMS
OPEN SINCE	1980		VEGETARIAN MENU ITEMS
CUISINE	NORTHERN ITALIAN		HANDICAPPED ACCESSIBLE
SPECIALTY	GRILLED PIZZAS		TAKE-OUT ORDERS AVAILABLE
PRICE RANGE	APPETIZERS $7 TO $17		PRIVATE DINING ROOM
	ENTREES $18 TO $40		FIREPLACE
CREDIT CARDS	MAJOR CREDIT CARDS ACCEPTED	DRESS CODE	CASUAL
RESERVATIONS	NO	PARKING	AVAILABLE IN PARKING LOT
HOURS:	TUESDAY THROUGH SATURDAY		ON THE PREMISES AND ON
	FOR DINNER		THE STREET
LIQUOR	FULL LIQUOR		

APPETIZERS

GRILLED PIZZA MARGARITA

CLAMS AL FORNO

PROSCIUTTO DI PARMA AND SPRING PEAS IN BED

GRASS SALAD WITH LEMON, VIRGIN OLIVE OIL, GORGONZOLA,
    ROASTED BEETS AND FRESH SAGE

ENTREES

BAKED PASTA IN THE PINK WITH TOMATOES, FRESH HERBS, CREAM
    AND FIVE CHEESES

TAGLIATELLE WITH ASPARAGUS PESTO

LASAGNETTE WITH VEAL RAGU

CRISPY OYSTER "PO'BOY" SANDWICH WITH SHOESTRING POTATOES,
    FRESH HORSERADISH AND LEMON AIOLI

OVEN-ROASTED COD LOIN WITH ROASTED SPRING RISOTTO CAKE,
    ONIONS, LEMON AND VIRGIN OLIVE OIL

GRILLED LAMB LOIN CHOP WITH ROASTED ASPARAGUS AND ROSEMARY
    MASHED POTATOES

Angelo's Civita Farnese

141 Atwells Avenue (Federal Hill), Providence | 401-621-8171 | www.angelosonthehill.com

SOUTHERN ITALIAN SOUL FOOD

Dining at the award-winning Angelo's Civita Farnese is much like traveling through time, back to 1924 when this Federal Hill restaurant opened. Dedicated to providing an Old World dining experience, at bargain prices, Angelo's offers large communal tables where newspaper reporters sit elbow-to-elbow with politicians, construction workers next to lawyers. They are all there for the same thing – honest, old-fashioned, comforting Italian food (especially the famous Veal Parmigiana grinder). The walls are covered with marinara-splattered photographs, and for 25 cents, you can make the model railroad run along its overhead track through the big, airy dining room. Get the picture?

INSIDE SCOOP

CHEF	JOE LOPES
OWNER	ROBERT ANTIGNANO
OPEN SINCE	1924
CUISINE	ITALIAN
SPECIALTY	STEWED VEAL AND PEPPERS
PRICE RANGE	APPETIZERS $4 TO $6.95
	ENTREES $4.60 TO $13.45
CREDIT CARDS	CASH OR TRAVELER'S CHECKS ONLY
RESERVATIONS	OFFERED ONLY ON MONDAY THROUGH THURSDAY; ON WEEKENDS, CALL TO GET ON LIST
HOURS	OPEN SEVEN DAYS A WEEK FOR LUNCH AND DINNER MAY TO SEPTEMBER: CLOSED SUNDAYS
LIQUOR	FULL LIQUOR
SMOKING	PERMITTED IN DESIGNATED AREAS
SERVICES	CHILDREN'S MENU
	HEALTHY/LOW-FAT MENU ITEMS
	VEGETARIAN MENU ITEMS
	HANDICAPPED ACCESSIBLE
	TAKE-OUT ORDERS AVAILABLE
	CATERING TO GO
DRESS CODE	CASUAL
PARKING	AVAILABLE ON THE STREET, IN A NEARBY PARKING LOT, AND THROUGH THE VALET SERVICE

APPETIZERS

ANTIPASTO
STRING BEAN SALAD
SNAIL SALAD
GRILLED CHICKEN ENSALATA
MOZZARELLA STICKS

ENTREES

MACARONI AND BEANS
BRACIOLA
CHICKEN PARMIGIANA
EGGPLANT PARMIGIANA
SPAGHETTI AGLIO E OLIO
BAKED VEAL CHOPS
LASAGNA
SPAGHETTI WITH CLAM SAUCE

Atlantic Inn

AS GOOD AS IT GETS

The Atlantic Inn sits high on a bluff overlooking Block Island Sound. Sipping a cocktail on the porch at sunset is a lovely way to begin an evening there. Heading in for dinner in the warm pink-hued Victorian dining room is the perfect way to spend the rest of the night. The food here matches the view, with a constantly changing, always fresh menu. With a chef who comes from L'Espalier in Boston, the food is classically prepared using stocks and reductions. It's a four-course, prix fixe dinner. The Atlantic Inn offers beautifully prepared seafood, but if you're a meat eater, go for the rack of lamb in the balsamic reduction.

GRAPEVINE GEM: We asked diners around Block Island where to eat, and the Atlantic Inn usually topped the list of recommendations.

INSIDE SCOOP

CHEF	EDWARD MOON	LIQUOR	FULL LIQUOR
OWNERS	BRAD AND ANNE MARTHENS	SMOKING	NOT ALLOWED
OPEN SINCE	1978	SERVICES	BANQUET FACILITIES
CUISINE	CONTEMPORARY AMERICAN		HEALTHY/LOW-FAT MENU ITEMS
	REGIONAL WITH FRENCH INFLUENCE		VEGETARIAN MENU ITEMS
SPECIALTY	SEAFOOD		HANDICAPPED ACCESSIBLE
PRICE RANGE	TAPAS $3 TO $10		OUTDOOR DINING AVAILABLE
	PRIX FIXE FOUR-COURSE DINNER	DRESS CODE	BUSINESS/CASUAL
	$44 (RESERVATIONS ONLY)	PARKING	AVAILABLE ON THE PREMISES
CREDIT CARDS	MAJOR CREDIT CARDS ACCEPTED		
RESERVATIONS	RECOMMENDED		
HOURS	FROM MEMORIAL DAY		
	THROUGH COLUMBUS DAY		
	DINNER ONLY, 6 TO 9:30 P.M.		

APPETIZERS

ROASTED GAME CONSOMME

CHILLED ASIAN-STYLE BEEF SALAD WITH CELLOPHANE NOODLE SALAD AND
ASIAN PEARS

SEARED TILAPIA WITH CUCUMBER YOGURT SALAD, MELON AND PRESERVED
LEMON

SAUTÉED QUAIL WITH ALMOND COUSCOUS STRUDEL AND TAHINI SAUCE

FOIE GRAS WITH HOMEADE DUCK PROSCIUTTO, HAZELNUT ONION SALAD AND
POMEGRANATE MOLASSES

ENTREES

GRILLED STRIPED BASS WITH AMARANTH GRAIN, GRAPEFRUIT, ONION AND
BEET SALAD, AND WATERMELON BROTH

SAUTÉED HALIBUT WITH SUGAR SNAP PEAS, CELERY ROOT, AND ROASTED
CARROT AND GINGER PUREE

SEARED SALMON WITH POLENTA CAKE AND WARM SALAD OF LOBSTER, FENNEL
AND GREEN BEANS, TOMATO AND SPINACH CREAM

ROASTED DUCK WITH A CORN AND TOMATILLO SALSA, ROASTED SHALLOT HUSH
PUPPIES AND ANCHO CHILE CREME FRAICHE

SAUTÉED RIB-EYE STEAK WITH A POTATO PARMESAN NAPOLEON, ZUCCHINI
CAKE, CARROTS AND BEEF JUS

SEARED SCALLOPS WITH RADICCHIO

Serves 4

Olive oil, as needed	1 tablespoon sugar
1 small onion, sliced thin	Orange juice, as needed
1/4 jalapeno pepper, seeded and sliced	Salt and pepper, to taste
1 teaspoon chopped garlic	20 medium-size scallops
2 ripe mangos, peeled, seeded and rough chopped	2 heads radicchio, sliced thin
	1 teaspoon chopped garlic
1 cup dark rum	Freshly chopped chives and parsley, for garnish

For the sauce:
Lightly oil a sauté pan over medium high heat; add onion, jalapeno and garlic, and cook until slightly browned. Add the mango and cook for about 5 minutes until the mango begins to break down. Remove the pan completely from the stove and add the dark rum. Return to heat. (Be careful to avoid flame up of rum.)

Once the alcohol has burned off, add the sugar, and simmer an additional 5 to 10 minutes until the mango and onion are very soft. Puree the mixture in a blender until smooth. Thin with orange juice if necessary. Season with salt and pepper.

For the scallops:
Season the scallops with salt and pepper. Brown in a non-stick pan.

For the radicchio.
Place a sauté pan over high heat. Add 3 tablespoons of olive oil. Toss in the radicchio and garlic. Sauté until radicchio starts to wilt. Season with salt and pepper; remove from heat.

Place radicchio in center of plate. Drizzle the sauce around and place the scallops in a star pattern. Garnish with freshly chopped chives and parsley.

Bay Voyage

ROOM WITH A VIEW

Award-winning Chef Brian Ruffner says his style of cooking is based on classic French technique with an infusion of the freshest seasonal ingredients available. The results? A menu that offers escargots as well as a venison tenderloin hand-rubbed with juniper, sage and rosemary and served with herbed mashed potatoes and espresso demiglace, one of the chef's signature dishes. All this in a beautiful old inn, meticulously restored, overlooking the harbor at Jamestown with Newport and its magnificent bridge in the near distance – a spectacular view especially at night. The Sunday brunch at the Bay Voyage Inn is one of the very best offered anywhere in Rhode Island.

GRILLED THAI SHRIMP

Serves 4

16 extra-large shrimp
1/3 cup sesame oil
1/3 cup Thai red curry paste
2 cups vegetable oil
Zest of 3 oranges
1 pound baby greens
Extra virgin olive oil, as needed to dress greens

Peel and devein shrimp.

Combine sesame oil, Thai red curry paste, vegetable oil and orange zest to make marinade. Place shrimp in marinade. Marinate shrimp in the refrigerator 24 to 72 hours.

Soak 4 bamboo skewers in water overnight.

Remove shrimp from marinade and place 4 on each skewer. Remove excess marinade to avoid flame up on grill.

Prepare grill. Grill shrimp until opaque in center. Serve shrimp on top of lightly dressed baby greens.

INSIDE SCOOP

CHEF	BRIAN RUFFNER	SMOKING	PERMITTED AT THE BAR
OWNER	CONDANT CORPORATION	SERVICES	BANQUET FACILITIES
OPEN SINCE	NOBODY REALLY KNOWS,		HEALTHY/LOW-FAT MENU ITEMS
	THEY SAY IN THE 1980S		VEGETARIAN MENU ITEMS
CUISINE	NEW AMERICAN		AVAILABLE ON REQUEST
SPECIALTY	JUNIPER SAGE, AND		HANDICAPPED ACCESSIBLE
	ROSEMARY-RUBBED VENISON		CATERING (ON-SITE)
	WITH ESPRESSO DEMIGLACE		PRIVATE DINING ROOM
PRICE RANGE	APPETIZERS $7 TO $11		SUNDAY BRUNCH
	ENTREES $23 TO $33	DRESS CODE	TASTEFUL
CREDIT CARDS	MAJOR CREDIT CARDS ACCEPTED	PARKING	AVAILABLE ON THE PREMISES
RESERVATIONS	RECOMMENDED		
HOURS	OPEN MONDAY THROUGH		
	SATURDAY FOR DINNER		
LIQUOR	FULL LIQUOR		

APPETIZERS

THAI SHRIMP WITH SAFFRON RISOTTO, THAI SAUCE AND ASIAN GREENS

NARRAGANSETT OYSTERS ON THE HALF SHELL WITH MIGNONETTE SAUCE

SAUTÉED CRAB CAKES SERVED OVER BABY GREENS WITH MANGO JICAMA SALAD AND SPICY SAFFRON AIOLI

ENTREES

BAKED SALMON SERVED OVER A CANNELLINI BEAN RAGOUT WITH FIG GLAZE

GRILLED CHILEAN SEA BASS WITH OLIVE COUSCOUS AND ARTICHOKE TOMATO-GARLIC RAGOUT

RACK OF LAMB WITH A PISTACHIO PINE NUT GLAZE, SERVED WITH ARUGULA SALAD AND POTATOES

VENISON TENDERLOIN WITH A JUNIPER, SAGE AND ROSEMARY RUB, SERVED WITH MASHED POTATOES AND ESPRESSO DEMIGLACE

The Black Pearl

ANCIENT MARINER

Since 1983, Chef Daniel Knerr has been creating the New American Cuisine for which the beautiful Black Pearl is so famous. His food has deep classical roots and strong New England influences. Earlier in his stellar career, Knerr worked in France and at the nationally known restaurants La Cote Basque and Le Bec Fin. His personal favorite dish is cassoulet, which will warm your bones on a snowy winter night. Located on famed Bannister's Wharf, the Black Pearl is the epitome of this city-by-the-sea and, with quaint nautical elegance, it's especially popular with the local yachting crowd. Make sure you try Chef Knerr's award-winning clam chowder.

ARUGULA SALAD
WITH MARINATED WILD MUSHROOMS AND PARMIGIANO-REGGIANO

Serves 6

1/2 cup extra virgin olive oil
1 tablespoon minced garlic
3 to 4 cups assorted wild mushrooms (honshimjii or Japanese honey mushrooms, chanterelle, oyster
    mushrooms, pleurotte, black trumpet, cepes, hedgehog, shiitake, etc.)
1/4 cup raspberry vinegar
1 large rosemary sprig
Salt and pepper, to taste
1/2 pound arugula, washed and trimmed
Parmigiano-Reggiano cheese, as needed

Heat olive oil in large sauté pan. Add garlic and stir until golden brown. Add mushrooms, vinegar, rosemary, salt and pepper. Cook for 3 to 4 minutes.

Arrange arugula on 6 plates. Spoon warm mushroom mixture in center of each plate. Garnish with shavings of Parmigiano-Reggiano cheese.

INSIDE SCOOP

CHEF	J. DANIEL KNERR
OWNER	NOT AVAILABLE
OPEN SINCE	1966
CUISINE	CLASSICAL SEAFOOD, AMERICAN AND NEW ENGLAND FARE
SPECIALTY	CASSOULET
PRICE RANGE	APPETIZERS $5 TO $10.50
	ENTREES $17.50 TO $35
CREDIT CARDS	MAJOR CREDIT CARDS ACCEPTED
RESERVATIONS	RECOMMENDED
HOURS	OPEN SEVEN DAYS A WEEK FOR LUNCH AND DINNER, SATURDAY/SUNDAY BRUNCH
LIQUOR	FULL LIQUOR
SMOKING	NO
SERVICES	VEGETARIAN MENU ITEMS
DRESS CODE	TASTEFUL
PARKING	AVAILABLE IN NEARBY LOTS

APPETIZERS

CLAM CHOWDER
WELLFLEET OYSTERS ON THE HALF SHELL
COUNTRY PATE
FRIED BRIE
CLAMS CASINO
MANDARIN SWORDFISH BROCHETTE

ENTREES

JUMBO SHRIMP SCAMPI
NEW ENGLAND LOBSTER TAILS
BONELESS CHICKEN BREAST WITH TOMATO-BASIL BEURRE BLANC
MEDALLIONS OF VEAL WITH MORELS AND CHAMPAGNE SAUCE
BROCHETTE OF SHRIMP AND SEA SCALLOPS WITH LIME AND TEQUILA
    MARINADE, BEURRE BLANC

Bob & Timmy's

IT'S NO TOSS-UP

A bit hard to find but definitely worth the hunt is Bob & Timmy's, a wonderful hole-in-the-wall family restaurant that has been kicking around Providence since 1988. Those in the know food-wise have been going to Bob & Timmy's especially for their wood-grilled pizza and signature pasta dishes. Chef Jose Sanchez changes his menu annually and offers a special menu every summer, when a stroll through the city's "Little Italy" can be just delightful. Far from fancy, this little restaurant is perfect for a quick business lunch, a hearty dinner, or a late-night snack with a date. You just might fall in love there.

INSIDE SCOOP

CHEF	JOSE SANCHEZ	HOURS	OPEN SEVEN DAYS A WEEK
OWNER	TIM DOYLE		FOR LUNCH AND DINNER
OPEN SINCE	1988	LIQUOR	FULL LIQUOR
CUISINE	ITALIAN FAMILY-STYLE	SMOKING	PERMITTED
SPECIALTY	WOOD-GRILLED PIZZA,	SERVICES	HEALTHY/LOW-FAT MENU ITEMS
	SPECIALTY PASTA DISHES		VEGETARIAN MENU ITEMS
PRICE RANGE	APPETIZERS $2 TO $8		HANDICAPPED ACCESSIBLE
	ENTREES $5 TO $13		TAKE-OUT ORDERS AVAILABLE
CREDIT CARDS	MAJOR CREDIT CARDS ACCEPTED	DRESS CODE	CASUAL
RESERVATIONS	NO	PARKING	AVAILABLE ON NEARBY STREETS

GRILLED SPECIALTY PIZZAS

GREAT WHITE PIZZA WITH OLIVE, OIL, GARLIC, OREGANO, MOZZARELLA AND PARMESAN

LASAGNA PIZZA WITH SPINACH, RICOTTA CHEESE, MOZZARELLA AND TOMATO SAUCE

WOOD-GRILLED CHICKEN BREAST PIZZA WITH GRILLED YELLOW ONIONS, PARMESAN, GORGONZOLA AND ROASTED RED PEPPERS

WILD MUSHROOM PIZZA WITH PORTABELLO, CRIMINI AND SHIITAKE MUSHROOMS WITH DICED TOMATOES, GRILLED ONIONS, PARMESAN, ROMANO, GARLIC AND OLIVE OIL

PASTAS

LINGUINE WITH WHITE CLAM SAUCE

PAULI'S PASTA WITH GRILLED CHICKEN, SUN-DRIED TOMATOES AND WILD MUSHROOMS IN A SMOKED GOUDA CREAM SAUCE

SATURDAY PASTA WITH SPINACH, ARTICHOKE HEARTS AND SUN-DRIED TOMATOES IN A LEMON-WHITE WINE SAUCE

Brick Alley Pub

140 Thames Street, Newport | 401-849-6334 | www.brickalley.com

RIGHT UP YOUR ALLEY

For more than two decades, the award-winning Brick Alley Pub with its trademark yellow awnings has been a favorite of locals and tourists alike. And why not? Brick Alley has it all – a cozy fireplace in winter, an air-conditioned dining room on hot summer days, and a tree-shaded outdoor courtyard for warm-weather enjoyment. Chefs Ronald Silvia and Gary Mathias have the proverbial "something for everyone" on their huge seasonal menu which features eclectic and traditional American cuisine. Not to be missed: the Steak au Poivre, a New York sirloin in a sauce of cognac, fresh cream, Dijon mustard and black peppercorns.

BLACK BEAN AND MANGO SALSA

Makes 2 cups or 6 to 8 servings as topping

1/2 cup dried black beans, washed
1/3 teaspoon sea salt
2 mangoes, diced
1/2 red bell pepper, diced
1 tablespoon hot sauce
1 tablespoon fresh lime juice

Cook the beans for 90 minutes, adding sea salt after 60 minutes. Drain the beans and let cool. Transfer beans to mixing bowl; add the other ingredients and gently stir together. Use as a topping for broiled fish.

INSIDE SCOOP

CHEFS	RONALD J. SILVIA AND GARY MATHIAS	LIQUOR	FULL LIQUOR
		SMOKING	PERMITTED
OWNERS	RALPHY AND PAT PLUMB	SERVICES	BANQUET FACILITIES
OPEN SINCE	1980		CHILDREN'S MENU
CUISINE	ECLECTIC AND TRADITIONAL AMERICAN		HEALTHY/LOW-FAT MENU ITEMS
			VEGETARIAN MENU ITEMS
SPECIALTY	STEAK AU POIVRE		HANDICAPPED ACCESSIBLE
PRICE RANGE	APPETIZERS $7 TO $11		TAKE-OUT ORDERS AVAILABLE
	ENTREES $7 TO $22		PRIVATE DINING ROOM
CREDIT CARDS	MAJOR CREDIT CARDS ACCEPTED		FIREPLACE
RESERVATIONS	RECOMMENDED	DRESS CODE	TASTEFUL
HOURS	OPEN SEVEN DAYS A WEEK FOR LUNCH AND DINNER SUNDAY BRUNCH	PARKING	AVAILABLE ON THE STREET AND IN NEARBY MUNICIPAL PARKING LOTS

APPETIZERS

PORTABELLO FRIES WITH PARMIGIANO AND RED PEPPER BREADING, SERVED WITH HORSERADISH SOUR CREAM DIPPING SAUCE
CALIFORNIA NORI ROLL

ENTREES

BUFFALO SHRIMP PASTA IN A RED PEPPER CREAM SAUCE OVER RED PEPPER RIGATONI
CREAMY LOBSTER AND SCALLOP SAUTÉ IN A PARMESAN CREAM SAUCE ON SPINACH FETTUCCINE
SEDONA BURGER SMOTHERED WITH PEPPER-JACK CHEESE, BACON AND SLICED JALAPENOS
SOUTHWESTERN TILAPIA WITH A CHIPOTLE CILANTRO SAUCE ON A BED OF BLACK BEANS AND RICE
SIRLOIN AU POIVRE IN A COGNAC MUSTARD CREAM SAUCE

Dining al fresco

Cafe Fresco

301 Main Street, East Greenwich | 401-398-0027 | www.cafefrescori.com

ITALIAN, DONE RIGHT

Everyone has been talking about Cafe Fresco since it opened. What's the buzz all about? Really good Italian food with many modern twists at very reasonable prices. Billing itself as "a wood grill and bar," Cafe Fresco is smart looking with a comfy lounge filled with loveseats. The menu offers raw seafood on the half shell, zesty appetizers, thin and crisp wood-grilled pizzas, a variety of bruschettas and salads, several risottos and pastas, and main courses that are simply a bargain. The menu at Cafe Fresco seems to offer some dishes made famous by other restaurants in the state, proving once and for all that imitation is the sincerest form of flattery.

FRESH FRUIT TART

Serves 5

2 1/2 cups all-purpose flour
1/2 cup granulated sugar
1/2 cup frozen butter, cut into small cubes
1/4 cup ice cold water
Fresh fruit, cut into thin slices
Sugar, as needed
Whipped cream, to garnish

In food processor, blend flour, sugar and butter. Slowly add water and blend for 3 to 5 seconds to incorporate. Roll dough into ball, wrap and freeze overnight. Cut dough into 5 equal pieces, and roll out each piece onto floured surface until 1/8 inch thick.

Add thin slices of fresh fruit to center of dough; sprinkle sugar on fruit. Fold edges of dough up around fruit, about 1 inch from center. Place on sheet pan and bake at 350 degrees for approximately 8 to 10 minutes, or until golden brown.

Garnish with fresh whipped cream.

INSIDE SCOOP

CHEF	TONY MORALES	LIQUOR	FULL LIQUOR
OWNERS	TONY MORALES AND	SMOKING	PERMITTED
	JACK WALROND	SERVICES	BANQUET FACILITIES
OPEN SINCE	2001		CHILDREN'S MENU
CUISINE	ITALIAN		HEALTHY/LOW-FAT MENU ITEMS
SPECIALTY	LOCAL SEAFOOD,		VEGETARIAN MENU ITEMS
	GRILLED PIZZAS, STEAKS		HANDICAPPED ACCESSIBLE
PRICE RANGE	APPETIZERS $4 TO $12		TAKE-OUT ORDERS AVAILABLE
	ENTREES $12 TO $19		CATERING
CREDIT CARDS	MAJOR CREDIT CARDS ACCEPTED		PRIVATE DINING ROOM
RESERVATIONS	RECOMMENDED	DRESS CODE	CASUAL
HOURS	OPEN SEVEN NIGHTS	PARKING	AVAILABLE ON THE STREET
	A WEEK FOR DINNER		

APPETIZERS

PASTA FAGIOLI
SAUTÉED SHRIMP AND SPINACH CROSTINI
OYSTERS AND CREAM SHALLOT SAUCE
BLACK AND BLUE TUNA WITH SOY, SESAME OIL AND WASABI
PIZZA BIANCO WITH HOT ITALIAN SAUSAGE, ROASTED PEPPERS AND
    SPICY OIL

ENTREES

VEGETABLE RISOTTO
PAN-SEARED CHICKEN BREAST WITH GRILLED VEGETABLES AND
    MASHED POTATOES
CLAMS AND SAUSAGE IN TOMATO, ONION AND GARLIC SAUCE WITH
    MASHED POTATOES
PAN-SEARED SEA SCALLOPS WITH SPICY CARROT PUREE, MIXED GREENS
    AND MASHED POTATOES
WOOD-GRILLED SIRLOIN WITH GRILLED VEGETABLES AND MASHED
    POTATOES

Cafe Nuovo

STILL SO STYLISH

When we first visited Cafe Nuovo shortly after it opened in 1994, we were blown away by the creative cuisine, especially the towering desserts. Today, Cafe Nuovo lives up to its name – still new and fresh and in the lead when it comes to the latest culinary trends. Why go to New York to dine when you can enjoy New World Cuisine right here in Rhode Island with a panoramic view of the city, simply spectacular on a WaterFire night? Chef Tim Kelly, who has been there since the start, has described his style of cooking as "evolutionary" – we can't wait to see what he has planned for the future.

GRAPEVINE GEM: On warm summer nights, you can watch the city's beautiful gondolas glide by as you dine outside under Cafe Nuovo's Arabian-like tents right on the Riverwalk.

INSIDE SCOOP

CHEF	TIMOTHY KELLY	LIQUOR	FULL LIQUOR
OWNER	DIMITRI KRITICOS	SMOKING	PERMITTED AT THE BAR
OPEN SINCE	1994	SERVICES	BANQUET FACILITIES
CUISINE	NEW WORLD CUISINE		CHILDREN'S MENU
SPECIALTY	TALL "ARCHITECTURAL" DESSERTS		HEALTHY/LOW-FAT MENU ITEMS
PRICE RANGE	APPETIZERS $9 TO $14		VEGETARIAN MENU ITEMS
	ENTREES $18 TO $30		HANDICAPPED ACCESSIBLE
CREDIT CARDS	MAJOR CREDIT CARDS ACCEPTED		TAKE-OUT ORDERS AVAILABLE
RESERVATIONS	RECOMMENDED		PRIVATE DINING ROOM
HOURS	OPEN SIX NIGHTS A WEEK		OUTDOOR DINING
	FOR DINNER, CLOSED SUNDAY	DRESS CODE	BUSINESS/CASUAL
	MONDAY THROUGH THURSDAY,	PARKING	AVAILABLE IN NEARBY PARKING LOTS AND
	5 TO 10:30 P.M.		THROUGH THE VALET SERVICE
	FRIDAY AND SATURDAY, 5 TO 11 P.M.		

APPETIZERS

ESCARGOTS BOURGUIGNONNE, PERNOD-SCENTED GARLIC-HERB BUTTER AND
    PIGNOLI NUTS, WITH A HOT BAGUETTE AND A WEDGE OF BRIE

WARM PARMESAN CUSTARD WITH ENGLISH PEAS, WILD MUSHROOM
    BRUSCHETTA, SHAVED PARMIGIANO-REGGIANO AND BASIL OIL

LOBSTER NIME CHOW WITH LEMON GRASS DIPPING SAUCE, SPICY PEANUTS
    AND KIMCHI SLAW

HAWAIIAN KING PRAWNS AND TUNA TARTARE TEMPURA WITH ASIAN MIXED
    GREENS AND LEMON TAMARI DIPPING SAUCE

CHOPPED SALAD WITH TOMATO, CUCUMBER, ASPARAGUS, SUGAR SNAP PEAS,
    SWEET RED PEPPERS, BERMUDA ONION, FETA CHEESE, FRESH HERBS AND
    SHERRY VINAIGRETTE

ENTREES

LOBSTER RAVIOLI WITH SWEET LOBSTER CREAM, BUTTER-BRAISED HALF TAIL OF
    LOBSTER, AND FRESH SUCCOTASH

PAN-FRIED SPAGHETTI AND SHRIMP SCAMPI WITH TOMATOES, SWEET PEPPERS,
    POBLANO CHILE, RED ONION, OLIVES AND FRESH BASIL

LINGUINE AND SESAME SWORDFISH WITH SHIITAKE MUSHROOMS, CARROT
    AND LEEK STIR-FRY AND GINGERED TAMARI BROTH

UDON NOODLES AND SPICY STIR-FRIED TENDERLOIN WITH SHIMEJI, MAITAKE
    AND SHIITAKE MUSHROOMS, JERUSALEM ARTICHOKE, CARROT AND SWEET
    PEPPERS, IN A GINGER AND MUSHROOM REDUCTION

DUCK BREAST WITH GINGERED RHUBARB MARMALADE, SPICY PEANUTS, ASIAN
    GREENS AND SWEET POTATO TEMPURA

JERK-RUBBED PORK TENDERLOIN WITH MAPLE MUSTARD SAUCE, GREEN
    PEPPERCORNS, COLLARD GREENS AND SWEET POTATO FLAN

SIX-HOUR LAMB SHANKS
Serves 4

4 Frenched* lamb shanks, about 1 pound each	1 tablespoon imported dry Greek oregano
Kosher salt and freshly ground black pepper, to taste	3/4 pound Misko orzo**
1/4 cup canola oil	1 cup grated Parmigiano-Reggiano cheese
2 (30-ounce) cans tomatoes, peeled, ground	1/4 cup chopped fresh parsley

Preheat oven to 300 degrees. Generously season the shanks with the kosher salt and black pepper. Heat the canola oil in a large, heavy-bottomed skillet until it just about smokes, then brown the shanks two at a time until they are browned on all sides.

Transfer the shanks to 6-quart covered casserole dish, and add the tomatoes and oregano. Cover the shanks with water; add a little kosher salt and black pepper. Stir so all the ingredients are well mixed and loose in the casserole dish.

Cover and place in the oven. The shanks will take about 6 hours to cook; however, check them after the first 2 hours and add more water to cover if the cooking liquid falls below the level of the shanks, leaving them exposed.

Check periodically and add water as needed. At the 5-hour mark, the shanks should just begin falling off the bone. At this point, uncover them, check the seasoning, adjust with salt and add the orzo, gently stirring it into the cooking liquid. At the 6-hour mark, the orzo should be tender. Check by tasting it. Be careful. It will be very hot.

When the orzo is fully cooked, there should be only a little visible liquid. Sprinkle the top with the cheese and set the oven to "Broil." Cook just 5 or so more minutes so the cheese can form a crust. Sprinkle the top with parsley and serve at once.

Note: Serve extra cheese at the table to sprinkle on top.

* Frenched shanks have all the excess fat removed, the hoof bone removed and the tendons trimmed, leaving an inch of bone showing. A good butcher shop will be able to do this for you.

** Misko is a brand available at Middle Eastern markets. A good hard orzo will work; however, most basic grocery store brands do not fare as well.

Cafe Paragon

THE VIRTUES OF PARAGON

This high-energy, always-crowded restaurant with its European atmosphere seems to match the constant hustle and bustle out on Thayer Street. Co-owner Mario Panagos is usually on the premises, greeting regular customers and making sure newcomers are satisfied. What's not to like at Cafe Paragon? The trendy menu offers incredibly fresh salads, contemporary pizzas and hearty burgers, but the best dish in the the cafe's repertoire just might be the Pappardelle Pasta with chunks of lobster meat in a light pink herb sauce. No wonder this place is always packed with people.

GRAPEVINE GEM: And now the suburbs are also getting a taste of this successful restaurant via its sister restaurant, Paragon, in East Greenwich near the Warwick line.

INSIDE SCOOP

CHEF	MICHAEL BACCARI	LIQUOR	FULL LIQUOR
OWNERS	MARIO PANAGOS	SMOKING	PERMITTED
	AND ANDREW MITRELIS	SERVICES	BANQUET FACILITIES, UP TO 40 POEPLE
OPEN SINCE	1994		HEALTHY/LOW-FAT MENU ITEMS
CUISINE	NEW AMERICAN CUISINE		VEGETARIAN MENU ITEMS
SPECIALTY	SALADS AND BURGERS		HANDICAPPED ACCESSIBLE
PRICE RANGE	APPETIZERS $7 TO $8		TAKE-OUT ORDERS AVAILABLE
	ENTREES $11 TO $17		CATERING
CREDIT CARDS	MAJOR CREDIT CARDS ACCEPTED		PRIVATE DINING ROOM
RESERVATIONS	ONLY FOR LARGE PARTIES	DRESS CODE	CASUAL
HOURS	OPEN SEVEN DAYS A WEEK	PARKING	AVAILABLE ON NEARBY STREETS
	LUNCH AND DINNER		
	SUNDAY THROUGH THURSDAY,		
	11 A.M. TO 1 A.M.		
	FRIDAY AND SATURDAY,		
	11:30 A.M. TO 2 A.M.		

APPETIZERS

WILD MUSHROOM BRUSCHETTA ON CHARGRILLED FOCACCIA WITH A WHITE
    WINE CREAM SAUCE
MYKONOS-STYLE OCTOPUS IN AN HERB VINAIGRETTE
CRAB AND LOBSTER CAKES WITH PARAGON'S HOUSE MAYONNAISE

SPECIALTY SALADS

BABY SPINACH SALAD WITH LOBSTER MEAT, SMOKED APPLEWOOD BACON,
    VINE-RIPENED TOMATOES AND SCALLIONS IN A LEMON VINAIGRETTE
AVOCADO ROMA SALAD (ROMAINE LETTUCE, SLICED AVOCADOS, RED ONION,
    GORGONZOLA CHEESE AND TOMATOES IN A CITRUS VINAIGRETTE)
GRILLED SLICES OF BEEF TENDERLOIN TOSSED WITH DICED TOMATO,
    MONTEREY JACK CHEESE, ONION AND LETTUCE IN A CRISPY TORTILLA SHELL

ENTREES

GOURMET BURGERS WITH THE FULL ARRAY OF TOPPINGS AND AWARD-
    WINNING FRIES
LOBSTER RAVIOLI WITH SHRIMP AND SWORDFISH IN A LIGHT PINOT GRIGIO
    PINK SAUCE
CHARGRILLED LAMB CHOPS IN A LEMON OREGANO SAUCE
CAJUN DUCK BREAST WITH RICE PILAF OR SMASHED POTATOES
HONEY DIJON CHICKEN BREAST
CHARGRILLED SIRLOIN STEAK WITH A BURGUNDY WILD MUSHROOM SAUCE

CORNISH HEN
WITH CRANBERRY AND PORCINI STUFFING
Serves 2

3 cups chicken stock
Thyme, sage, rosemary and fresh garlic, to taste
1 cup wild rice
1/4 cup dried porcini mushrooms
1/4 cup dried cranberries
1 cup white wine
1/2 cup cranberry sauce
Cornstarch, as needed (optional)
2 Cornish game hens, rinsed clean
Salt, pepper and garlic powder, to taste

Preheat oven to 450 degrees.

Bring 2 cups chicken broth, flavored with fresh herbs, to a boil. Add the wild rice and reduce heat to a simmer. After 15 minutes, add mushrooms, cranberries and half of the white wine.

In another pot, combine the remaining wine with the cranberry sauce. Bring to a simmer, stir thoroughly, and hold. Add cornstarch to thicken, if desired.

After the rice has cooked for 30 minutes, set it aside and allow to cool. Stuff the cooled rice into the Cornish game hens. Place stuffed hens in baking dish and add the remaining cup of chicken stock. Season the hens completely with salt, pepper and garlic powder.

Bake in preheated 450-degree oven for 20 minutes. Then cover and reduce heat to 350 degrees, and continue cooking for an additional 30 to 40 minutes.

Remove hens from oven and serve at once. Pour drippings over the entrees. Serve with cranberry sauce and either additional rice, potatoes or roasted vegetables.

Caffe Itri

MANGE BENE

Greg Spremulli is the gracious chef-owner of the award-winning Caffe Itri, and his passion for southern Italian cuisine is most evident at this casual restaurant in the Knightsville section of Cranston. Everything is cooked to order, and the menu changes two to three times a year. Pasta rules at Caffe Itri, with more than 20 dishes offered. Signature dishes include Grilled Shrimp and Scallop Spiedini, Grilled Double Breast of Chicken over Gnocchi, and Wood-Grilled Double Thick Pork Chops. Don't be surprised if you're made to feel like you're part of the family when you dine at Caffe Itri.

PENNE ITRI

Serves 2

1/4 cup olive oil
1/8 cup proscuitto, cut into thin strips
1/2 cup wild mushrooms, chopped into bite-size pieces
1 tablespoon capers
8 Gaeta olives, pitted
1 tablespoon scallions
Pinch of salt
1 teaspoon black pepper
1 teaspoon red pepper
12 ounces marinara
1/2 pound penne, cooked
1 tablespoon extra virgin olive oil

Combine olive oil, proscuitto, wild mushrooms, capers, olives and scallions, and then sauté in a large frying pan. Add seasonings. Deglaze pan with marinara and simmer until sauce becomes thick. Add penne and drizzle with extra virgin olive oil. Serve in large bowl.

INSIDE SCOOP

CHEF-OWNER	GREGORY SPREMULLI	RESERVATIONS	RECOMMENDED
OPEN SINCE	1990	HOURS	MONDAY THROUGH FRIDAY
CUISINE	COOKED-TO-ORDER		FOR LUNCH AND DINNER
	SOUTHERN ITALIAN CUISINE		SATURDAYS – DINNER ONLY
SPECIALTY	GRILLED SHRIMP AND	LIQUOR	FULL LIQUOR
	SCALLOP SPIEDINI OVER BAKED	SMOKING	PERMITTED
	CAPELLINI AND SAUTÉED BABY	SERVICES	BANQUET FACILITIES
	SPINACH DRESSED WITH HONEY		HEALTHY/LOW-FAT MENU ITEMS
	BALSAMIC GLAZE		HANDICAPPED ACCESSIBLE
PRICE RANGE	APPETIZERS $7 TO $13		TAKE-OUT ORDERS AVAILABLE
	ENTREES $11 TO $21		CATERING
CREDIT CARDS	MAJOR CREDIT CARDS ACCEPTED		

APPETIZERS

GRILLED PIZZA

CANNELLINI BEANS, PROSCIUTTO AND RED ONIONS OVER GRILLED FOCACCIA

TRIPE STEWED IN A SPICY NEAPOLITAN RAGU

ABRUZZESE SAUSAGE WITH AGED PARMIGIANO, GAETA AND CERIGNOLA OLIVES

ENTREES

LONG-SHELLED PASTA WITH A SAUCE OF PANCETTA, RED ONIONS, RED PEPPERS, TOMATOES, BASIL AND GARLIC

GNOCCHI GORGONZOLA WITH CREAM, CRACKED PEPPER AND GRATED PECORINO ROMANO OVER POTATO DUMPLINGS

PENNE WITH PROSCIUTTO, WILD MUSHROOMS, OLIVES, CAPERS, SCALLIONS, GARLIC AND TOMATOES

LINGUINE WITH LITTLENECKS, SHRIMP, SCALLOPS, CALAMARI AND MUSSELS IN A TOMATO BROTH

BREADED BABY VEAL CHOPS WITH A FOREST MUSHROOM TOMATO SAUCE OVER GARLIC MASHED POTATOES

VEAL SCALOPPINE WITH ROCK CRAB, SHALLOTS AND DICED PLUM TOMATOES IN A SHERRY CREAM SAUCE WITH GRILLED VEGETABLE RAVIOLI

GRILLED DOUBLE-THICK PORK CHOPS WITH BRANDIED APPLE AND RAISIN CHUTNEY OVER MASHED SWEET POTATO

Canfield House

5 Memorial Boulevard, Newport | 401-847-0416 | www.canfieldhouse.com

IN SHARP CONTRAST

You can't judge a book by its cover nor a restaurant by its overall appearance. The staid, historical Canfield House in Newport is home to some of the most exciting food being offered in that city-by-the-sea. Chef Michael Quattrucci dazzles his guests with "nouveau eclectic cuisine" – dishes with French, Italian, Asian, and Cajun influences. It's a contradiction in terms to sit in the resplendent lounge with its soaring ceiling and nautical prints on the walls, and at the same time dine on the Rock Crab Cakes with Tomato-Basil-Corn Salad and Habanero Aioli. But we did, and we would do it again, anytime.

GRAPEVINE GEM: The history behind the Canfield House and its namesake Richard Canfield is fascinating. From 1897 to 1905, the Canfield House was a highly successful gambling casino, where the Vanderbilts are said to have lost millions. Canfield is considered the most famous of American gamblers and is the man who invented the card game known as Solitaire.

INSIDE SCOOP

CHEF	MICHAEL QUATTRUCCI	LIQUOR	FULL LIQUOR
OWNERS	PATRICK AND LYNNE MAHER	SMOKING	CIGAR-FRIENDLY EAT-IN LOUNGE,
OPEN SINCE	1995, WITH CURRENT OWNER		NON-SMOKING DINING ROOMS
CUISINE	NOUVEAU, ECLECTIC	SERVICES	BANQUET FACILITIES
SPECIALTY	HALIBUT WITH SAFFRON RISOTTO		CHILDREN'S MENU
PRICE RANGE	APPETIZERS $7 TO $12		VEGETARIAN MENU ITEMS
	ENTREES $12 TO $38		TAKE-OUT ORDERS AVAILABLE
CREDIT CARDS	MAJOR CREDIT CARDS ACCEPTED		CATERING
RESERVATIONS	RECOMMENDED		PRIVATE DINING ROOM
HOURS	APRIL TO DECEMBER:		FIREPLACES
	OPEN SEVEN NIGHTS A WEEK	DRESS CODE	CASUAL
	FOR DINNER AND	PARKING	AVAILABLE ON THE PREMISES AND
	WEDNESDAY THROUGH SUNDAY		THROUGH THE VALET SERVICE
	FOR LUNCH		
	JANUARY TO MARCH:		
	OPEN WEDNESDAY THROUGH		
	SUNDAY FOR DINNER		

APPETIZERS

ROCK CRAB CAKES WITH TOMATO-BASIL-CORN SALAD AND HABANERO AIOLI

GRILLED SKEWERED JUMBO SHRIMP DUSTED WITH CAJUN SPICES OVER SAUTÉED SPINACH AND TOMATO WITH GARLIC

ESCARGOTS WITH CHORIZO, FENNEL, TOMATO AND PERNOD HERB BUTTER

STEAMED LITTLENECKS WITH PANCETTA, ROASTED CORN, PLUM TOMATOES AND SPINACH IN CHAMPAGNE GARLIC BROTH

ENTREES

PAN-SEARED SEA SCALLOPS WITH SCALLION RISOTTO CAKE, JULIENNE OF VEGETABLES AND ORANGE-GINGER BUTTER SAUCE

SMOKED DUCK BREAST OVER SWEET POTATO MASH, SOY SESAME VEGETABLES WITH ASIAN PEPPER JELLY SAUCE

BAKED LOBSTER STUFFED WITH ROCK SHRIMP, BAY SCALLOPS AND LIGHT GINGER BUTTER

ROASTED CHICKEN BREAST WITH GARLIC CHICKEN DEMIGLACE

BEEF TENDERLOIN AU POIVRE WITH WILD MUSHROOM DEMIGLACE

Capital Grille

STILL THE ONE

Restaurants come and go, but the Capital Grille obviously has staying power. Since 1990, this upscale, classic steakhouse has defied the skeptics and established itself as one of the finest, most successful restaurants in the city. Walk into the cavernous dining room, and the feeling of money and power is palpable. The steak is the thing at Capital Grille, dry-aged to perfection on the premises. Chops and fresh seafood of the highest quality are also available. The award-winning wine list features more than 300 selections. Prepare to be pampered by the well-trained professional waitstaff.

GRAPEVINE GEM: The Capital Grille is owned by Rare Hospitality Inc., which also owns Hemenway's, another great Providence restaurant that specializes in seafood.

INSIDE SCOOP

CHEF	FRED BARRIGA	LIQUOR	FULL LIQUOR
OWNER	RARE HOSPITALITY	SMOKING	PERMITTED (CIGARS ARE
	INTERNATIONAL, INC.		QUITE POPULAR HERE)
OPEN SINCE	1992 (OWNED BY RARE SINCE 1997)	SERVICES	BANQUET FACILITIES
CUISINE	TRADITIONAL NEW YORK		HEALTHY/LOW-FAT MENU ITEMS
	STEAKHOUSE		VEGETARIAN MENU ITEMS, ON
SPECIALTY	DRY-AGED STEAKS		REQUEST
PRICE RANGE	APPETIZERS $10 TO $35		HANDICAPPED ACCESSIBLE
	ENTREES $18 TO $33		TAKE-OUT ORDERS AVAILABLE
CREDIT CARDS	MAJOR CREDIT CARDS ACCEPTED		CATERING
RESERVATIONS	HIGHLY RECOMMENDED		PRIVATE DINING ROOM
HOURS	MONDAY THROUGH FRIDAY	DRESS CODE	BUSINESS/CASUAL
	FOR LUNCH AND DINNER	PARKING	COMPLIMENTARY VALET PARKING
	SATURDAY AND SUNDAY		AFTER 5 P.M. AND VALIDATED
	DINNER ONLY		SELF-PARKING IN ADJACENT LOT

APPETIZERS

SMOKED NORWEGIAN SALMON
LOBSTER AND CRAB CAKES
COLD BABY LOBSTER WITH CONFETTI MAYONNAISE
COLD SHELLFISH PLATTER
STEAK TARTARE
FRENCH ONION SOUP
PAN-FRIED CALAMARI WITH HOT CHERRY PEPPERS

ENTREES

14-OUNCE SIRLOIN STEAK
24-OUNCE PORTERHOUSE STEAK
STEAK AU POIVRE WITH COGNAC CREAM SAUCE
VEAL CHOP WITH ROQUEFORT BUTTER SAUCE
GRILLED SALMON WITH WHITE BEAN FRICASSEE
SHRIMP SCAMPI WITH ROASTED TOMATOES OVER LINGUINE
2-POUND LOBSTER

Capriccio

IF ONLY THOSE WALLS COULD TALK

A Rhode Island institution, Capriccio is a high-end, white-linen dining establishment offering candlelight sophistication and European elegance. Master Chef Gaetano "Nino" D'Urso gives his continental menu an Italian accent. The award-winning, Italian-born chef says he loves to work with fresh seafood and veal. His current menu also includes quail, ostrich and pheasant dishes, prime beef, and skillful tableside presentations of Steak Diane, Scampi alla Gino, and Cherries Jubilee. Open since 1976, Capriccio is a subterranean restaurant located one flight down from street level, a popular gathering spot for the rich, the powerful and the beautiful.

CAPELLINI CARDINALE
Serves 4

4 chicken lobsters, 1 1/4 pounds each	1/4 cup butter
1/4 cup brandy	12 ounces capellini
2 cups crushed plum tomatoes	Salt and pepper, to taste
1 pint heavy cream	Fresh basil, as needed

For the lobster:
In a very large pot, bring water to a boil and add lobsters. Maintain boil for 12 minutes or until lobsters turn bright red. Remove lobsters and split shells. Remove and clean lobster meat. Set aside.

For the sauce:
Pour brandy into hot skillet or sauté pan to burn off the alcohol. Add crushed tomatoes, and simmer for 12 to 15 minutes on low heat. Add heavy cream; increase heat and simmer, stirring regularly, for an additional 12 to 15 minutes. Add butter and lobster meat.

For the pasta:
Bring a large pot of salted water to a boil. Add capellini and maintain boil for 4 to 5 minutes or until pasta becomes tender to the bite.

For the final dish:
Toss sauce and pasta together. Garnish with fresh basil.

INSIDE SCOOP

CHEF	GAETANO "NINO" D'URSO	LIQUOR	FULL LIQUOR
OWNER	VINCENZO IEMMA	SMOKING	PERMITTED
OPEN SINCE	1976	SERVICES	BANQUET FACILITIES
CUISINE	CONTINENTAL WITH		HEALTHY/LOW-FAT MENU ITEMS
	NORTHERN ITALIAN ACCENT		VEGETARIAN MENU ITEMS
SPECIALTY	FRESH SEAFOOD AND VEAL		TAKE-OUT ORDERS AVAILABLE
PRICE RANGE	APPETIZERS $10 TO $50		CATERING
	ENTREES $18 TO $54		PRIVATE DINING ROOM
CREDIT CARDS	MAJOR CREDIT CARDS ACCEPTED		FIREPLACE
RESERVATIONS	RECOMMENDED	DRESS CODE	TASTEFUL, NO JEANS OR SNEAKERS
HOURS	OPEN WEEKDAYS FOR LUNCH	PARKING	AVAILABLE ON NEARBY STREETS,
	AND SEVEN NIGHTS A WEEK		IN PARKING LOTS AND THROUGH
	FOR DINNER		THE VALET SERVICE

APPETIZERS

BEEF CARPACCIO IN A SEASONED MARINADE OVER MIXED GREENS
MOZZARELLA IN CARROZZA (A SPICY MARINARA SAUCE WITH FRESH BAKED BREAD)
FRESH BABY ARTICHOKES STUFFED WITH SEASONED BREAD CRUMBS, ROASTED PEPPERS AND PARMIGIANO CHEESE

ENTREES

LINGUINE PRIMAVERA
ORECCHIETTE SAUTÉED WITH BROCCOLI, SUN-DRIED TOMATOES, WHITE WINE, BASIL AND GARLIC
CHAMPAGNE RISOTTO WITH SHRIMP, ASPARAGUS, RADICCHIO AND PARMIGIANO CHEESE
SHRIMP SCAMPI SERVED OVER CAPELLINI
VEAL SCALOPPINE WITH PROSCIUTTO AND SAGE, TOPPED WITH MUSHROOMS AND FRESH MOZZARELLA, FINISHED IN A WHITE WINE SAUCE
GRILLED VEAL CHOP WITH SAUTÉED MUSHROOMS, ONION AND CROSTINI OF POLENTA

Cassarino's

177 Atwells Avenue (Federal Hill), Providence | 401-751-3333

RED SAUCE AND MORE

Cassarino's is a classic Federal Hill restaurant, popular with college kids on dates and especially with families at graduation, and often busy with bus loads of senior citizens visiting Providence for the day. One taste of Chef-owner Richard Cassarino's veal parmigiana and you understand why. Stir in reasonable prices, and you have this restaurant's recipe for success. But wait there's more – try the littlenecks steamed in champagne with scallions and prosciutto. Cassarino's is especially appealing on a warm summer evening when the floor-to-ceiling windows open up for a bit of al fresco dining.

INSIDE SCOOP

CHEF-OWNER	RICHARD CASSARINO	SERVICES	BANQUET FACILITIES
OPEN SINCE	1993		CHILDREN'S MENU
CUISINE	ITALIAN		HEALTHY/LOW-FAT MENU ITEMS
SPECIALTY	VEAL AND SEAFOOD		VEGETARIAN MENU ITEMS
PRICE RANGE	APPETIZERS $7 TO $20		HANDICAPPED ACCESSIBLE
	ENTREES $13 TO $38		TAKE-OUT ORDERS AVAILABLE
CREDIT CARDS	MAJOR CREDIT CARDS ACCEPTED		PRIVATE DINING ROOM
RESERVATIONS	RECOMMENDED	DRESS CODE	CASUAL
HOURS	MONDAY THROUGH SATURDAY	PARKING	AVAILABLE ON THE STREET AND
	FOR LUNCH AND DINNER		THROUGH THE VALET SERVICE
LIQUOR	FULL LIQUOR		
SMOKING	PERMITTED IN DESIGNATED AREAS		

APPETIZERS

COMBINATION PLATTER WITH CALAMARI, BRUSCHETTA, STUFFED
   MUSHROOM CAPS AND CLAMS CASINO
BALSAMIC CALAMARI WITH HOT PEPPERS
TORTELLINI CARBONARA WITH SCALLIONS, PROSCIUTTO AND BACON
   IN AN ALFREDO SAUCE
LITTLENECKS STEAMED IN CHAMPAGNE WITH SCALLIONS AND
   PROSCIUTTO
SNAIL SALAD

ENTREES

GRILLED MARINATED CHICKEN BREAST OVER A BED OF BROCCOLI RABE
   WITH PROSCIUTTO, PORTABELLO MUSHROOMS, ASPARAGUS, RED
   AND YELLOW PEPPERS
SIRLOIN STRIPS SAUTÉED WITH GARLIC, HOT PEPPERS, DICED
   TOMATOES, ONIONS, OLIVES AND ROASTED POTATOES
VEAL CUTLET WITH EGGPLANT, HAM, PEPPERS AND MUSHROOMS
   GLAZED WITH CHEESE AND MARINARA SAUCE
PENNE BOLOGNESE
SHRIMP, SCALLOPS, MUSHROOMS, BROCCOLI AND TOMATOES IN A
   LIGHT CHEESE CREAM SAUCE OVER FETTUCCINE NOODLES

The Grapevine Guide | 23

Castle Hill Inn

NEWPORT'S GRAND DAME

One of the most impressive destination restaurants in the state, Castle Hill Inn and Resort is simply spectacular in its setting and in its cuisine, imaginatively designed by the award-winning chef, Casey Riley. Riley is devoted to original modern American cuisine and dedicated to using regional ingredients in season. For example: native littleneck clams steamed in Sakonnet Vidal Blanc with ripe local tomatoes, fennel, potatoes and fava beans. Riley's dinner menu changes eight times a year, ensuring his regular guests with something new and exciting at all times. This is a special occasion restaurant, most definitely.

GRAPEVINE GEM: This 19th-century shingle-style inn sits like a grand old lady on an emerald-green slope looking out over Narragansett Bay at the constant parade of ships in and out of Newport Harbor.

INSIDE SCOOP

CHEF	CASEY RILEY	LIQUOR	FULL LIQUOR
OWNER	NEWPORT HARBOR CORPORATION	SMOKING	NOT PERMITTED
OPEN SINCE	30+ YEARS AGO	SERVICES	BANQUET FACILITIES
CUISINE	ORIGINAL MODERN AMERICAN		HEALTHY/LOW-FAT MENU ITEMS
	CUISINE WITH A STRONG FOCUS ON		VEGETARIAN MENU ITEMS
	REGIONAL INGREDIENTS IN SEASON		HANDICAPPED ACCESSIBLE
SPECIALTY	VANILLA-SCENTED LOBSTER AND	DRESS CODE	TASTEFUL
	REALLY CHUNKY LOBSTER STEW	PARKING	AVAILABLE ON THE PREMISES
PRICE RANGE	APPETIZERS $6 TO $15		
	ENTREES $25 TO $39		
CREDIT CARDS	MAJOR CREDIT CARDS ACCEPTED		
RESERVATIONS	RECOMMENDED		
HOURS	LUNCH		
	MONDAY THROUGH SATURDAY,		
	NOON TO 3 P.M., APRIL-OCTOBER		
	FRIDAY AND SATURDAY, NOON TO 3 P.M.,		
	NOVEMBER-MARCH		
	DINNER		
	SUNDAY THROUGH THURSDAY,		
	6 TO 9 P.M., YEAR ROUND		
	FRIDAY AND SATURDAY,		
	6 TO 10 P.M., YEAR ROUND		
	SUNDAY BRUNCH		

APPETIZERS

NEW ENGLAND CLAM CHOWDER, CARAWAY AND RED CHILE CRACKER

SPRING NAGE OF BRAISED FREE-RANGE CHICKEN, SWEET PEAS, TOMATO AND
HERBS WITH VIDALIA ONION FRITTERS

POLENTA TERRINE OF CHANTERELLE AND PORCINI MUSHROOMS WITH
SAUTÉED TENDER SPINACH AND TARRAGON LEMON VINAIGRETTE

ROASTED HALF ARTICHOKE STUFFED WITH SPICY GROUND VEAL, WRAPPED IN
SHAVED PARMA HAM WITH BASIL AIOLI AND BLACK OLIVE SOUR CREAM

NATIVE LOBSTER POTATO CAKES WITH GRILLED CORN, SPRING PEA AND HOT
PEPPER SALAD WITH TARRAGON-HORSERADISH CREAM MAYONNAISE

ENTREES

CITRUS-GLAZED ATLANTIC SALMON WITH ALMOND, FAVA BEAN, ARUGULA AND
POTATO PANCAKES; LOBSTER AND TOMATO BUTTER SAUCE

SEARED YELLOWFIN TUNA WITH JONAH CRAB SPRING ROLL, STEAMED JASMINE
RICE, BOK CHOY, PICKLED GINGER RELISH, PAPAYA WASABI AND HOT SAKE

WOOD-GRILLED FREE-RANGE CHICKEN BREAST WITH TOASTED PORCINI, RABE-
SWEET PEPPER SALAD, ROASTED FINGERLING POTATOES AND BALSAMIC-RED
WINE SAUCE

WOOD-GRILLED MAPLE-ONION GLAZED PORK TENDERLOIN WITH GRILLED
YUKON POTATOES, ROASTED VIDALIA ONION, MUSTARD GREENS AND
TOMATILLO KETCHUP

WOOD-GRILLED PRIME BEEF TENDERLOIN FILET WITH POTATO AU GRATIN OF
CHEDDAR, WALNUT AND FOIE GRAS, BACON-BUNDLED SPRING ASPARAGUS
AND PORT-CURRANT DEMIGLACE

ROASTED RACK OF LAMB
WITH CHEVRE CRUST AND ROSEMARY REDUCTION

Castle Hill Inn

Serves 2

1 rack of lamb, split, Frenched and cap fat removed	Salt and coarse black pepper, to taste
1/2 cup marinade (minced garlic, splash of balsamic vinegar, fresh chopped rosemary, pinch of hot chile flakes and mild olive oil)	2 shallots, chopped
	6 cloves garlic, smashed
	1 tablespoon dry rosemary
1/2 cup fresh unripened goat cheese	1/2 cup ruby port wine
6 cloves garlic, roasted to golden brown and smashed or roughly chopped	1 cup dry heavy-bodied red wine
	1 cup veal or beef demiglace (can be purchased at gourmet shops)
2 tablespoons fine breadcrumbs	
2 tablespoons extra virgin olive oil	2 tablespoons fresh chopped rosemary
2 tablespoons finely chopped herbs (thyme, basil, rosemary and fennel)	Splash of lemon juice
	Salt and ground black pepper, to taste
Grated rind of 1 orange	

Rub the rack of lamb with the marinade; refrigerate overnight.

For the crust:

In a mixing bowl, combine goat cheese with roasted garlic, breadcrumbs, oil and herbs. With a fork, incorporate by pressing along the sides of the bowl until well blended. Season with orange zest, salt and coarse pepper.

For the sauce:

In a sauce pan, sauté the shallots until golden brown. Add the garlic and rosemary; cook for 2 minutes. Add the port wine and reduce by half. Add the red wine; reduce by half. Add the demiglace and reduce to sauce consistency. Strain the sauce through a fine mesh strainer. When ready to serve, place sauce in clean pan; bring to a simmer and season with fresh rosemary, lemon juice, salt and pepper.

For the lamb:

Preheat oven to 450 degrees. In a large sauté pan, sear the lamb on all sides to golden brown. Place foil over the exposed bones and spread goat cheese crust thickly on the top flesh. Place on a sheet pan with a rack and roast to desired temperature, with medium rare (120 degrees) taking about 12 minutes.

Slice between the bones and fan 4 chops onto each plate and serve with the sauce. For a side dish, risotto or herbed roasted potatoes are excellent choices.

CAV

TALK ABOUT HIDDEN TREASURES

Without a doubt, CAV is the most magical restaurant in Rhode Island, especially at night when the tiny white lights twinkle and the candlelight glows in the beautiful dining room. Filled with antiques and artifacts from around the world, CAV offers some of the most extraordinary food imaginable. This is fine dining at its best, with an exciting cutting-edge seasonal menu that features contemporary and fusion cuisine. Owner Sylvia Moubayed is devoted to not only satisfying your hunger, but restoring your spirit as well. Simply enchanting.

GRAPEVINE GEM: If you see it and like it, it's probably for sale and can be yours to take home. Really.

INSIDE SCOOP

OWNER	SYLVIA MOUBAYED	LIQUOR	FULL LIQUOR
OPEN SINCE	1990	SMOKING	NOT PERMITTED
CUISINE	CONTEMPORARY FUSION	SERVICES	HEALTHY/LOW-FAT MENU ITEMS
	WITH FRENCH, ITALIAN,		VEGETARIAN MENU ITEMS
	AMERICAN AND		HANDICAPPED ACCESSIBLE
	ASIAN INFLUENCES		TAKE-OUT ORDERS ON WEEKDAYS
SPECIALTY	PAN-SEARED DIVER SCALLOPS		CATERING
	WITH SHAD ROE, POTATO LATKES		PRIVATE DINING ROOM
	AND STAR ANISE-INFUSED		SUNDAY BRUNCH
	RED WINE REDUCTION	DRESS CODE	CASUAL
PRICE RANGE	APPETIZERS $7 TO $17	PARKING	AVAILABLE ON THE STREET AND
	ENTREES $15 TO $26		IN A NEARBY LOT
CREDIT CARDS	MAJOR CREDIT CARDS ACCEPTED		
RESERVATIONS	RECOMMENDED		
HOURS	LUNCH AND DINNER		
	MONDAY THROUGH THURSDAY,		
	11:30 A.M. TO 10 P.M.		
	FRIDAY AND SATURDAY,		
	11:30 A.M. TO 1 A.M.		
	SUNDAY (INCLUDING BRUNCH),		
	10:30 A.M. TO 10 P.M.		

APPETIZERS

SEARED HUDSON VALLEY FOIE GRAS ON TOASTED BRIOCHE AND SLOW-
   ROASTED CORTLAND APPLES
MUSSELS WITH LEMON GRASS
SEARED SEA SCALLOPS WITH SUGAR BEET MOUSSELINE, ASPARAGUS AND FRISEE
MARYLAND BLUE CRAB CAKE WITH CURRIED BUTTERCUP SQUASH PUREE
ARUGULA SALAD WITH ROASTED PANCETTA, ORANGE, WARM SHERRY
   VINAIGRETTE AND GOAT CHEESE FONDUE

ENTREES

FARFALLE WITH SMOKED DUCK BREAST, BLACK TRUMPET MUSHROOMS AND PEA
   TENDRILS IN A LIGHT SHERRY SAUCE
PAN-SEARED CHICKEN BREAST, RED WINE-POACHED PEARS AND A GINGER PEAR
   SAUCE, SERVED WITH SAUTÉED ASIAN CHIVE DUMPLINGS
BRAISED LAMB SHANK WITH MOROCCAN COUSCOUS AND ACORN SQUASH
   CUSTARD IN A RED WINE RAISIN SAUCE
PACIFIC HALIBUT BRAISED IN VERJUS BLANC WITH SPRING VEGETABLE RAGOUT
   AND SEA BEANS

ACORN SQUASH CUSTARD

Serves 12

1 acorn squash	Salt and pepper, to taste
1 pint heavy cream	4 whole eggs
1/4 cup brown sugar	Sprigs of thyme, to garnish

Peel acorn squash. Remove seeds, and cut squash into large dice. Place cut-up squash in a large pot. Cover with cold water, and bring to a boil. Simmer for 15 to 30 minutes, or until tender. Drain off water.

Add heavy cream to pot. Bring to a boil, lower heat and reduce cream slightly. Add brown sugar, salt and pepper. Mix well, remove from heat, and allow to cool.

When cool, puree the mixture with a hand blender or food processor, adding the eggs one at a time, and equally distribute the mixture into (4-ounce) greased custard cups or ramekins.

Place filled custard cups in a baking pan with sides. Add water to the baking pan three-quarters up the sides of the custard cups. Cover the baking pan tightly with parchment paper and double foil. Bake in preheated 350-degree oven for exactly 1 1/2 hours. When done, remove from oven and allow to cool to room temperature, still covered in the baking pan.

You can serve this custard after it has cooled for 20 to 30 minutes, or you can refrigerate them for later use (within 3 days).

When ready to serve, place the chilled custard cups into a 400-degree oven for about 3 minutes. Gently run a steak knife around the edge of the cup and invert custard onto the plate. Place a sprig of thyme to garnish, sticking straight up in the middle of the custard.

The kitchen heats up at Adesso

Chan's

EGG ROLLS AND JAZZ

Since 1905, Chan's has been offering fine Oriental dining, This is the place for no-nonsense Chinese food: pu pu platters, egg drop soup, sweet and sour dishes, chow mein, chop suey, and roast pork fried rice. The massive menu also offers Szechuan, Mandarin and Polynesian cuisine as well as special combination plates that are an absolute bargain. Our favorite dish: See Gyp Littlenecks with Black Bean Sauce. Over the decades, Chan's has evolved into an attractive mecca for music lovers with well-known singers and musicians appearing there on a regular basis, everyone from Diana Krall to Leon Redbone to Bellevue Cadillac. Owner John Chan is the consummate host.

CHAN'S CHICKEN WINGS

Serves 8

4 pounds chicken wings
1 teaspoon salt
2 tablespoons light soy sauce
2 tablespoons cooking sherry
2 tablespoons sugar
2 tablespoons ground fresh ginger
1/2 teaspoon white pepper
1/2 teaspoon five-spice powder

Cut chicken wings between joints; save tips for soup or discard. Mix remaining ingredients until smooth. Pour over wing pieces and marinate for 1 hour. Preheat fryer or oven to 350 degrees. In fryer, cook 15 minutes, or until tender. In oven, cook at least 30 minutes, or until tender.

INSIDE SCOOP

CHEF	GENE MUI	SMOKING	PERMITTED IN LOUNGE
OWNER	JOHN CHAN	SERVICES	BANQUET FACILITIES
OPEN SINCE	1905 (PURCHASED BY THE		HEALTHY/LOW-FAT MENU ITEMS
	CHAN FAMILY 35 YEARS AGO)		VEGETARIAN MENU ITEMS
CUISINE	CHINESE		HANDICAPPED ACCESSIBLE
SPECIALTY	SZECHWAN, MANDARIN		TAKE-OUT ORDERS AVAILABLE
	AND POLYNESIAN DISHES		CATERING
PRICE RANGE	APPETIZERS $3 TO $21		PRIVATE DINING ROOM
	ENTREES $3.50 TO $11.25	DRESS CODE	CASUAL
CREDIT CARDS	MAJOR CREDIT CARDS ACCEPTED	PARKING	AVAILABLE ON THE STREET AND
RESERVATIONS	RECOMMENDED ONLY		IN PARKING LOTS IN FRONT
	FOR JAZZ SHOWS		AND TO THE REAR OF CHAN'S
HOURS	OPEN SEVEN DAYS A WEEK		
	FOR LUNCH AND DINNER		
LIQUOR	FULL LIQUOR		

APPETIZERS

PUPU PLATTER — EGG ROLLS, GOLD FINGERS, BONELESS RIBS, CHICKEN
    WINGS, BEEF TERRIYAKI
PEKING RAVIOLI
CRAB RANGOON/WONTONS
FRIED JUMBO SHRIMP
CLAMS WITH BLACK BEAN SAUCE
SPRING ROLLS
SCALLION PANCAKE
HOT AND SOUR SOUP

ENTREES

SHRIMP WITH LOBSTER SAUCE
SINGAPORE RICE NOODLES WITH SPICY CURRY FLAVOR, SHRIMP, PORK
    AND SHREDDED VEGETABLES
MONGOLIAN STEAK MARINATED IN ORIENTAL SEASONING WITH
    SAUTÉED ONIONS
CASHEW CHICKEN WITH MUSHROOMS, CELERY AND CARROTS IN A
    LIGHT SAUCE
MU-SHI PORK, BEEF OR CHICKEN
KUNG PAU GAI DING — DICED CHICKEN WITH SPICY SAUCE AND
    PEANUTS

Cheeky Monkey Cafe

YES, WE HAVE NO BANANAS

Leave it to owner Hank Kates to create one of the most original restaurants in the state. Where else will you see portraits of famous monkeys that are sure to make you smile? You'll also be grinning from ear to ear with the fabulous, inventive food created by Chef Jeffrey Cruff and his talented staff. This is American regional cuisine at its best. The Cheeky Monkey's signature dish is Sesame Seared Yellowfin Tuna with jasmine rice, stir-fried Asian vegetables, tamari dipping sauce, wasabi and pickled ginger. We also recommend the Duck Confit Spring Rolls and the Panko-Crusted Tuna Nori Roll, all served in handsome surroundings on the waterfront in downtown Newport.

GRAPEVINE GEM: If you like the whimsical look of the Cheeky Monkey, you can thank Manager Maggie Gordon who designed the stylish restaurant.

INSIDE SCOOP

CHEF	JEFFREY CRUFF	LIQUOR	FULL LIQUOR
OWNER	HENRY KATES	SMOKING	PERMITTED IN LOUNGE
OPEN SINCE	1995	SERVICES	BANQUET FACILITIES
CUISINE	AMERICAN REGIONAL CUISINE		HEALTHY/LOW-FAT MENU ITEMS
SPECIALTY	CREATIVE DISHES,		VEGETARIAN MENU ITEMS
	MANY WITH ASIAN FLAIR		HANDICAPPED ACCESSIBLE
PRICE RANGE	APPETIZERS $7 TO $9		CATERING
	ENTREES $20 TO $30		PRIVATE DINING ROOM
CREDIT CARDS	MAJOR CREDIT CARDS ACCEPTED	DRESS CODE	CASUAL
RESERVATIONS	RECOMMENDED	PARKING	AVAILABLE ON PERRY MILL
HOURS	OPEN SEVEN DAYS A WEEK		WHARF AND IN NEARBY LOTS
	FOR DINNER ,		
	5:30 P.M. TO 1 A.M.		
	FRIDAY AND SATURDAY,		
	11:30 P.M. TO 1 A.M.		
	(CALL TO CHECK HOURS		
	DURING WINTER MONTHS)		

APPETIZERS

CHEEKY SALAD WITH BABY GREENS, GOAT CHEESE CROUTONS, TOMATOES IN A
BASIL BALSAMIC DRESSING

SZECHUAN PEPPERCORN SIRLOIN SALAD OVER SCALLIONS, RED ONIONS AND
CUCUMBERS WITH A SPICY GARLIC DRESSING

DUCK CONFIT SPRING ROLLS WITH PASSION FRUIT AND TAMARI DIPPING
SAUCE

STEAMED MUSSELS IN A COCONUT-GINGER SCENTED BROTH

THAI CODFISH CAKES WITH CURRY LOBSTER CREAM, CHILI OIL AND ASIAN COLE
SLAW

ENTREES

FIVE-SPICE SEARED CHICKEN BREAST WITH DUCK SAUCE, SNOW PEAS AND LO
MEIN

GRILLED MOROCCAN BARBECUED SALMON OVER CURRIED POTATOES AND
SMOKY SPINACH

CREOLE MUSTARD AND GOAT CHEESE CRUSTED PORK TENDERLOIN WITH A
WILD MUSHROOM DEMIGLACE, HERBED MASHED POTATOES AND SEASONAL
VEGETABLES

RIBEYE STEAK WITH GRILLED VIDALIA ONIONS AND CHEEKY STEAK SAUCE WITH
MASHED POTATOES AND ASPARAGUS

LOBSTER PAELLA WITH SEA SCALLOPS, MUSSELS AND CHORIZO OVER PAELLA
RICE

CRISPY TEMPURA RED SNAPPER OVER BABY BOK CHOY WITH STEAMED BROWN
RICE AND DRIZZLED WITH SWEET CHILI GLAZE

CILANTRO LIME VINAIGRETTE

1/3 cup minced ginger
2 teaspoons minced garlic
1/3 cup honey
1/2 cup cilantro, chopped slightly
3/4 cup fresh lime juice
1/3 cup soy sauce
4 dashes Tabasco sauce
1 teaspoon kosher salt
1/4 cup sesame oil
3 cups canola oil

In a blender or food processor, combine all ingredients except for sesame oil and canola oil. Pulse machine until well incorporated. Slowly drizzle oils into blender while machine is running.

Use as a marinade for tuna or chicken or to dress salad greens.

Chez Pascal

TRES BIEN

If you can't go to France this year, then make sure you visit Chez Pascal, where an authentic French dining experience awaits you. Chef Pascal Leffray, who formerly worked at the famous La Cote Basque and other New York City restaurants, and his wife Lynn are the proud owners of this East Side bistro. By all means, sample the fabulous Soupe de Poisson, garlicky escargots, fresh foie gras, sautéed frog legs, and the roasted duck, which the chef considers his best dish. Even the salads are memorable. Open for lunch and dinner, Chez Pascal is especially known for its wine dinners and special events. A quiet intimate *boite* for a quiet intimate evening.

CHOCOLATE MOUSSE WITH GRIOTTE

Serves 4

5 ounces semi-sweet chocolate
1/4 cup butter
Pinch of salt
1/3 cup sugar
6 egg yolks
3/4 cup heavy cream, whipped
6 egg whites
1/2 cup cherries, pitted

Melt the chocolate, butter and salt in the top part of a double boiler. Beat half the sugar with the egg yolks. Remove the chocolate from heat and add the sugar-egg yolk mixture. Gently add the whipped cream. Whip the egg whites with the remaining sugar. Add to chocolate and stir. Add cherries.

Pour into individual ramekins and chill for at least 4 hours before serving.

INSIDE SCOOP

CHEF-OWNER	PASCAL LEFFRAY	LIQUOR	FULL LIQUOR
OPEN SINCE	1998	SMOKING	NO
CUISINE	BISTRO-STYLE FRENCH	SERVICES	BANQUET FACILITIES
SPECIALTY	DUCK		VEGETARIAN MENU ITEMS
PRICE RANGE	APPETIZERS $7 TO $22		TAKE-OUT ORDERS AVAILABLE
	ENTREES $10 TO $32		PRIVATE DINING ROOM
CREDIT CARDS	MAJOR CREDIT CARDS	DRESS CODE	CASUAL
	ACCEPTED	PARKING	AVAILABLE ON THE STREET
RESERVATIONS	RECOMMENDED		
HOURS	TUESDAY THROUGH FRIDAY		
	FOR LUNCH		
	TUESDAY THROUGH SATURDAY		
	FOR DINNER		

APPETIZERS

FISH BROTH WITH TOMATOES, GARLIC AND SAFFRON SERVED WITH
    ROUILLE, GRUYERE CHEESE AND CROUTONS
SNAILS IN PUFF PASTRY WITH ROQUEFORT
FRESH DUCK FOIE GRAS
CRAB CAKE WITH MUSTARD SAUCE

ENTREES

VEAL SWEET BREADS
LAMB CHOP WITH FRESH FENNEL
CHICKEN BREAST WITH MUSTARD SAUCE
HALF ROASTED DUCK IN A RED WINE, BLACK CURRANT, BLACK PEPPER
    AND BRANDY SAUCE
ROASTED LOBSTER TAIL WITH ROSEMARY, TOMATO AND BRANDY SAUCE

Clarke Cooke House

ISN'T IT ROMANTIC?

The historical Clarke Cooke House in the heart of scenic Newport is a special destination restaurant, where you go for fine dining on American contemporary cuisine prepared by the masterful chef, Ted Gidley. On a snowy winter night, you can warm youself by the crackling fireplace. In warmer months, you can dine by an open window or up on the top level, high above the bustling crowds. Whether it's a birthday, anniversary or simply the end of the work week, the Clarke Cooke House is the perfect place to celebrate all that's good in life. And do it with champagne.

INSIDE SCOOP

CHEF	TED GIDLEY	LIQUOR	FULL LIQUOR
OWNER	DAVID RAY	SMOKING	PERMITTED ON FIRST
OPEN SINCE	1973		FLOOR ONLY
CUISINE	AMERICAN CONTEMPORARY	SERVICES	BANQUET FACILITIES
SPECIALTY	SEAFOOD, AS WELL AS AN		CHILDREN'S MENU
	ECLECTIC MIX OF CUISINES		HEALTHY/LOW-FAT MENU ITEMS
PRICE RANGE	APPETIZERS $9 TO $100		VEGETARIAN MENU ITEMS
	ENTREES $28 TO $36		HANDICAPPED ACCESSIBLE
CREDIT CARDS	MAJOR CREDIT CARDS ACCEPTED		PRIVATE DINING ROOM
RESERVATIONS	RECOMMENDED		FIREPLACE
HOURS	APRIL 1 TO NOVEMBER 1:	DRESS CODE	DOWNSTAIRS –
	OPEN SEVEN DAYS A WEEK		COLLARED SHIRTS
	FOR LUNCH AND DINNER		FORMAL DINING ROOM –
	NOVEMBER 2 TO APRIL 1:		UPSCALE BUSINESS
	DINNER ONLY – LUNCH SERVED		CASUAL (JACKETS REQUIRED)
	ONLY ON WEEKENDS	PARKING	AVAILABLE IN NEARBY LOTS
	SATURDAY/SUNDAY BRUNCH		

APPETIZERS

RAVIOLI OF LOBSTER AND WILD MUSHROOMS WITH LEEKS, MORELS
   AND BEURRE DE CHAMPIGNON
PAN-SEARED BREAST OF SQUAB WITH A ROAST CORN PANCAKE, FOIE
   GRAS, BLACK MISSION FIGS AND A PHYLLO PASTILLE
SEARED DUCK FOIE GRAS
BELUGA CAVIAR WITH BLINI AND CRÈME FRAICHE

ENTREES

PEPPERED TUNA STEAK WITH A SWEET AND SOUR SHERRY VINEGAR
   GLAZE AND POMMES ALLUMETTES
WOOD-GRILLED FILET MIGNON WITH BRAISED SHORT RIBS, SALSIFY,
   PORCINI MUSHROOMS AND A RED WINE BORDELAISE
FILET OF SOLE LYONNAISE WITH SPINACH, CARAMELIZED ONION,
   OYSTER MUSHROOMS AND BEURRE MEUNIERE
TWIN LOBSTERS STEAMED IN AN AROMATIC COURT BOUILLON

Coast Guard House

A SHORE THING

If you have time to visit only one restaurant in Narragansett, make it the Coast Guard House. Steeped in history and set on the rocky coastline in the shadow of the magical Narragansett Towers, this popular restaurant serves mostly seafood – on the half shell, appetizers, soups and chowders, and all the classics, from Baked Stuffed Shrimp to various surf-and-turf combinations. Salads, pasta, beef and chicken dishes round out the menu. On a perfect summer day, when the humidity is low and expectations are high, you'll want to be on the big deck at the Coast Guard House, with an ocean view that stretches from Newport to Block Island. Where's my pina colada?

INSIDE SCOOP

CHEF	TOM DUFFY
OWNER	DEBORAH KELSO
OPEN SINCE	1979
CUISINE	SEAFOOD-BASED
	AMERICAN MENU
SPECIALTY	SEAFOOD STEW
PRICE RANGE	APPETIZERS $4 TO $12
	ENTREES $13 TO $22
CREDIT CARDS	MAJOR CREDIT CARDS ACCEPTED
RESERVATIONS	RECOMMENDED FOR
	PARTIES OF 8 OR MORE
HOURS	OPEN SEVEN DAYS A WEEK
	FOR LUNCH AND DINNER
	CLOSED IN JANUARY
	SUNDAY BRUNCH
LIQUOR	FULL LIQUOR

SMOKING	PERMITTED IN LOUNGE ONLY
SERVICES	BANQUET FACILITIES
	CHILDREN'S MENU
	HEALTHY/LOW-FAT MENU ITEMS
	VEGETARIAN MENU ITEMS
	HANDICAPPED ACCESSIBLE
	TAKE-OUT ORDERS AVAILABLE
	FIREPLACE
	SEASONAL OUTDOOR DINING
DRESS CODE	CASUAL
PARKING	AVAILABLE ON THE PREMISES

APPETIZERS

CRAB CAKE WITH REMOULADE AND FIELD GREEN SALAD

MUSSELS SIMMERED IN SAFFRON, FENNEL AND TOMATO BROTH

MUSHROOM MEDLEY AND CARAMELIZED ONION BRUSCHETTA WITH
ROSEMARY, OLIVE OIL, BALSAMIC SYRUP AND BABY GREENS

CRAB BISQUE WITH SHERRY AND CREAM

GRILLED VEGETABLE SALAD WITH BABY GREENS IN A BASIL GARLIC
VINAIGRETTE

ENTREES

LEMON CHICKEN WITH ROASTED GARLIC, BLACK OLIVES, WHITE WINE
AND ROSEMARY ON RICE PILAF

LINGUINE WITH CLAM SAUCE

GRILLED TENDERLOIN WITH ROASTED GARLIC AND MUSHROOM
DEMIGLACE WITH CRISPY FRIED ONIONS AND CHEF'S VEGETABLE

BAKED LOBSTER STUFFED WITH SHRIMP, CRAB MEAT, SCALLOPS AND
LOBSTER CLAW MEAT, THEN FINISHED IN THE OVEN

Costantino's Ristorante

THE REAL DEAL

Undoubtedly one of the most beautiful and elegant places for food and drink in Providence, Costantino's Ristorante on Federal Hill is decorated in soft shades of celadon green, gold and apricot. The first-floor lounge – perfect for pre-dinner cocktails and appetizers, as well as after-dinner drinks, coffee and desserts – is filled with love seats, wingback chairs, and a stunning pink marble bar, imported from Italy. Crystal chandeliers, gilded mirrors, and romantic works of art complete the picture. A mural of the Italian countryside by Ron Dabelle graces the stairway wall. The upper level, as well as the outdoor cafe in warm weather, serves traditional Italian cuisine.

GRAPEVINE GEM: Wine lovers will be delighted with the reasonably priced vintages on Costantino's wine list. In addition to more than 20 wines by the glass, Costantino's is also known for its authentic Bellini cocktail, the same as the one served at the famous Harry's Bar in Venice.

INSIDE SCOOP

CHEF	ALBERTO LOPEZ	LIQUOR	FULL LIQUOR
OWNER	ALAN COSTANTINO		EXTENSIVE WINE LIST WITH BOTTLES
OPEN SINCE	2002		RANGING FROM $15 TO $300
CUISINE	TRADITIONAL ITALIAN	SMOKING	ALLOWED ONLY ON
SPECIALTY	VEAL RIB EYE CHOP STUFFED		THE OUTDOOR PATIO
	WITH CIAMBELLA AL ALIO	SERVICES	BANQUET FACILITIES
PRICE RANGE	APPETIZERS $8 TO $17		HEALTHY/LOW-FAT MENU ITEMS
	ENTREES $12 TO $22		VEGETARIAN MENU ITEMS
CREDIT CARDS	MAJOR CREDIT CARDS ACCEPTED		HANDICAPPED ACCESSIBLE
RESERVATIONS	RECOMMENDED		PRIVATE DINING ROOM
HOURS	MONDAY THROUGH THURSDAY,	DRESS CODE	CASUAL TO DRESSY
	5 TO 10 P.M.	PARKING	ON THE STREET, IN NEARBY LOTS
	FRIDAY AND SATURDAY,		AND THROUGH THE VALET SERVICE
	5 TO 11 P.M.		

APPETIZERS

PORTOBELLO MUSHROOM CAP OVER SAUTÉED BROCCOLI RABE AND TOPPED
WITH SMOKED MOZZARELLA

BRUSCHETTA (HOMEMADE GRILLED BREAD) TOPPED WITH A PATE OF
EGGPLANT, BLACK OLIVES, PUREE OF CANNELLINI BEANS, WITH EXTRA
VIRGIN OLIVE OIL AND SHAVED PARMIGIANO-REGGIANO

BEEF CARPACCIO WITH TRADITIONAL TOPPINGS OVER BABY ARUGULA, SHAVED
PARMIGIANO-REGGIANO AND EXTRA VIRGIN OLIVE OIL

BABY SPINACH LIGHTLY SAUTÉED IN EXTRA VIRGIN OLIVE OIL, WITH ROASTED
GARLIC, TOPPED WITH IMPORTED GOAT CHEESE AND CRUMBLED PANCETTA

ENTREES

HOMEMADE RIGATONI WITH BABY ARUGULA, GARLIC, EXTRA VIRGIN OLIVE OIL,
WHITE WINE, AND IMPORTED SPECK, FINISHED WITH PECORINO-ROMANO

HOMEMADE GNOCCHI WITH FRESH MOZZARELLA, BASIL AND PLUM TOMATOES

FRESH PENNETTA WITH SWEET SAUSAGE IN AGLIO E OLIO SAUCE WITH FRESH
DICED TOMATOES AND BABY SPINACH

PROVIMI VEAL POUNDED THIN AND GRILLED WITH EXTRA VIRGIN OLIVE OIL,
GARLIC, WILD MUSHROOMS, TOMATOES AND WHITE WINE

PAN-SEARED FILET MIGNON RUBBED WITH A BLACK TRUFFLE BUTTER

YELLOWFIN TUNA, MARINATED IN GREEN ONION, BASIL, EXTRA VIRGIN OLIVE
OIL, BALSAMIC VINEGAR AND LEMON, THEN GRILLED AND TOPPED WITH
CHERRY TOMATOES AND CAPER BERRIES

VEAL RIB EYE CHOP
STUFFED WITH CIAMBELLA AL ALIO

Serves 1

1 (10-ounce) rib eye veal chop
4-ounce wedge ciambella al alio (cow's milk cheese infused with garlic)
Kosher salt and freshly ground black pepper, to taste
Olive oil, as needed
1 tablespoon unsalted butter
1 shallot, chopped very fine
1 cup red wine (Barolo or Burgundy is recommended)
1 sprig fresh thyme
1/2 cup veal stock

With a very sharp knife, make an incision through the eye of the veal chop, forming a pocket. Stuff the cheese wedge into the veal chop. Season the veal chop with salt and pepper. In a hot skillet, sear the veal chop in a little olive oil until golden brown on both sides. Remove the veal chop from the pan and place in a preheated 375-degree oven until well done, approximately 20 minutes.

In the same skillet, combine the butter and shallots. Cook until the shallots are translucent. Add the wine. Simmer until wine is reduced by three-quarters. Add the fresh thyme and veal stock. Reduce by half. Season to taste with more salt and pepper.

Remove veal chop from oven. Pour sauce over veal chop just before serving. This recipe can easily be doubled.

Venda Ravioli storefront

Don Jose Tequilas

SOUTH OF THE BORDER

Authentic upscale Mexican cuisine at affordable prices is offered at Don Jose Tequilas, one of the few non-Italian restaurants in the Federal Hill section of Providence. Owner Jaime Gaviria often greets his guests and makes sure they are totally satisfied. Chef Raquel Diaz comes from a restaurant family in Yucatan, Mexico, and worked at La Golondina in Los Angeles. One of the best dishes on the menu is the Pork in Green Sauce with Cactus. Open for lunch and dinner, the dining room at Don Jose Tequilas is warm and friendly, just like the restaurants down Mexico way.

PORK IN GREEN SAUCE WITH CACTUS

Serves 4

2 tablespoons vegetable oil

1 1/4-pound pork shoulder, cut into 1-inch cubes

1 onion, finely chopped

2 garlic cloves, crushed

1 teaspoon dried oregano

3 fresh jalapeno chiles, seeded and chopped

2 cups canned tomatillos (green tomatoes), drained

2/3 cup vegetable stock

11-ounce jar nopalitos (cactus), drained

Salt and freshly ground black pepper, to taste

Fresh corn tortillas, warmed

Heat the oil in a large saucepan. Add the pork cubes and cook over high heat, turning several times, until browned all over. Add the onion and garlic; sauté gently until soft, then stir in the oregano and chopped jalapenos. Cook for 2 more minutes.

Place the tomatillos in a blender, add the stock and process until smooth. Add to the pork mixture; cover and cook for 30 minutes.

Meanwhile, soak the nopalitos in cold water for 10 minutes. Drain, then add to the pork; continue cooking for about 10 minutes or until the pork is cooked through and tender.

Season the mixture with salt and plenty of freshly ground black pepper. Serve with fresh corn tortillas.

INSIDE SCOOP

CHEF	RAQUEL DIAZ	SMOKING	NO
OWNER	JAIME GAVIRIA	SERVICES	CHILDREN'S MENU
OPEN SINCE	2000		HEALTHY/LOW-FAT MENU ITEMS
CUISINE	AUTHENTIC UPSCALE MEXICAN		VEGETARIAN MENU ITEMS
SPECIALTY	SHRIMP IN TEQUILA		HANDICAPPED ACCESSIBLE
	SAUCE, PAELLA		TAKE-OUT ORDERS AVAILABLE
PRICE RANGE	APPETIZERS $4 TO $11		CATERING
	ENTREES $10 TO $18	DRESS CODE	CASUAL
CREDIT CARDS	MAJOR CREDIT CARDS ACCEPTED	PARKING	AVAILABLE ON THE STREET
RESERVATIONS	RECOMMENDED		
HOURS	OPEN SEVEN DAYS A WEEK		
	FOR LUNCH AND DINNER		
	SATURDAY/SUNDAY BRUNCH		
LIQUOR	FULL LIQUOR		

APPETIZERS

QUESO FUNDIDO — A BLEND OF BAKED CHEESES WITH MEXICAN CHORIZO

CEVICHE — MEXICAN SEAFOOD COCKTAIL

NACHOS MACHOS — TORTILLA CHIPS WITH BEANS, CHEESE, PICO DE GALLO, SOUR CREAM, GUACAMOLE AND SPICY SALSA

BURRITO WITH SHRIMP

ENTREES

ENCHILADAS TAPATIAS — FILLED WITH CHICKEN, GUAJILLO SAUCE, GOAT CHEESE AND SOUR CREAM

YUCATAN-STYLE ROAST PORK SLOW-COOKED IN PLANTAIN LEAVES, SERVED IN A MILD ACHIOTE SAUCE

CHIMICHANGAS FILLED WITH CHICKEN, TOPPED WITH RED AND GREEN SALSA AND MONTEREY JACK CHEESE

CHILE RELLENO DE QUESO

CHICKEN BREAST WITH CHORIZO, POBLANO PEPPERS AND MONTEREY CHEESE, SERVED IN A MOLE SAUCE

BRAISED GOAT SHANKS IN A GUAJILLO SAUCE

IT ADDS UP

Generous servings of contemporary world cuisine is what's on the menu at Downcity Food + Cocktails, where chef-owners Anthony Salemme and Paul Shire constantly outdo one another in their tiny kitchen. These guys really know how to cook. Their slightly wacky menu is seasonally inspired with Mediterranean and Caribbean influences. Mom's Meatloaf is so good, it's served year round. Our personal favorite: the Buffalo Chicken Salad – positively addictive. We recommend you begin your festive dining experience with one of the signature cocktails while you give the creative menu serious consideration. All the desserts, including the award-winning Lemon Blueberry Cheesecake, are prepared in-house. The artsy decor is American eclectic, and so is the fun-loving staff who make every customer feel most welcome. Don't be surprised if you get a great big sincere hug from a certain waitress.

GRAPEVINE GEM: Downcity also offers a full-service catering menu, one of the best in the state.

INSIDE SCOOP

CHEFS-OWNERS:	ANTHONY SALEMME AND PAUL SHIRE	LIQUOR:	FULL LIQUOR
OPEN SINCE:	1990	SMOKING:	PERMITTED AT BAR
CUISINE:	CONTEMPORARY WORLD CUISINE	SERVICES:	HEALTHY/LOW-FAT MENU ITEMS
SPECIALTY:	LOOSELY MADE RAVIOLI		VEGETARIAN MENU ITEMS
PRICE RANGE:	APPETIZERS $6 TO $10		HANDICAPPED ACCESSIBLE
	ENTREES $14 TO $24		CATERING
CREDIT CARDS:	MAJOR CREDIT CARDS ACCEPTED		SATURDAY/SUNDAY BRUNCH
RESERVATIONS:	RECOMMENDED ON WEEKENDS	DRESS CODE:	CASUAL
HOURS:	LUNCH:	PARKING:	AVAILABLE ON THE STREET AND IN NEARBY PARKING LOTS
	MONDAY THROUGH FRIDAY,		
	DINNER:		
	TUESDAY AND WEDNESDAY, 5:30 TO 9 P.M.		
	THURSDAY TO SATURDAY. 5:30 TO 10 P.M.		
	SUNDAY DINNER, 4:30 TO 8 P.M.		
	SATURDAY AND SUNDAY BRUNCH		
	(DURING THE SUMMER, THE RESTAURANT WILL BE CLOSED ON SUNDAY EVENINGS.)		

APPETIZERS

FINNAN HADDIE SEAFOOD CHOWDER WITH CLAM AND LEEK FRITTERS

VIDALIA ONION AND GRUYERE TART WITH ROASTED PEPPER COULIS AND MIXED
GREENS

SPICY BEEF AND PEPPER JACK CHEESE QUESADILLA WITH SALSA VERDE

MUSSELS STEAMED WITH LEMON GRASS AND RED CURRY SAUCE

PANKO-CRUSTED TUNA LOLLIPOPS WITH HOISIN AND WASABI DRIZZLE

ENTREES

CORIANDER-CRUSTED FILET MIGNON WITH JALAPENO DEMIGLACE AND POTATO
WITH TRUFFLE CHIVE BUTTER

GRILLED ROSEMARY LAMB TENDERLOINS WITH CITRUS GREMOLATA OVER WILD
MUSHROOM/PARMESAN RISOTTO

VEAL SAUTÉED WITH BABY SPINACH, GRILLED RADICCHIO, PINE NUTS AND
FRESH MOZZARELLA OVER CAPELLINI

FRENCH RACK OF PORK WITH GREEN PEPPERCORN SAUCE AND GREEN APPLE,
WALNUT AND STILTON STRUDEL

BLACKENED FARM-RAISED CATFISH WITH ROCK CRAB GRITS AND COOL LIME
AIOLI

CODFISH BAKED WITH PLUM TOMATOES, PEPPER, SPRING ONIONS AND
VERMOUTH OVER LOBSTER BRANDADE

LOBSTER/CHANTERELLE MUSHROOM RISOTTO
Serves 4

1 tablespoon butter
1 garlic clove minced
1 small tomato, peeled, seeded and chopped
15 chanterelle mushrooms, chopped
1 cup cooked lobster meat, from about 3 chicken lobsters
3 tablespoons olive oil
2 tablespoons diced shallots
2 tablespoons finely diced carrot
2 tablespoons diced celery
1 1/2 cups arborio rice
1/2 cup dry white wine
5 cups lobster broth
1 tablespoon butter
1/2 cup grated Parmesan cheese
1 tablespoon chopped parsley

Heat butter in a small skillet over moderat heat. Add the garlic and tomato; cook about 1 minute. Add chanterelle mushrooms and cook until soft. Add lobster meat and as soon as it is heated through, remove pan from heat; set aside.

Pour olive oil into large sauté pan, add shallots, carrots and celery; sauté for 1 to 2 minutes to soften, but don't brown them. Add rice to sauté pan; stir with a wooden spoon for about 1 minute. Add wine and stir until evaporated. Add the lobster broth 1/2 cup at a time, stirring until broth is almost totally absorbed before adding the next batch.

After all liquid is absorbed (approximately 18 minutes), add ingredients from small skillet, folding them in. Add butter, grated cheese and chopped parsley. Stir well and serve immediately.

Eclectic Grille

RUSTIC, ROMANTIC CHARM

This stylish Federal Hill restaurant offers upscale fine dining with a Mediterranean flair. In warm weather, the large front windows open, allowing guests to gaze at window boxes overflowing with flowers while they dine on food that has been cooked to order. The chef changes the menu quarterly. Year after year, the handmade giant tortelloni has won awards. This popular restaurant is much larger than it appears to be from the street. The bar area glows in shades of yellow and gold, offset with dark woods and a rough-hewn floor. The main dining room exudes European warmth with its exposed brick walls and offers patrons a view of the busy, open kitchen.

GRAPEVINE GEM: The Eclectic Grille had such success in its early days, it had to move to larger quarters. Even in the larger space, it's often hard to get a table.

INSIDE SCOOP

OWNERS	JOSEPH, KAREN AND ANTHONY ROCCHIO	LIQUOR	FULL LIQUOR
		SMOKING	PERMITTED
OPEN SINCE	1994	SERVICES	VEGETARIAN MENU ITEMS
CUISINE	MADE-TO-ORDER UPSCALE FUN FOOD WITH A MEDITERRANEAN FLAIR		HANDICAPPED ACCESSIBLE
			TAKE-OUT ORDERS AVAILABLE
		DRESS CODE	CASUAL
SPECIALTY	GRILLED FILET MIGNON WITH A PORCINI MUSHROOM DEMIGLACE	PARKING	AVAILABLE ON THE STREET AND THROUGH THE VALET SERVICE
PRICE RANGE	APPETIZERS $9 TO $15 ENTREES $14 TO $35		
CREDIT CARDS	MAJOR CREDIT CARDS ACCEPTED		
RESERVATIONS	RECOMMENDED		
HOURS	OPEN SEVEN DAYS A WEEK FOR DINNER MONDAY THROUGH THURSDAY, 5 TO 10 P.M. FRIDAY AND SATURDAY, 5 TO 11 P.M. SUNDAY, 4:30 TO 9 P.M.		

APPETIZERS

PORTABELLO WITH POLENTA, GREENS, DRIED CHERRIES AND BLUE CHEESE
CRISP LOBSTER WITH WATERCRESS AND SWEET CHILI OIL
CLAMS AND MUSSELS WITH GREEN ONION, LINGUICA AND FRIED GARLIC
ANTIPASTO OF CURED MEATS, AGED CHEESES AND SEASONED OLIVES
GREENS WITH HARICOTS VERTS, HAZELNUTS, TOMATO AND LEMON SOY
ARUGULA WITH CANDIED WALNUTS, GOAT CHEESE, DATES AND FENNEL

ENTREES

LINGUINE WITH LITTLENECKS, PANCETTA, FRIED GARLIC AND PARSLEY
SWEET RED PEPPER LINGUINE WITH CHICKEN, SAUSAGE, RED PEPPERS AND
    MADEIRA WINE
VEAL CHOP WITH CARAMELIZED FENNEL, SOFT POLENTA, FIG JAM, AND
    CITRUS GASTRIQUE
PAELLA WITH LOBSTER, MUSSELS, SCALLOPS, LINGUICA AND SAFFRON RICE
HALIBUT WITH LOBSTER FRIED RICE, ORANGE SYRUP AND BASIL OIL
OLIVE-RUBBED TUNA WITH WHITE BEAN, SWISS CHARD, BALSAMIC EMULSION
    AND SAFFRON
OSSO BUCO WITH TINY ONIONS, LARDONS, TRUFFLE MAC AND CHEESE
PORK LOIN WITH APPLE BRANDY BUTTER, POTATO AND HARICOTS VERTS
PRIME FILET WITH GRILLED ASPARAGUS, TOMATO GINGER JAM AND PORT GLAZE

PORTABELLO AND WILD MUSHROOM CROSTINI

Serves 4

4 large portabello mushrooms, roasted
1 pound wild mushrooms (shiitake, morel, etc.)
3 garlic cloves
10 sage leaves
2 plum tomatoes
4 sprigs flat parsley
1 French baguette, sliced 1/2-inch thick (12 pieces)
Olive oil, as needed
Kosher salt, to taste
Freshly ground black pepper, to taste
1 cup dry sherry wine
1 cup chicken stock (salt-free canned chicken stock may be used)
1 stick unsalted butter

Remove stems and clean gills of portabello mushrooms. Clean wild mushrooms; remove stems and slice. Peel and slice garlic cloves. Remove stems of sage leaves. Cut plum tomatoes in half; remove seeds and chop into 1/2-inch pieces. Wash, dry, and chop parsley.

Grill or roast baguette slices; place 3 pieces on each plate.

Brush portabello mushroom caps with olive oil; lightly season with salt and pepper, and set one on each plate. Bring a large sauté pan to medium heat. Add 1/3 cup olive oil and garlic; sauté garlic until lightly browned. Add wild mushrooms and sage; sauté until olive oil coats the mushrooms. Add sherry and chicken stock; reduce the liquid by half. Add the butter, salt and pepper. When the butter is almost melted, add the chopped tomato and parsley. Distribute cooked mushroom mixture evenly on each plate. Serve immediately.

EMPIRE IN THE SUN

In the heart of the downtown Arts District, this Providence restaurant has an atmosphere that is simultaneously cool and sophisticated, warm and welcoming. The regional Italian cuisine tends to be sublime. Empire's Grand Antipasto is clearly the grandest around. Yes, that ever-popular calamari is on the menu, but here it's served with spicy pumpkin seed sauce. Less is often more, so consider Empire's Fluffy Gnocchi, served with browned butter and Parmigiano. The Spaghetti Carbonara is authentic, topped with a fried egg. The made-to-order desserts are truly extraordinary, especially the Roasted Peach Pie and the Chocolate-Filled Bomboloncino.

GRAPEVINE GEM: Chef Loren Falsone asks her guests to enjoy her creations as she intended, so no substitutions, please. This is one chef you can completely trust.

INSIDE SCOOP

CHEF-OWNER	LOREN FALSONE	LIQUOR	FULL LIQUOR
OPEN SINCE	1999	SMOKING	NOT ALLOWED
CUISINE	REGIONAL ITALIAN CUISINE	SERVICES	BANQUET FACILITIES
SPECIALTY	FOOD AND WINE PAIRINGS		CHILDREN'S ENTREES
PRICE RANGE	APPETIZERS $8 TO $16		VEGETARIAN MENU ITEMS
	ENTREES $16 TO $38		HANDICAPPED ACCESSIBLE
CREDIT CARDS	MAJOR CREDIT CARDS ACCEPTED		TAKE-OUT ORDERS AVAILABLE – PIZZA ONLY
RESERVATIONS	RECOMMENDED		PRIVATE DINING ROOM
HOURS	CLOSED MONDAY		OUTDOOR DINING
	TUESDAY THROUGH THURSDAY,	DRESS CODE	BUSINESS /CASUAL
	5 TO 10 P.M.	PARKING	FREE VALET PARKING OR IN NEARBY
	FRIDAY AND SATURDAY,		LOT AVAILABLE FOR TRINITY REPERTORY
	5 P.M. TO CLOSING		THEATER TICKET HOLDERS
	SUNDAY BRUNCH, 10:30 A.M. TO 2 P.M.		
	SUNDAY DINNER, 4 TO 9 P.M.		
	WEDNESDAYS ONLY – LUNCH		
	SERVED FROM 11:30 A.M. TO 2 P.M.		

APPETIZERS

GRAND ANTIPASTO (CRAB CAKES, PROSCIUTTO, SWEET SOPPRESSATA, OLIVES,
   MOZZARELLA, RED PEPPERS, CREAMY POLENTA, TORTA CARMELLA, BABY
   ARTICHOKES, ROASTED FIGS, SQUID AND WHITE BEAN SALAD AND
   CROSTINI)
FRIED CALAMARI WITH SPICY PUMPKIN SEED SAUCE
CRISPY SCALLOP STECCHI WITH SPICY CARAMELIZED CARROT DIPPING SAUCE
FRIED CREAMY POLENTA WITH FOUR CHEESES AND SAUCE SCIUE-SCIUE
EMPIRE FRENCH FRIES WITH HOMEMADE KETCHUP AND LEMONY MAYONNAISE
CHEESE FONDUE WITH GARLIC CROSTINI

ENTREES

GRIDDLED SIRLOIN STEAK WITH CHIMICHURRI SAUCE, TOMATO AND RED
   ONION SALAD, GUACAMOLE AND FRENCH FRIES
BOUILLABAISSE WITH COD, SCALLOPS, SHRIMP, MUSSELS AND CALAMARI IN A
   SPICY AROMATIC SAFFRON BROTH WITH ROASTED RED PEPPER ROUILLE AND
   GARLIC CROSTINI
SEARED SCALLOP GRATIN WITH CARAMELIZED ONIONS, CARROT PUREE AND
   MUSHROOM RAVIOLI
MARINATED PORK PAILLARD WITH FRENCHED PORK CHOP, HOMEMADE
   SAUERKRAUT AND WHOLE GRAIN MUSTARD WITH CORN MEAL-BEER
   BATTERED ONION RINGS
SEARED DUCK BREAST AND FOIE GRAS WITH CRISPY POTATO CAKE, ENDIVE AND
   GORGONZOLA SALAD WITH FRESH MACHE

DESSERTS

DEEP CHOCOLATE POT DE CREME WITH WHIPPED CREAM AND TORCHETTA
LAVENDER PANNA COTTA WITH PISTACHIO BROYAGE, CARAMEL SAUCE AND
   WHIPPED CREAM
QUEEN BEE-ROSEWATER AND HONEY MOUSSE ON A CHOCOLATE HONEYCOMB
   WITH BARENJAGER CHOCOLATE SAUCE AND BEE POLLEN, LEMON
   SHORTBREAD AND HONEY DRIZZLE

SPAGHETTI CARBONARA
WITH SWEET ENGLISH PEAS, FRIED EGG AND PARMIGIANO
Serves 4

1/4 cup bacon, coarsely chopped
1 teaspoon pure olive oil
2 cups fresh heavy cream
2 tablespoons chopped parsley
1 teaspoon chopped rosemary
1 teaspoon chopped thyme
1/4 cup pasteurized egg yolks or 4 egg yolks

1 pound spaghetti (Empire uses Delverde)
1 cup sweet English peas (can be frozen)
Kosher salt and black pepper, to taste
1 tablespoon unsalted butter
4 large eggs
3/4 cup Parmigiano-Reggiano, freshly grated

Fry the bacon in the oil over medium heat until the bacon is well browned and the fat is complete rendered, lowering the heat as the bacon browns to continue the rendering without burning. Add heavy cream and scald over low heat. Remove from heat and allow the bacon to steep in the cream for about 20 minutes to infuse the cream with flavor.

Combine the chopped parsley, rosemary and thyme; set aside.

In a stainless steel bowl, whisk the egg yolks well. In a trickle, pour all the cream into the yolks while stirring constantly. Strain the bacon cream through a fine mesh strainer into a large saucepan to remove the bacon. Discard the bacon and set the bacon cream aside.

Bring 4 quarts of salted water to a boil. Add the spaghetti to the boiling water and cook, stirring occasionally for 9 minutes or until the pasta is soft but still firm (al dente). Drop the peas in to the boiling water when the pasta has been cooking for 5 minutes. Remove the cooked pasta with the peas to the saucepan containing the bacon cream. Fold the spaghetti into the cream with a large rubber spatula. The heat from the spaghetti will thicken the sauce a bit. Taste a strand of pasta and stir in a little kosher salt and black pepper, if necessary.

Add the butter to a large non-stick frying pan, big enough to fry 4 eggs, and begin to heat the pan over low to medium heat. Just before serving, fry the 4 eggs.

Divide the spaghetti and any extra bacon cream among 4 warm pasta bowls. Top each mound of spaghetti with a fried egg and sprinkle each with the Parmigiano-Reggiano and chopped herbs.

Estrela Do Mar

ETHNIC ELEGANCE

We are so fortunate to have several excellent Portuguese restaurants in Rhode Island. Quite possibly the most fancy is Estrela do Mar, offering fine Portuguese cuisine in a beautiful dining room, often filled with people of Portuguese descent – a good sign that this restaurant offers the real thing. Several classic dishes stand out: Chourico a Bombeiro, flamed grilled sausage; Caldo Verde, kale and chorizo in a potato broth; and Carne de Porco Alentejana, marinated pork with potatoes and littlenecks. Our favorite is the Bife a Casa, a sirloin steak topped with a slice of ham and egg, served with Portuguese fries in a clay pot. Now that's intriguing.

AMEIJOAS A BULHAO PATO
LITTLENECKS IN OLIVE OIL, GARLIC AND WINE SAUCE

Serves 2 to 4

1/3 cup olive oil
15 small littlenecks
10 cloves garlic, finely minced
1/2 cup dry white wine
1 tablespoon margarine
1 teaspoon mustard
1/4 cup chopped fresh cilantro
Lemon wedges, for garnish

In a large sauté pan over medium heat, warm the olive oil. Add littlenecks; cover and cook 5 to 8 minutes until clams open. Add garlic; cover and cook for 5 minutes. Add wine, margarine, mustard and fresh cilantro. Bring to a complete boil. Transfer the clams to a serving bowl and serve immediately. Garnish with lemon wedges.

INSIDE SCOOP

CHEFS	SEVERAL	SMOKING	PERMITTED IN BAR AREA ONLY
OWNER	GEORGE RODRIGUES	SERVICES	BANQUET FACILITIES
OPEN SINCE	1982		CHILDREN'S MENU
CUISINE	PORTUGUESE		HEALTHY/LOW-FAT MENU ITEMS
SPECIALTY	PAELHA AND BIFE A CASA		VEGETARIAN MENU ITEMS
PRICE RANGE	APPETIZERS $7 TO $9		HANDICAPPED ACCESSIBLE
	ENTREES $12 TO $22		TAKE-OUT ORDERS AVAILABLE
CREDIT CARDS	MAJOR CREDIT CARDS ACCEPTED		CATERING
RESERVATIONS	RECOMMENDED		PRIVATE DINING ROOM
HOURS	MONDAY THROUGH SUNDAY,	DRESS CODE	CASUAL
	11:30 A.M. TO 10 P.M.	PARKING	AVAILABLE ON THE PREMISES
LIQUOR	FULL LIQUOR		

APPETIZERS

LITTLENECKS IN OLIVE OIL, GARLIC AND WINE SAUCE
SAUTÉED SHRIMP IN BUTTER, WINE, GARLIC AND SPICES
FLAME-GRILLED PORTUGUESE SAUSAGE
FRIED CHICKEN WINGS
SEAFOOD BISQUE WITH SHRIMP, SCALLOPS AND CRABMEAT
KALE, CHORIZO IN POTATO BROTH

ENTREES

BAKED STUFFED JUMBO SHRIMP WITH SEAFOOD STUFFING
LOBSTER, SHRIMP, MUSSELS, SQUID, CRABMEAT AND FISH IN A SPICY
    RED SAUCE
PAELHA – LOBSTER, SHRIMP, MUSSELS, LITTLENECKS, SQUID,
    CRABMEAT, FISH, CHORIZO AND PORK WITH SAFFRON RICE IN A
    MILD RED SAUCE
GRILLED DRIED CODFISH IN OLIVE OIL AND GARLIC
BIFE A CASA – SIRLOIN STEAK TOPPED WITH A SLICE OF HAM AND
    EGG, SERVED WITH PORTUGUESE FRIES IN A CLAY POT
GRILLED MARINATED PORK CUTLETS TOPPED WITH ROASTED GARLIC
    AND RED WINE SAUCE

Ferns & Flowers Teahouse

1094 Centerville Road, Warwick | 401-821-1447 | www.ftd.com/fernsand

TEA FOR TWO

What a delight! With its lace-laden atmosphere, this is one restaurant that might appeal more to "the ladies who lunch." Nestled in a shady grove, Ferns & Flowers is a rambling 1860s farmhouse offering beautiful gifts, elegant home decor items, seasonal plants and pottery, as well as quaintly decorated rooms for quiet conversation and fine dining. Since Ferns & Flowers opened, it has been a very special destination restaurant, particularly for generations of mothers and daughters at breakfast, lunch or tea time. Dinner is also offered, but only on Thursday and Friday nights. The menu changes monthly, inspired by what local farmers, fishermen and wineries have to offer.

ROASTED VEGETABLE TORTA

Serves 8

1 (12-ounce) package polenta, refrigerated
24 ounces mascarpone cheese
6 eggs
1 cup shredded cheddar cheese
1 tablespoon garlic and herb seasoning
1 large eggplant

3 eggs, beaten
Bread crumbs, as needed
Olive oil, as needed
1 large jar roasted red peppers
1 large jar marinated artichoke hearts

Preheat oven to 350 degrees.

Spray 10-inch spring form pan with cooking spray. Line bottom with slices of polenta.

In a mixer, combine mascarpone, 6 eggs, cheddar cheese and seasoning; blend until smooth.

Peel eggplant and slice thinly. Dip in beaten eggs, then bread crumbs and sauté in olive oil over medium heat until tender.

Layer eggplant, roasted red peppers and artichokes in pan on top of polenta. Pour in cheese mixture. Bake at 350 degrees for 45 minutes until puffed.

INSIDE SCOOP

CHEF	MARK ROGERS	LIQUOR	WINE AND BEER ONLY
OWNER	MONICA GERARD	SMOKING	NO
OPEN SINCE	2000	SERVICES	HEALTHY/LOW-FAT MENU ITEMS
CUISINE	SIGNATURE DISHES INSPIRED		VEGETARIAN MENU ITEMS
	BY THE EARTH UTILIZING		HANDICAPPED ACCESSIBLE
	LOCAL AND REGIONAL		TAKE-OUT ORDERS AVAILABLE
	FARMERS, FISH AND WINERIES		PRIVATE DINING ROOM
SPECIALTY	ROASTED VEGETABLE TORTA		FIREPLACE
PRICE RANGE	APPETIZERS $5 TO $11	DRESS CODE	CASUAL
	ENTREES $11 TO $17	PARKING	AVAILABLE ON THE PREMISES
CREDIT CARDS	MAJOR CREDIT CARDS ACCEPTED		
RESERVATIONS	RECOMMENDED		
HOURS	TUESDAY THROUGH SATURDAY		
	FOR BREAKFAST AND LUNCH		
	SUNDAY – BREAKFAST ONLY		
	DINNER SERVED ONLY ON		
	THURSDAY AND FRIDAY NIGHTS		
	SATURDAY/SUNDAY BRUNCH		

APPETIZERS

ROASTED VEGETABLE TORTA
MEDITERRANEAN PIZZA WITH GRILLED CHICKEN, ARTICHOKES
    AND MASCARPONE CHEESE IN A POLENTA CRUST
MUSHROOM STRUDEL
CASHEW CHICKEN CREPE

LUNCH ENTREES

ROASTED DUCK SALAD WITH RASPBERRIES AND ORANGES ON ARUGULA
    AND BABY GREENS
ROASTED CHICKEN IN PUFF PASTRY WITH ARTICHOKE HEARTS,
    SPINACH, RED PEPPERS AND PARMESAN CHEESE

DINNER ENTREES

SEAFOOD CREPES WITH LOBSTER, SCALLOPS AND SHRIMP IN A SHERRY
    CREAM SAUCE
COCONUT SHRIMP
GRILLED PORK TENDERLOIN WITH BLACKBERRY BARBECUE SAUCE

15 Point Road

A POINT WELL TAKEN

Classical music plays softly in the background at this waterfront American bistro, where the food also leans toward the classical. Chef-owner Steven Renshaw has been in restaurant kitchens since 1970, honing his skills as the executive chef at Bailey's Beach and the White Horse Tavern in Newport, and as the sous chef at the Palm Beach Polo and Country Club. The man clearly knows how to please an upscale audience. His award-winning restaurant – overlooking the Sakonnet River at the Old Stone Bridge in Island Park – may be on the road less traveled, but 15 Point Road is very much worth the trip.

SEAFOOD MEDLEY

Serves 1

1/4 cup clarified butter
4 large scallops
4 extra-large shrimp
Seasoned flour, as needed
1/4 cup lobster
1/4 cup peeled and chopped tomatoes
1/4 cup dry white wine
1/2 cup heavy cream
1/4 cup broccoli flowerets
1 tablespoon chopped scallions
1 tablespoon chopped fresh basil
Salt and pepper, to taste

Heat the butter in a 12-inch sauté pan.

Dredge scallops and shrimp in seasoned flour; place in the sauté pan. Sauté for 30 seconds; add the lobster and tomatoes. Add the wine and bring to a boil; then add the heavy cream, broccoli, scallions and basil. Reduce to desired consistency and season with salt and pepper to taste.

To serve, pour into a puff pastry shell or over fresh pasta.

INSIDE SCOOP

CHEF	STEVEN RENSHAW	LIQUOR	FULL LIQUOR
OWNERS	LIZ AND STEVEN RENSHAW	SMOKING	PERMITTED ONLY IN THE LOUNGE
OPEN SINCE	1992 (CURRENT CHEF AND OWNERS TOOK OVER IN 1999)	SERVICES	BANQUET FACILITIES, LIMITED CHILDREN'S MENU, LIMITED
CUISINE	AMERICAN WITH AN OCCASIONAL CLASSICAL FLAIR		HEALTHY/LOW-FAT MENU ITEMS VEGETARIAN MENU ITEMS ON
SPECIALTY	BEEF WELLINGTON, DUCK A L'ORANGE		REQUEST HANDICAPPED ACCESSIBLE
PRICE RANGE	APPETIZERS $7 TO $9 ENTREES $14 TO $22		TAKE-OUT ORDERS AVAILABLE PRIVATE DINING ROOM
CREDIT CARDS	MAJOR CREDIT CARDS ACCEPTED	DRESS CODE	CASUAL BUT NO BEACH
RESERVATIONS	RECOMMENDED FOR PARTIES OF 6 OR MORE AND FOR SPECIAL OCCASIONS		ATTIRE ALLOWED
		PARKING	AVAILABLE ON THE PREMISES
HOURS	OPEN SEVEN DAYS A WEEK FOR DINNER		

APPETIZERS

STEAMED LITTLENECKS WITH A WHITE WINE AND GARLIC SAUCE

WILD MUSHROOMS IN A THYME BRANDY DEMIGLACE, SERVED IN A PUFF PASTRY SHELL

HOT AND SPICY SHRIMP WITH CRUSHED RED PEPPERS, CAJUN SPICES AND WHITE WINE

ENTREES

SHRIMP, SCALLOPS AND LITTLENECKS WITH MARINARA SAUCE OVER FETTUCCINE

LOBSTER MEAT AND VEAL MEDALLIONS IN A SHERRY CREAM SAUCE OVER FETTUCCINE

CHICKEN BREAST SAUTEED WITH APPLES, CELERY, LINGONBERRIES AND CHOPPED WALNUTS

CASSEROLE OF SEA SCALLOPS IN A WHITE WINE AND BUTTER CRUMB TOPPING

STEAK AU POIVRE

Florentine Grille

LOYAL FOLLOWING

Since 1992, Nick Iannuccilli has been pleasing people with his authentic Italian cooking at the Florentine Grille. Born in Bologna, Italy, and trained as a chef in Florence, Iannuccilli has many fans who go to his restaurant regularly for the upscale, yet rustic Italian regional cuisine. Often working the grill, the chef always has time to say hello to guests being seated. The award-winning menu offers many of the classic dishes from northern Italy. This North Providence restaurant is dark and romantic – you almost feel like you are in a "Godfather" movie when you dine there.

GRAPEVINE GEM: Over the years, Chef Nick Iannuccilli has cooked for famous and powerful people, including Frank Sinatra and Oscar Luigi Scalfaro, president of Italy.

INSIDE SCOOP

CHEF-OWNER	NICHOLAS LANNUCCILLI JR.	SMOKING	PERMITTED IN LOUNGE
OPEN SINCE	1992	SERVICES	BANQUET FACILITIES
CUISINE	TRUE REGIONAL ITALIAN COOKING,		CHILDREN'S MENU
	PREDOMINANTLY NORTHERN		HEALTHY/LOW-FAT MENU ITEMS
SPECIALTY	STEAKS AND VEAL CHOPS, PASTA		VEGETARIAN MENU ITEMS
	AND ANTIPASTO		HANDICAPPED ACCESSIBLE
PRICE RANGE	APPETIZERS $7 TO $12		TAKE-OUT ORDERS AVAILABLE
	ENTREES $12 TO $27		CATERING
CREDIT CARDS	MAJOR CREDIT CARDS ACCEPTED		PRIVATE DINING ROOM
RESERVATIONS	RECOMMENDED, ESPECIALLY ON		FIREPLACES
	WEEKENDS	DRESS CODE	CASUAL
HOURS	OPEN SEVEN NIGHTS A WEEK	PARKING	AVAILABLE IN A NEARBY LOT
	FOR DINNER		AND THROUGH THE VALET SERVICE
LIQUOR	FULL LIQUOR		

APPETIZERS

SAUTEED PORTABELLO, CRIMINI, PORCINI AND SHIITAKE MUSHROOMS WITH TRUFFLE OIL ATOP PROSCIUTTO AND GOAT CHEESE

JUMBO SHRIMP, GRILLED AND SERVED OVER SAUTEED SPINACH AND PROSCIUTTO

CARPACCIO OF FILET MIGNON, ROLLED WITH HERBS AND MIXED CHEESE, LIGHTLY SEARED, OVER SAUTEED SPINACH

PIZZA WITH TOMATO SAUCE, JALAPENOS AND RED ONION

CALAMARI WITH TOMATOES, GARLIC, RED ONION, MASCARPONE CHEESE AND AGED BALSAMIC VINEGAR

ENTREES

SPAGHETTI WITH SAUTEED BABY GREENS, OLIVE OIL, GARLIC AND PARMIGIANO

PAPPARDELLE WITH VEAL TOMATO SAUCE

CAPELLINI PASTA WITH SHRIMP, ASPARAGUS, DELICATE TOMATO SAUCE, MASCARPONE AND BASIL

GRILLED T-BONE STEAK PREPARED WITH OLIVE OIL, LEMON AND ROSEMARY

EXTRA-THICK VEAL CHOP WITH OLIVE OIL, PINOT GRIGIO AND HERBS

SALMON FILET TOPPED WITH COOL TOMATO SALAD

THE BEST JUST GOT BETTER

For years, The Gatehouse has been looked upon as one of the best and certainly one of the most romantic restaurants in the state. Thanks to new owner Jaime D'Oliveira, The Gatehouse is now more beautiful than ever with a breathtaking renovation by Jaime's wife, Kim Nathanson D'Oliveira. With one of the city's rare waterviews, the new Gatehouse offers seafood as its specialty with the creative team of Chefs Steve Marsella and Holly Dion in the kitchen. This multi-level jewel of a restaurant also offers up a jazz club late at night. How cool is that?

GRAPEVINE GEM: Located in the Richmond Square area on the East Side of Providence, The Gatehouse has plenty of free parking – a real novelty in any city.

INSIDE SCOOP

CHEFS	STEVE MARSELLA AND HOLLY DION	LIQUOR	FULL LIQUOR
OWNER	PROVIDENCE HOSPITALITY GROUP	SMOKING	PERMITTED IN BAR ONLY
OPEN SINCE	2003	SERVICES	BANQUET FACILITIES
CUISINE	AMERICAN REGIONAL SEAFOOD		HEALTHY/LOW-FAT MENU ITEMS
SPECIALTY	CIOPPINO		VEGETARIAN MENU ITEMS
PRICE RANGE	APPETIZERS $5 TO $10		TAKE-OUT ORDERS AVAILABLE
	ENTREES $16 TO $24		CATERING
CREDIT CARDS	MAJOR CREDIT CARDS ACCEPTED		PRIVATE DINING ROOM
RESERVATIONS	RECOMMENDED		FIREPLACES
HOURS	OPEN SEVEN DAYS A WEEK FOR DINNER	DRESS CODE	CASUAL
	SUNDAY THROUGH THURSDAY,	PARKING	AVAILABLE IN A LARGE PARKING
	5 TO 10 P.M.		LOT IN THE IMMEDIATE AREA
	FRIDAY AND SATURDAY, 5 TO 11 P.M.		
	SATURDAY AND SUNDAY BRUNCH		

APPETIZERS

RAW SELECT OYSTERS ON THE HALF SHELL WITH CHAMPAGNE MIGNONETTE

CHILLED LOBSTER COCKTAIL

NEW ORLEANS-STYLE BARBECUED SHRIMP

FRIED CLAM TART WITH SPICY GARLIC AIOLI

BUTTERNUT SQUASH BISQUE WITH SHERRY SPICE BUTTER

WOOD-GRILLED TUNA NICOISE SALAD

FRISEE AND POACHED SECKEL PEAR SALAD WITH ROQUEFORT AND ROASTED
   PECAN VINAIGRETTE

ENTREES

FRIED OYSTER AND SHRIMP PO'BOY SANDWICH

WOOD-GRILLED CHIMICHURRI SKIRT STEAK

BLACKENED AHI TUNA STEAK FRITES

ANGEL HAIR PASTA AND LITTLENECK CLAMS ARRABBIATA

SLOW-ROASTED BONELESS DUCK

WOOD-GRILLED PORK TENDERLOIN AND LITTLNECK CLAMS

WOOD-GRILLED VEGETABLES WITH SAGE GNOCCHI

CREAMY SCALLOP, CORN AND GARLIC SOUP

Serves 6

1 large head garlic, separated into about 20 large cloves with any green parts removed
4 cups rich fish stock or clam juice
2 large russet potatoes, peeled and cut into 1/2-inch cubes
1 cup heavy cream
2 cups fresh yellow corn, cut from the cob (about 3 ears) and blanched for 1 minute
1 pound bay scallops or sea scallops (if using sea scallops, cut in half crosswise)
Salt, to taste
6 pats unsalted butter
Cayenne pepper, to taste
1 tablespoon finely minced Italian parsley
1 tablespoon separated chive flowers

Place the garlic cloves in a large heavy-bottomed saucepan and cover with 2 cups of fish stock. Bring to a boil over medium heat. Reduce heat to low and cook garlic, covered, until soft, about 10 minutes. Add the potatoes and cook, covered, until soft, about 15 more minutes.

Puree the mixture in a food processor or blender and return to the saucepan. Add the remaining 2 cups of fish stock and the cream; cook over medium heat, whisking slowly but steadily, until slightly thickened, about 10 minutes. Do not let the soup boil. Add the scallops. Cook until the scallops are tender, about 4 minutes. Season the soup with salt.

To assemble: Place a spoonful of corn in the center of each bowl. Using a slotted spoon, arrange the scallops on top of the corn. Pour the broth around. Place a pat of butter on top of the scallops in the middle of the bowl, then sprinkle with the cayenne pepper, chopped parsley and chive flowers.

Gracie's Bar & Grille

409 Atwells Avenue (Federal Hill), Providence | 401-272-7811 | www.gracie'sprov.com

AMAZING GRACE

This is the kind of neighborhood restaurant we're always looking for, the romantic corner eatery you might frequent several times a week. Owner Ellen Gracyalny wants to make her guests feel welcome, and Chef Champe Speidel's food keeps everyone coming back for more. Speidel has left his culinary calling card at some of the best restaurants in Providence as well as the Ritz-Carlton in St. Thomas and Clio in Boston. His diverse seasonal menu offers Italian and French influences with a new American twist. Highly recommended is the Boneless Lamb Wrapped in Phyllo Pastry, which serves two people. You'll see stars when you dine at Gracie's.

One of the best dishes to come out of the kitchen at Gracie's is the Boneless Lamb Rib, wrapped in phyllo, with diced vegetables, goat cheese, potato puree and mint jus. The potato puree is absolute perfection and so easy to make. Here is the recipe:

POTATO PUREE

Serves 2

1 pound Yukon gold potatoes, peeled and quartered
3/4 cup cream
2 tablespoons butter

Boil the Yukon gold potatoes in water until tender; drain and push through a strainer to ensure all pieces are the same size. Add the cream and butter. Using a food processor, puree. Keep warm.

INSIDE SCOOP

CHEF	CHAMPE SPEIDEL	CREDIT CARDS	MAJOR CREDIT CARDS ACCEPTED
OWNER	ELLEN GRACYALNY	RESERVATIONS	RECOMMENDED
OPEN SINCE	1999	HOURS	TUESDAY THROUGH SUNDAY FOR
CUISINE	SEASONAL PRODUCE		DINNER
	WITH A VARIETY OF MEATS	LIQUOR	FULL LIQUOR
	AND SEAFOOD, EMPHASIZING	SMOKING	PERMITTED AT THE BAR
	A VERY MODERN BUT	SERVICES	BANQUET FACILITIES
	AUSTERE PRESENTATION		HEALTHY/LOW-FAT MENU ITEMS
SPECIALTY	BONELESS RIB OF LAMB		VEGETARIAN MENU ITEMS
	WRAPPED IN PHYLLO WITH		TAKE-OUT ORDERS AVAILABLE
	DICED VEGETABLES, POTATO	DRESS CODE	CASUAL
	PUREE AND MINT JUS	PARKING	AVAILABLE ON THE STREET
PRICE RANGE	APPETIZERS $7 TO $10		
	ENTREES $16 TO $27		

APPETIZERS

TRUFFLE AGNOLOTTI WITH BROWN BUTTER, BALSAMIC AND
    PARMIGIANO-REGGIANO
SEARED SEA SCALLOPS WITH LOBSTER RAVIOLI, LEEK CREAM AND BASIL
SALAD OF GRILLED BEEF TENDERLOIIN, ROASTED ONIONS, POTATO
    PUREE AND FRESH GREEN BEANS

ENTREES

GRILLED TENDERLOIN OF PORK WITH A SUMMER SALSA OF WHITE
    BEANS, PEACHES, LOCAL CORN AND RED PEPPERS
ROASTED NEW YORK STRIP LOIN WITH WILD MUSHROOM RAGOUT, RED
    BLISS POTATO AND WILD THYME JUS
ROASTED VEAL CHOP WITH CHANTERELLE MUSHROOMS AND
    ROSEMARY POTATOES WITH SHALLOTS
GRILLED SWORDFISH LOIN AND SUMMER RATATOUILLE WITH A
    PARSLEY AND LEMON EMULSION
SHELLFISH RISOTTO WITH SHRIMP, JUMBO SCALLOPS, LOBSTER,
    CALAMARI, SAFFRON, FRESH PEAS AND SPRING ONION

Hanson's Landing

MARGARITAVILLE

Hanson's Landing is one of Rhode Island's best-kept secrets, the kind of quaint waterside restaurant and pub you're reluctant to rave about for fear crowds will come and prevent you from getting your favorite seat at the bar. Hanson's Landing is especially popular in the summer with the boating crowd that keeps its vessels docked nearby at the head of Salt Pond. Many a good time has been had here, especially on the deck where Jimmy Buffett tunes can usually be heard. The food on the seasonal menu, especially the seafood, is quite good. If you have nothing else, make sure you try the Lobster Cheesecake, the signature appetizer at Hanson's Landing.

CHICKEN MR. JOE
Serves 4

4 boneless, skinless chicken breasts
Flour, as needed
Clarified butter or oil, as needed
4 mild Italian sausage links, sliced
1 tablespoon chopped shallots
1/2 tablespoon chopped garlic
1 cup white wine
1 cup chicken stock
2 cups spinach, stems removed
1 cup chopped tomatoes
1/2 cup Parmesan cheese

Dredge chicken breasts in flour and sauté in large hot pan using clarified butter or oil. When golden brown, add sliced Italian sausage, shallots and garlic. Deglaze pan with white wine; reduce and add chicken stock. Cook for 1 minute and add spinach and tomatoes. Cook for 2 minutes and finish with Parmesan cheese.

Variation: Shrimp and scallops can be used in place of chicken.

INSIDE SCOOP

CHEFS	MATHEW AND ELLEN BOYLE	HOURS	OPEN SEVEN DAYS A WEEK
OWNERS	RICHARD NAGLE AND		FOR LUNCH AND DINNER
	SARAH BLIVEN	LIQUOR	FULL LIQUOR
OPEN SINCE	1996	SMOKING	PERMITTED
CUISINE	NON-TRADITIONAL, SEAFOOD-	SERVICES	CHILDREN'S MENU
	ORIENTED NUOVO CUISINE		HEALTHY/LOW-FAT MENU ITEMS
SPECIALTY	POACHED SALMON ARUGULA		VEGETARIAN MENU ITEMS
	WITH WHITE WINE GARLIC SAUCE		HANDICAPPED ACCESSIBLE
	ASIAN-MARINATED TUNA STEAK		TAKE-OUT ORDERS AVAILABLE
PRICE RANGE	APPETIZERS $3 TO $8		FIREPLACE
	ENTREES $4 TO $26	DRESS CODE	CASUAL
CREDIT CARDS	MAJOR CREDIT CARDS ACCEPTED	PARKING	AVAILABLE ON THE PREMISES
RESERVATIONS	RECOMMENDED		

APPETIZERS

RED OR WHITE CLAMS ZUPPA IN WHITE WINE WITH GARLIC, BUTTER AND FRESH BASIL
LOBSTER CHEESECAKE
HOISIN-GLAZED SHRIMP AND SCALLOP BROCHETTES
SONOMA SALAD – ROASTED VEGETABLES AND BLACK BEANS SERVED OVER SPINACH AND MESCLUN, WITH FETA CHEESE IN A BALSAMIC DRESSING

ENTREES

ASIAN-MARINATED TUNA WITH SESAME OIL, BLACK SOY, GARLIC AND SCALLIONS
FISHERMAN'S STEW WITH COD, MUSSELS, CLAMS, SHRIMP, SCLLOPS AND NEW POTATOES IN A SPICY TOMATO BROTH
MEDALLIONS OF PORK LOIN WITH AN HERB CRUST AND A TARRAGON DIJON SAUCE
CHICKEN STUFFED WITH PROSCIUTTO AND WILD MUSHROOMS IN A WHITE WINE-CAPER-LEMON ZEST BUTTER
STEAK WITH CAJUN BLUE CHEESE SAUCE

Haruki

BRING ON THE WASABI

Owner Haruki Kibe claims to have the largest sushi bar in Rhode Island, and his Cranston restaurant is known for using only the freshest ingredients. In fact, Haruki, the restaurant, has one of the finest reputations in the state. Chefs Yuji Suzuki and Alen Sung were trained in Japan, and their authentic menu – which includes vegetarian items – reflects their decades of experience. The open and airy restaurant has a definite Asian atmosphere. Offering lunch and dinner, Haruki has plenty of free parking, a nice surprise for anyone used to dining out in major cities.

INSIDE SCOOP

CHEFS	YUJI SUZUKI AND ALEN SUNG	LIQUOR	FULL LIQUOR
OWNER	HARUKI KIBE	SMOKING	NO
OPEN SINCE	1986	SERVICES	CHILDREN'S MENU
CUISINE	JAPANESE		VEGETARIAN MENU ITEMS
SPECIALTY	SUSHI		HANDICAPPED ACCESSIBLE
PRICE RANGE	APPETIZERS $4 TO $7		TAKE-OUT ORDERS AVAILABLE
	ENTREES $14 TO $19		CATERING
CREDIT CARDS	MAJOR CREDIT CARDS ACCEPTED		PRIVATE DINING ROOM
RESERVATIONS	ONLY TAKEN ON WEEKDAYS	DRESS CODE	CASUAL
HOURS	LUNCH ON WEEKDAYS	PARKING	AVAILABLE ON THE PREMISES
	DINNER SEVEN NIGHTS A WEEK		

APPETIZERS

MISO SOUP

WAKAKYU – CUCUMBER AND WAKAMI SEAWEED WITH SANBAI
SU SAUCE

SUNOMO – CUCUMBER WAKAME WITH SAUCE AND MACKEREL
OR OCTOPUS

SHRIMP TEMPURA

PORK LOIN IN A LIGHT BREAD CRUMB BATTER, DEEP-FRIED
AND SERVED WITH SPECIAL SAUCE

CHICKEN TERIYAKI

GRILLED THIN SIRLOIN SLICES ROLLED WITH CHEESE AND
SCALLIONS IN A TERIYAKI SAUCE

ENTREES

FISH KATSU – WHITE FISH DIPPED IN A LIGHT BATTER, DEEP-FRIED
WITH A SPECIAL SAUCE

CRISPY CATFISH

SCALLOPS TERIYAKI

THICK NOODLES SERVED IN A LIGHT SOY BROTH WITH SHRIMP
TEMPURA, CHICKEN, SCALLOPS AND ASSORTED VEGETABLES TOPPED
WITH AN EGG

SUSHI AND SASHIMI COMBINATION

SUKI YAKI – THINLY SLICED PRIME RIB WITH FRESH SEASONAL
VEGETABLES AND TOFU SIMMERED IN SWEETENED SHOYU BROTH

HONEY BARBECUE PORK RIB

Hot Point

31 State Street, Bristol | 401-254-7474 | www.hotpointbistro.com

COOL FOOD

Foodies have been buzzing about Hot Point ever since it opened, and no wonder. This small casual bistro in quaint Bristol proudly claims to have "its own style of cooking." Chef-owner James Reardon learned how to cook on the job at some of the best restaurants around – Adesso, Cafe Nuovo, Clarke Cooke House, and Raphael Bar-Risto. With a menu that changes at least four times a year, Reardon prepares everything from scratch, even smoking his own bacon for his famous BLTs. He says he likes to serve comfort food, "comfortably twisted." What's not to like about that refreshing approach?

SANGRIA

Serves 20

2 cups freshly squeezed, pulp-free ruby red grapefruit juice
2 cups pulp-free pure orange juice
1 cup cranberry juice cocktail
1/2 cup freshly squeezed pulp-free lime juice
4 cups flat mineral water
1 3/4 cups granulated sugar
1 large bunch mint, freshly washed
1-foot cinnamon stick (or 6 regular-size)
1 cup fresh raspberries

3 liters Burgundy wine
10 pounds ice

Garnishes:
Maraschino cherries
Orange slices
Lime wedges

Bring all ingredients, except wine and ice, to a boil in a non-reactive container (such as stainless steel). Strain through a fine strainer. Allow liquid (sangria base) to cool. Chill sangria base overnight.

Fill large red wine glasses to the brim with ice. Fill glass almost full with Burgundy wine. Top off with sangria base. Stir well. Add garnishes.

Chef's tip: It's best to make the sangria ahead of time to chill overnight so the flavors come together. William Wycliff Burgundy jug wine is highly recommended.

INSIDE SCOOP

CHEF-OWNER	JAMES REARDON	LIQUOR	FULL LIQUOR
OPEN SINCE	1998	SMOKING	PERMITTED
CUISINE	COMFORT FOOD,	SERVICES	CHILDREN'S MENU
	COMFORTABLY TWISTED		HEALTHY/LOW-FAT MENU ITEMS
SPECIALTY	SEA SCALLOPS WITH		VEGETARIAN MENU ITEMS
	POLENTA, STEAK AU		TAKE-OUT ORDERS AVAILABLE
	POIVRE, MARINATED	DRESS CODE	CASUAL
	PORK TENDERLOIN	PARKING	AVAILABLE ON THE STREET
PRICE RANGE	APPETIZERS $9 TO $11		
	ENTREES $12 TO $35		
CREDIT CARDS	MAJOR CREDIT CARDS ACCEPTED		
RESERVATIONS	RECOMMENDED		
HOURS	TUESDAY THROUGH FRIDAY		
	FOR LUNCH		
	TUESDAY THROUGH SUNDAY		
	FOR DINNER		

APPETIZERS

MOZZARELLA CHEESE AND TOMATO SALAD

ANTIPASTO

BABY SPINACH SALAD WITH GREAT HILL BLUE CHEESE, PECANS, YELLOW AND RED TOMATOES WITH ORANGE-WALNUT SHERRY VINAIGRETTE

SESAME SHRIMP SALAD WITH GREEN BEANS, TOMATO, ORANGE SESAME RICE WINE VINAIGRETTE, SESAME SEEDS AND FIELD GREENS

LOBSTER BISQUE

ENTREES

CRISPY SEA SCALLOPS AND FRENCH FRIES

GRILLED SIRLOIN AND SHRIMP WITH A CHANTERELLE-PORTABELLO MUSHROOM SAUCE, GARLIC MASHED POTATOES AND VEGETABLE

BONELESS CHICKEN BREAST SAUTÉED WITH GARLIC, SAGE, PORTABELLO MUSHROOMS, MADEIRA WINE AND VEAL DEMIGLACE, TOPPED WITH PROSCIUTTO AND PROVOLONE, SERVED WITH FRESH FETTUCCINE AND WILTED SPINACH

SEA SCALLOPS SIMMERED IN A SPICY TOMATO SAUCE WITH CAPERS, GREEN OLIVES, CHIPOTLE, OREGANO, BASIL AND GARLIC

Il Fornello

16 Josephine Street, North Providence | 401-722-5599

OLD BLUE EYES WOULD APPROVE

On a side street in North Providence is Il Fornello, an unpretentious Italian restaurant with seriously good, authentic Italian food at very affordable prices. You'll dine by candlelight in a room filled with Italian music, from opera to Dino. Lovers of seafood, take note – the Linguine a la Pescatore is outstanding.

LINGUINE A LA PESCATORE

Serves 4

Olive oil, as needed
1 large onion, chopped
4 garlic cloves, minced
12 littlenecks
1 pound mussels
1 cup white wine
1 can (28 ounces) plum tomatoes

1/2 pound squid rings
8 large shrimp, shelled and cleaned
Salt, to taste
Pepper, to taste
Hot pepper flakes, to taste
1 pound linguine
Fresh basil, for garnish

In a sauce pan, heat the olive oil and sauté onions and garlic. Add littlenecks and mussels; simmer over meduim until garlic has browned. Add wine and plum tomatoes. Continue to cook until shellfish start to open, add squid and shrimp. Reduce heat to low; stir frequently, and remove when shrimp turns pink. Add salt, pepper and hot pepper flakes.

Cook linguine in boiling water until al dente. Serve the cooked linguine in a large pasta bowl, topped with the sauce and seafood. Garnish with fresh basil.

INSIDE SCOOP

CHEF	PHILIP NASISI	LIQUOR	FULL LIQUOR
OWNER	ANTHONY LANNI	SMOKING	PERMITTED
OPEN SINCE	1997	SERVICES	BANQUET FACILITIES
CUISINE	OLD WORLD MENU WITH		HEALTHY/LOW-FAT MENU ITEMS
	CONTEMPORARY FLAIR		VEGETARIAN MENU ITEMS
SPECIALTY	LINGUINE PESCATORE		HANDICAPPED ACCESSIBLE
PRICE RANGE	APPETIZERS $6 TO $10		TAKE-OUT ORDERS AVAILABLE
	ENTREES $11 TO $19		CATERING
CREDIT CARDS	MAJOR CREDIT CARDS ACCEPTED	DRESS CODE	UPSCALE/CASUAL
RESERVATIONS	RECOMMENDED	PARKING	AVAILABLE ON THE PREMISES
HOURS	OPEN MONDAY THROUGH		
	SATURDAY FOR DINNER		

APPETIZERS

CALAMARI FRITTI WITH GARLIC BUTTER, WHITE WINE AND HOT PEPPER RINGS

BRUSCHETTA WITH CANNELLINI BEANS SAUTÉED IN GARLIC BUTTER WITH RED ONIONS

GRILLED EGGPLANT STUFFED WITH PROSCIUTTO AND PROVOLONE CHEESE WITH BALSAMIC VINAIGRETTE

BATTERED GRILLED CHEESE AND PROSCIUTTO, DEEP FRIED AND TOPPED WITH MARINARA SAUCE

MUSSELS SAUTÉED WITH ONIONS AND WHITE WINE IN A SPICY MARINARA SAUCE

ENTREES

FETTUCCINE TOSSED WITH PANCETTA, RED ONIONS, BASIL, GARLIC AND MARINARA

GRILLED BONELESS CENTER-CUT PORK WITH SAUTÉED MUSHROOMS, MARSALA WINE DEMIGLACE, POTATO AND VEGETABLE

SWORDFISH GRILLED WITH HERB DRESSING WITH POLENTA AND VEGETABLE

SCROD BAKED IN WHITE WINE AND LEMON BUTTER

VEAL MEDALLIONS WITH ROASTED PEPPERS, ONIONS AND MUSHROOMS IN A RED WINE-MARINARA SAUCE

CHICKEN BREAST SAUTÉED WITH BLACK OLIVES, RED PEPPERS, MUSHROOMS AND SUN-DRIED TOMATOES IN A PINK SAUCE

The Grapevine Guide | 56

Il Piccolo

ECLECTIC AND ECCENTRIC

That's how chef-owner Wayne Clark describes the food at his Johnston restaurant, which opened in 1989. Il Piccolo may be located in a small strip mall, but one step inside this romantic restaurant and you are swept away by its charming decor. The fine dining menu, which changes with the seasons, is decidedly Northern Italian in nature, with French and American flourishes. Clark is most proud of one dish in particular, a veal T-bone with a mushroom, shallot and green peppercorn sauce, served with Yukon gold mashed potatoes. When the "eclectic and eccentric" Clark isn't in the kitchen, he relaxes by refurbishing antique military rifles. Now that's different.

ZUCCHINI FRITTERS

Makes approximately 18

6 medium-size zucchini, sliced
3/4 cup flour
3/4 cup polenta (instant)
1/2 teaspoon salt
1/4 teaspoon cayenne pepper

1 egg
1/2 cup buttermilk
1 teaspoon baking powder
Oil, as needed for frying

In a preheated 350-degree oven, roast the zucchini until soft. Drain and mash. Mix together with the flour, polenta, salt and cayenne.

In a separate bowl, lightly beat the egg. Add the buttermilk and squash. Stir well. Add to the dry mixture. Heat the oil to 375 degrees. Drop spoonfuls of the mix into the hot oil. Cook about 2 1/2 minutes per side.

Drain on paper towels. Serve warm as an appetizer with your favorite marinara sauce for dipping.

INSIDE SCOOP

CHEF-OWNER	WAYNE L. CLARK
OPEN SINCE	1989
CUISINE	NORTHERN ITALIAN WITH FRENCH AND AMERICAN FLOURISHES
SPECIALTY	NODINO AI FERRI (VEAL T-BONE) WITH A MUSHROOM, SHALLOT AND GREEN PEPPERCORN SAUCE AND YUKON GOLD MASHED POTATOES
PRICE RANGE	APPETIZERS $5 TO $9 ENTREES $12 TO $27
CREDIT CARDS	MAJOR CREDIT CARDS ACCEPTED
RESERVATIONS	RECOMMENDED
HOURS	OPEN WEEKDAYS FOR LUNCH OPEN MONDAY THROUGH SATURDAY FOR DINNER
LIQUOR	FULL LIQUOR
SMOKING	PERMITTED AT THE BAR
SERVICES	BANQUET FACILITIES HEALTHY/LOW-FAT MENU ITEMS VEGETARIAN MENU ITEMS HANDICAPPED ACCESSIBLE, WITH ONE SMALL STEP TAKE-OUT ORDERS AVAILABLE CATERING PRIVATE DINING ROOM
DRESS CODE	CASUAL
PARKING	AVAILABLE ON THE PREMISES

APPETIZERS

BRUSHCHETTA WITH MASHED EGGPLANT, TOMATOES AND PECORINO CHEESE

BRUSCHETTA WITH CANNELLINI BEANS, TOMATOES AND PECORINO CHEESE

CLAMS STEAMED WITH SPICED GARLIC, LEMON, TOASTED SEMOLINA AND TOMATO BROTH, SERVED WITH GARLIC TOAST

CHIVE RICOTTA GNOCCHI WITH BUTTER SAUCE, SAGE AND FRESH MOZZARELLA

ENTREES

HOUSE-MADE VEAL AND GOAT CHEESE RAVIOLI IN A PORCINI MUSHROOM SAUCE

ANGEL-HAIR PASTA SAUTÉED WITH SHRIMP BAY SCALLOPS, DICED TOMATOES, LEMON AND GARLIC

GRILLED VEAL T-BONE STEAK WITH ROASTED SHALLOTS, MUSHROOMS, GREEN PEPPERCORNS AND FRESH HERBS

PAN-ROASTED SEA BASS WITH SHAVED FENNEL, SHIITAKE MUSHROOMS, FRESH HERBS, DICED TOMATOES AND SEAFOOD STOCK

GRILLED SIRLOIN ON A BED OF CHOPPED LOBSTER IN A SHERRY AND SHALLOT CREAM SAUCE

India

Multiple Locations | 401-278-2000 | www.indiarestaurant.com

TRANSCENDENTAL DINING

The decor at India is as beautiful as its food. Massive paintings depicting the people and places of India adorn the walls. Chef-owner Amar Singh, who meditates on a regular basis, says he strives for a very contemporary feel with a focus on warmth and coziness at all four of his restaurants, located in East Greenwich, Warren, and two in Providence. The menu is tailored to suit the American palate with an emphasis on healthy food. India is especially known for its Grilled Masala Lamb Chops, served with fragrant basmati rice, grilled peppers and mint chutney. On your next visit, check out their weekday specials and bargain bar menu.

MASALA GRILLED LAMB CHOPS

Serves 4

Marinade:
2 cups yogurt
1 bunch cilantro, plus extra to garnish
2 tablespoons garlic
2 tablespoons ginger paste
2 tablespoons vinegar
1 tablespoon garam masala (available in Indian markets)
1 tablespoon paprika powder
1 tablespoon coriander powder
1 tablespoon lemon juice, plus extra to dress
2 tablespoons canola oil

16 spring lamb chops (lean)
Fresh cilantro, chopped, as needed
Fresh lemons, quartered, as needed

Put all imarinade ngredients in a blender and puree to make a marinade. Coat the lamb chops and marinate them for 24 hours in the refrigerator.

Broil the chops to one's liking. Garnish with chopped cilantro. Serve with fresh lemon juice squeezed on top.

INSIDE SCOOP

LOCATION	PROVIDENCE	HOURS	OPEN SEVEN DAYS A WEEK

LOCATION: PROVIDENCE, 123 DORRANCE STREET, 1060 HOPE STREET, EAST GREENWICH, WARREN
CHEF-OWNER: AMAR SINGH
OPEN SINCE: HOPE STREET, 1995; DOWNTOWN PROVIDENCE, 1996; WARREN, 1997; EAST GREENWICH, 2000
CUISINE: INDIAN CUISINE TAILORED TO SUIT THE AMERICAN PALATE, WITH EMPHASIS ON HEALTHY FOOD
SPECIALTY: GRILLED MASALA LAMP CHOPS
PRICE RANGE: APPETIZERS $2 TO $7, ENTREES $10 TO $27
CREDIT CARDS: MAJOR CREDIT CARDS ACCEPTED
RESERVATIONS: RECOMMENDED

HOURS: OPEN SEVEN DAYS A WEEK FOR LUNCH AND DINNER, SUNDAY BRUNCH
LIQUOR: FULL LIQUOR
SMOKING: PERMITTED
SERVICES: BANQUET FACILITIES, HEALTHY/LOW-FAT MENU ITEMS, VEGETARIAN MENU ITEMS, HANDICAPPED ACCESSIBLE, TAKE-OUT ORDERS AVAILABLE, CATERING, PRIVATE DINING ROOM, ONLY AT THE WARREN LOCATION, FIREPLACE, ONLY AT THE HOPE STREET LOCATION
DRESS CODE: CASUAL
PARKING: AVAILABLE IN THE IMMEDIATE AREA

APPETIZERS

CUCUMBER AND YOGURT RAITA
VEGETABLE SAMOSA WITH POTATOES, GREEN PEAS, HERBS AND SPICES
PAPRI CHAT — INDIAN NACHOS TOPPED WITH CHICK PEAS, ONIONS, FRESH CILANTRO YOGURT AND TAMARIND CHUTNEY
SPICY STEAMED MUSSELS
CHICKEN KABOB SALAD

ENTREES

GRILLED MASALA LAMB CHOP KABOBS
SHRIMP SHEESH KABOBS
BIRYANI WITH MUSHROOMS, CHICKEN, LAMB, SHRIMP AND SCALLOPS
LAMB SAAG — CURRY WITH A MILD SPINACH-BASED SAUCE FLAVORED WITH GINGER AND GARLIC
CHICKEN MASALA IN A TOMATO AND CREAM CURRY SAUCE FLAVORED WITH CARDOMOM, FENUGREEK AND FRESH CILANTRO

Joe Marzilli's Old Canteen

120 Atwells Avenue (Federal Hill), Providence | 401-751-5544

IN THE PINK

The first restaurant you see upon entering Federal Hill in Providence is Joe Marzilli's Old Canteen, which has been in operation since 1956, making it one of the most famous restaurants in Rhode Island. The all-Italian menu seems to go on forever, with 15 spaghetti dishes, 21 veal entrees, chicken done 14 different ways, and so much more. Filled with Old World charm, the Old Canteen is also known for steaks and chops. Our favorite waiter, Andy, has been there for 25 years. He highly recommends the complete seven-course dinners. But don't ask him to rush – they cook to order at the Old Canteen.

INSIDE SCOOP

CHEF	SAL MARZILLI	LIQUOR	FULL LIQUOR
OWNER	JOE MARZILLI	SMOKING	PERMITTED IN LOUNGE
OPEN SINCE	1956	SERVICES	CHILDREN'S MENU
CUISINE	ITALIAN		HEALTHY/LOW-FAT MENU ITEMS
SPECIALTY	VEAL DISHES		VEGETARIAN MENU ITEMS
PRICE RANGE	APPETIZERS $3.75 TO $14.50		TAKE-OUT ORDERS AVAILABLE
	ENTREES $10.50 TO $34.50	DRESS CODE	CASUAL
CREDIT CARDS	MAJOR CREDIT CARDS ACCEPTED	PARKING	AVAILABLE ON THE STREET AND
RESERVATIONS	RECOMMENDED		THROUGH THE VALET SERVICE
HOURS	WEDNESDAY THROUGH MONDAY		
	FOR LUNCH AND DINNER		

APPETIZERS

SHRIMP COCKTAIL
BROILED SCAMPI
POLENTA WITH MARINARA SAUCE
STUFFED ARTICHOKE HEARTS
LITTLENECKS ZUPPA
MARINATED EELS

ENTREES

SPAGHETTI WITH CHICKEN, TOMATO SAUCE AND MUSHROOMS
SPAGHETTI AND MEATBALLS
VEAL AND SAUSAGE, HUNTER-STYLE
VEAL SCALOPPINE WITH MUSHROOMS IN MARSALA WINE
VEAL CHOP ZINGARELLA WITH MUSHROOMS AND PEPPERS
OSSO BUCO
SWORDFISH BROILED IN LEMON BUTTER
LOBSTER FRA DIAVOLO

Waterplace in Providence

Julian's

FUNKY, UNUSUAL, UNIQUE

Get the picture? That's what Julian's is all about. There's nothing ordinary here, whether it's the creative food, the wacky decor, the bohemian staff, or the quirky customers. The imaginative menu, which changes daily, offers New American Cuisine, including true vegetarian options. A small neighborhood restaurant, Julian's is quite popular with college students and artists. In warm weather, al fresco dining is offered on the sidewalk and on the brick patio in the rear, just past the café's award-winning bathroom (not to be missed). Intrigued? You should be, but Julian's hours are tricky so it's wise to call ahead.

BLEU CHEESE HASH

Serves 6

3 pounds red bliss potatoes
Chili powder, cajun spices, paprika, granulated garlic and salt, to taste
Vegetable oil, as needed for frying
2 red onions, chopped
4 to 5 handfuls of spinach
Bleu cheese dressing, to taste
Chunks of bleu cheese, optional

Parboil the potatoes whole. Cool with ice-cold water. Cut into thin slices about 1/4-inch thick. Season the potato slices with spices.

Heat a griddle or large sauté pan, preferably cast iron. Add vegetable oil, then the onions. When the onions become translucent, add the potatoes. Fry for about 15 minutes, allowing for the potatoes to become crisp. Drain any excess oil. Using 2 small spatulas, cut the potatoes into small pieces.

In a large serving bowl, place the spinach, tearing it apart with your hands. Add the cooked potatoes and the bleu cheese dressing; mix well. Chunks of bleu cheese make this dish even better. Serve immediately.

INSIDE SCOOP

CHEFS	ANDREW, JAMEZ, ILAN, MICHAEL, JAY, OSCAR AND JULIAN	SMOKING	PERMITTED AFTER 11 P.M.
OWNER	JULIAN FORGUE	SERVICES	HEALTHY/LOW-FAT MENU ITEMS
OPEN SINCE	1996		VEGETARIAN MENU ITEMS
CUISINE	NEW AMERICAN		HANDICAPPED ACCESSIBLE
SPECIALTY	VEGGIE BURGERS AND SOY BURGERS, VEAL, DUCK, SIRLOIN		TAKE-OUT ORDERS AVAILABLE
			CATERING
PRICE RANGE	APPETIZERS $4 TO $9	DRESS CODE	CASUAL AND PROPER
	ENTREES $3 TO $19	PARKING	AVAILABLE ON THE STREET
CREDIT CARDS	MAJOR CREDIT CARDS ACCEPTED		
RESERVATIONS	RECOMMENDED FOR PARTIES OF 6 OR MORE		
HOURS	OPEN MONDAY FOR BREAKFAST AND LUNCH ONLY TUESDAY THROUGH SUNDAY FOR BREAKFAST, LUNCH AND DINNER SATURDAY/SUNDAY BRUNCH		
LIQUOR	FULL LIQUOR		

APPETIZERS

DASHI BROTH WITH SOMEN NOODELS AND TOFU OR CHICKEN
QUESADILLA WITH PEPPERS, ONIONS, BLACK BEANS AND PEPPERJACK CHEESE WITH SOUR CREAM AND SALSA
ANTIPASTO WITH ROASTED RED PEPPERS, GRILLED ASPARAGUS, EGGPLANT, OLIVES, MOZZARELLA, PROVOLONE AND RED GRAPES

ENTREES

ROASTED RED PEPPER AND ROSEMARY GNOCCHI WITH SQUASH, ONION AND BASIL IN A TOMATO-RED WINE SAUCE
GRILLED SMOKED SALMON WITH SMOKED TOMATO LENTILS, GRILLED ASPARAGUS AND A RED PEPPER SAUCE
RIGATA PASTA WITH A SPICY PINK VODKA SAUCE AND TOMATO, FENNEL, ONION AND SAUSAGE
CHILI-RUBBED GRILLED SIRLOIN STEAK WITH RICE AND BEANS IN A MUSTARD-CHILI SAUCE
ROASTED TURKEY BREAST WITH BLACK BEANS, ONION, RED PEPPER AND SWEET POTATO WITH A MAPLE-CHIPOTLE SAUCE
COUSCOUS WITH SAUTÉED EGGPLANT, RED PEPPER AND TOMATO, TOPPED WITH GOAT CHEESE

Kabob and Curry

FLIGHTS OF FLAVOR

The recently renovated Kabob and Curry with its airy greenhouse design offers modern surroundings to well match its casual, eclectic Indian food, arguably the very best in the state, according to Meridith Ford, food critic for *The Providence Journal*. Chef-owner Sanjiv Dhar says he strives for freshness and flavor without the overpowering spices normally associated with Indian food. Dhar, who was honored as an outstanding visiting chef at nearby Brown University, changes his menu annually, often after one of his visits to his homeland. He considers Chicken Tikka Masala to be the best dish on his impressive menu. We agree.

GRAPEVINE GEM: Check out the weekend brunches — vegetarian on Saturday, omnivore on Sundays.

INSIDE SCOOP

CHEF-OWNER	SANJIV DHAR	LIQUOR	FULL LIQUOR
OPEN SINCE	1987	SMOKING	NOT PERMITTED
CUISINE	INDIAN CUISINE WITH AN	SERVICES	BANQUET FACILITIES
	EMPHASIS ON FRESHNESS		HEALTHY/LOW-FAT MENU ITEMS
	AND FLAVOR WITHOUT		VEGETARIAN MENU ITEMS
	OVERPOWERING SPICES		TAKE-OUT ORDERS AVAILABLE
SPECIALTY	CHICKEN TIKKA MASALA		CATERING
PRICE RANGE	APPETIZERS $3 TO $9		PRIVATE DINING ROOM
	ENTREES $7 TO $15		SATURDAY/SUNDAY BRUNCH
CREDIT CARDS	MAJOR CREDIT CARDS ACCEPTED	DRESS CODE	CASUAL
RESERVATIONS	RECOMMENDED	PARKING	AVAILABLE ON THE STREET
HOURS	OPEN SEVEN DAYS A WEEK FOR		
	LUNCH AND DINNER		
	LUNCH: 11 A.M. TO 3:30 P.M.		
	DINNER: 4:30 TO 10:30 P.M.		

APPETIZERS

SAMOSAS (PASTRY TURNOVERS FILLED WITH POTATO AND GREEN PEAS OR
WITH SEASONED MINCED LAMB)
PAPRI CHAT (WAFERS TOPPED WITH YOGURT, SWEET CHUTNEY, CHICK PEAS
AND DICED POTATOES)
PAKORAS (SEASONED FRITTERS OF MIXED VEGETABLE OR HOMEMADE
CHEESE)

BREADS

PARANTHA (WHOLE WHEAT PAN-FRIED BREAD, PLAIN OR STUFFED WITH
POTATOES AND GREEN PEAS)
HANDMADE NAN WITH CHOICE OF STUFFINGS INCLUDING GARLIC AND
CILANTRO, SEASONED LAMB, HONEY AND GINGER
POORI (DEEP-FRIED WHOLE WHEAT PUFFED BREAD)

ENTREES

TANDOOR MURGH (CORNISH HEN, MARINATED IN SPICED YOGURT, COOKED
ON A CHARCOAL FIRE)
TANDOORI SHRIMP IN A SPICY MARINADE
BIRYANI RICE WITH RAISINS, NUTS, HERBS AND A CHOICE OF LAMB,
CHICKEN, SEAFOOD OR VEGETABLES
CHICKEN TIKKA MASALA (CHICKEN BREAST COOKED IN A CREAMY TOMATO
SAUCE WITH SPICES)
COCONUT CHICKEN CURRY WITH PORTABELLO MUSHROOMS
LAMB ROGANJOSH COOKED IN SELECT KASHMIRI SPICES AND GARLIC
LAMB VINDALOO WITH POTATOES IN A VERY HOT, TANGY SAUCE
CHICK PEAS IN A CURRY WITH ONIONS, TOMATOES AND GINGER
SHRIMP AND SCALLOPS WITH GREEN PEPPPERS, ONIONS AND TOMATOES

BHOONA JHINGA
DRY MASALA SHRIMP

Serves 4

1/2 teaspoon cumin seeds
1/2 teaspoon coriander seeds
2 dry whole red chilies
1 green chili, chopped fine
1/2 cup finely chopped onions
2 tablespoons vegetable oil
1/4 teaspoon chopped ginger
1/4 teaspoon fenugreek seeds
1 pound jumbo shrimp deveined, with tails on
1/2 cup tomatoes, chopped fine
2 tablespoons freshly chopped cilantro
1/4 teaspoon tumeric
Salt, to taste
1 tablespoon low-fat yogurt

In a heavy-bottom skillet over low heat, dry roast cumin and coriander seeds for 2 to 3 minutes. Cool down and grind them together with the red chilies, green chilli and onions.

Heat the oil in a saucepan; add chopped ginger and fenugreek seeds.

As soon as they begin to sizzle, add the shrimp and sauté for a few minutes. Add the chopped tomatoes and half of the cilantro. After about 1 minute, add the ground mixture and tumeric. Coat the shrimp well with this mixture along with spices; season with salt. Add the yogurt. Garnish with remaining cilantro.

Serve with rice or pasta.

Kartabar

EAST SIDE GEM

Kartabar is a jewel of a restaurant, with wonderful food, friendly service, and an exciting late-night scene, especially with the local college crowd that keeps Thayer Street hopping. "Eclectic, casual and Mediterranean" is how owner Philippe Maatouk describes Kartabar, which is open for lunch and dinner seven days a week – now that's something you can always count on. Asked for the restaurant's number-one dish, Maatouk recommends the grilled Filet Mignon stuffed with Gorgonzola and topped off with a red wine glaze. Chef Julio Baptista, who changes his very tempting menu three to four times a year, suggests the Shrimp Barcelona.

BARCELONA SHRIMP

Serves 1

2 tablespoons olive oil
1 tablespoon chopped garlic
Fresh rosemary, chopped, to taste
Pinch of black pepper
Pinch of red crushed pepper
1 1/2 cups sherry wine
1/2 cup diced chorizo
8 large shrimp
1 tablespoon butter
Paprika, to taste
1 teaspoon kosher salt
1/4 cup chopped parsley

In a large frying pan, heat the oil. Sauté the garlic, rosemary, black and red peppers until garlic is light brown. Add the sherry wine and chorizo. Bring to a boil; add the shrimp, butter and paprika. Simmer until shrimp is red and cooked. Season with salt. Remove from heat. Sprinkle with parsley and serve.

INSIDE SCOOP

CHEF	JULIO BAPTISTA	HOURS	OPEN SEVEN DAYS A WEEK FOR
OWNER	PHILIPPE MAATOUK		LUNCH AND DINNER
OPEN SINCE	2001	LIQUOR	FULL LIQUOR
CUISINE	MEDITERRANEAN	SMOKING	PERMITTED
SPECIALTY	GRILLED FILET MIGNON STUFFED	SERVICES	HEALTHY/LOW-FAT MENU ITEMS
	WITH GORGONZOLA AND TOPPED		VEGETARIAN MENU ITEMS
	WITH RED WINE GLAZE		HANDICAPPED ACCESSIBLE
PRICE RANGE	APPETIZERS $5 TO $9		TAKE-OUT ORDERS AVAILABLE
	ENTREES $8 TO $18		CATERING
CREDIT CARDS	MAJOR CREDIT CARDS ACCEPTED	DRESS CODE	CASUAL
RESERVATIONS	RECOMMENDED	PARKING	AVAILABLE ON THE STREET

APPETIZERS

CHICKEN SKEWERS WITH A PEPPERY POMEGRANATE HONEY GLAZE
BARCELONA SHRIMP WITH GARLIC AND CHORIZO SAUTÉED IN A
    SHERRY WINE SAUCE
TUNA CARPACCIO WITH BABY GREENS, SHAVED ASIAGO CHEESE,
    CAPERS, LEMON AND EXTRA VIRGIN OLIVE OIL
MUSSELS SERVED IN A GARLIC, WHITE WINE, ROSEMARY, FRESH
    PARSLEY AND TOMATO SAUCE
BRUSCHETTA WITH SLICED GRILLED RIB-EYE STEAK, MOZZARELLA AND
    SHALLOT CREAM SAUCE
POACHED PEAR SALAD WITH WALNUTS, RAISINS, GOAT CHEESE, BABY
    GREENS, ONIONS AND RASPBERRY VINAIGRETTE

ENTREES

VEAL TENDERLOINS WITH A GARLIC, ROSEMARY AND PORT WINE
    DEMIGLACE
GRILLED CHICKEN BREAST WITH SWEETENED BALSAMIC
GLAZED SEA BASS ROASTED WITH CHAMPAGNE, PLUM TOMATOES,
    BASIL AND RED ONIONS
LOBSTER RAVIOLI WITH A PINK BASIL-MASCARPONE CREAM SAUCE
GNOCCHI WITH SAUTÉED GARLIC, CHICKEN AND TOMATOES IN A
    PESTO CREAM SAUCE
GRILLED FILET MIGNON STUFFED WITH GORGONZOLA IN A RED WINE
    GLAZE

La Moia Restaurant & Tapas Bar

292 Pocasset Avenue, Providence | 401-942-2505

LITTLE PLATES, BIG FLAVORS

As soon as La Moia Restaurant & Tapas Bar opened its doors, customers turned into avid fans who quickly spread the good word on this rustic eatery. Chef-owner Robert LaMoia describes his namesake restaurant as "my house," and all who enter are made to feel right at home. The menu features Mediterranean cuisine with three to five daily specials. The Salmon Relleno is considered the house specialty. It's one of the many tapas dishes on the menu. The best way to experience La Moia is to go with friends or family and order all kinds of tapas, hot and cold, for sharing.

INSIDE SCOOP

CHEF-OWNER	ROBERT LAMOIA	SMOKING	PERMITTED
OPEN SINCE	2001	SERVICES	BANQUET FACILITIES
CUISINE	MEDITERRANEAN		HEALTHY/LOW-FAT MENU ITEMS
SPECIALTY	SALMON RELLENO		VEGETARIAN MENU ITEMS
PRICE RANGE	APPETIZERS $4 TO $10		HANDICAPPED ACCESSIBLE
	ENTREES $5 TO $18		TAKE-OUT ORDERS AVAILABLE
CREDIT CARDS	MAJOR CREDIT CARDS ACCEPTED		CATERING
RESERVATIONS	RECOMMENDED	DRESS CODE	CASUAL
HOURS	TUESDAY THROUGH SATURDAY	PARKING	AVAILABLE ON THE PREMISES AND
	FOR LUNCH AND DINNER		THROUGH THE VALET SERVICE
LIQUOR	FULL LIQUOR		

TAPAS

GRILLED SHRIMP AND BLACK BEAN SALSA

BLACKENED SCALLOP WITH BLUE CHEESE, SPINACH, DEVILED WALNUTS AND WARM BACON VINAIGRETTE

MUFFALETTAS — CRUSTY BREAD FILLED WITH GRILLED CHICKEN, MOZZARELLA, AND REMOULADE SAUCE

JUMBO LOBSTER RAVIOLI

BEEF TENDERLOIN WITH BLUE CHEESE CRUST

PAELLA VALENCIANA WITH SHRIMP, CHICKEN AND CHORIZO

TORTILLA PAISANA — SPANISH FRITATTA WITH SPINACH, BLUE CHEESE, POTATOES AND ONIONS

MARINATED MUSHROOMS COOKED IN A LEMON AND PEPPERCORN BRINE

BACALAO — SALT-CURED COD WITH OLIVES, GARLIC AND OIL

SHISH KABOB OF BEEF TENDERLOIN, CHICKEN AND CHORIZO WITH PEPPERS AND CUMIN MAYO

Le Bistro

41 Bowen's Wharf, Newport | 401-849-7778 | www.lebistronewport.com

AWAY FROM THE MADDENING CROWD

There's something peaceful about climbing the stairs to Le Bistro and rising above the summer fray on Bowen's Wharf. During the winter, you can see the ocean beyond the tall masts of the ships in Newport Harbor. The quiet is delicious. So is the food. The offerings at lunch are creative, fresh and always tempting. Dinners are classic in preparation, contemporary in presentation. Not all the area restaurants do, but Le Bistro takes reservations, and that adds to your chance of getting away from it all. Definitely worth the climb.

CREOLE BREAD PUDDING
WITH BOURBON SAUCE

Serves 8 to 10

Bread pudding:
2 tablespoons butter
1 (12-ounce) loaf of stale French bread
1 quart milk

3 eggs
2 cups sugar
1/2 cup raisins
2 tablespoons vanilla extract

Spread the butter on the inside of a 10-inch (2-inch deep) cake pan.

Break the bread into chunks in a bowl, and pour in the milk. Crumble the bread into small pieces, and let it soak until all the milk is absorbed.

In another bowl, beat the eggs and sugar together until thick. Add the raisins and vanilla. Stir into the bread mixture. Mix well.

Pour into the buttered cake pan and spread it out evenly. Place the cake pan into a larger pan and add boiling water to a depth of 1 inch. Bake at 350 degrees for about 1 hour or until the pudding is set.

Bourbon sauce:
1/2 cup unsalted butter
1 cup sugar

1 egg
1/2 cup bourbon

Cut the butter into half-inch pieces and melt over very low heat. Combine the sugar and the egg, and add to the melted butter. Stir over low heat until the sugar dissolves and the mixture thickens. Do not allow the mixture to boil. Let it cool somewhat before adding the bourbon.

INSIDE SCOOP

CHEF	KEVIN WOOD	HOURS	OPEN SEVEN DAYS A WEEK
OWNER	JAMES J. BEAULIEU		FOR LUNCH AND DINNER
OPEN SINCE	1973		SUNDAY BRUNCH
CUISINE	AMERICAN BISTRO WITH A	LIQUOR	FULL LIQUOR
	PROVENCAL INFLUENCE	SMOKING	NOT PERMITTED
SPECIALTY	NEWPORT BOUILLABAISSE	SERVICES	BANQUET FACILITIES
	(SHRIMP, CLAMS, MUSSELS,		HEALTHY/LOW-FAT MENU ITEMS
	SCALLOPS AND FISH IN		VEGETARIAN MENU ITEMS
	A TOMATO LEEK BROTH		PRIVATE DINING ROOM
	SERVED WITH ROUILLES)	DRESS CODE	SMART/CASUAL
PRICE RANGE	APPETIZERS $7 TO $13	PARKING	AVAILABLE IN NEARBY LOTS
	ENTREES $17 TO $25		
CREDIT CARDS	MAJOR CREDIT CARDS ACCEPTED		
RESERVATIONS	RECOMMENDED		

APPETIZERS

CHILLED LOBSTER CLAWS WITH SALAD OF TOMATO, ARTICHOKE
    HEARTS, LEMON AND EXTRA VIRGIN OLIVE OIL ON BABY GREENS
SPINACH SALAD WITH CARAMELIZED PECANS, BACON AND
    PARMAGIANO-REGGIANO WITH A CITRUS VINAIGRETTE
OYSTERS ON THE HALF SHELL WITH MIGNONETTE SAUCE
ESCARGOTS IN GARLIC BUTTER
SCALLOPS AND WILD MUSHROOMS IN PUFF PASTRY

ENTREES

SOFT-SHELL CRAB SAUTÉ IN A SAUCE OF ASPARAGUS, SUN-DRIED
    TOMATOES, GARLIC AND FISH FUMET WITH CHIVE FETTUCCINE
TUNA SAUTÉ WITH FRESH STRAWBERRIES AND BALSAMIC VINEGAR
    WITH ROSEMARY ROASTED POTATOES
TENDERLOIN AND SHRIMP WITH SAGE BUTTER, ROSEMARY POTATOES
    AND ASPARAGUS
BOUILLABAISE WITH SHRIMP, CLAMS, MUSSELS, SCALLOPS AND FISH
    IN A TOMATO-LEEK BROTH WITH ROUILLES
SIRLOIN STEAK WITH ROASTED RED PEPPERS AND ONIONS WITH
    ROSEMARY MADEIRA DEMIGLACE, ROASTED POTATOES AND GRILLED
    ASPARAGUS

QUIET SOPHISTICATION

L'Epicureo is one of the city's cornerstone restaurants that helped put Providence on the nation's culinary map. Ever since it opened, this elegant spot on Federal Hill, with its warm, welcoming atmosphere, has been a favorite of both tourists and locals with discerning taste. The creative Italian menu from Chef Angel Cardona is simply dazzling. The service is as flawless as the food. Thanks to the high standards set by owners Tom and Rozann Buckner, L'Epicureo continues to be quite special.

GRAPEVINE GEM: Rozann DiGiglio Buckner lived out her father's dream by transforming his butcher shop into a restaurant. Two weeks after it opened, a very proud Joe DiGiglio died of a heart attack, but his memory lives on in his former butcher shop. To this day, the restaurant still cures and ages sides of beef and makes sausages and ravioli.

INSIDE SCOOP

CHEFS	TOM BUCKNER AND ANGEL CARDONA	LIQUOR	FULL LIQUOR
OWNERS	TOM AND ROZANN BUCKNER	SMOKING	PERMITTED AT BAR ONLY
OPEN SINCE	1994	SERVICES	PRIVATE DINING ROOM
CUISINE	ITALIAN		HEALTHY/LOW-FAT MENU ITEMS
SPECIALTY	PRIME MEATS		VEGETARIAN MENU ITEMS
PRICE RANGE	APPETIZERS $8 TO $12		HANDICAPPED ACCESSIBLE
	ENTREES $22 TO $32		TAKE-OUT ORDERS AVAILABLE
CREDIT CARDS	MAJOR CREDIT CARDS ACCEPTED		PRIVATE DINING ROOM
RESERVATIONS	RECOMMENDED		FIREPLACE
HOURS	TUESDAY THROUGH SATURDAY,	DRESS CODE	BUSINESS/CASUAL
	5 TO 9 P.M.	PARKING	AVAILABLE ON THE STREET AND
	FRIDAY AND SATURDAY,		THROUGH THE VALET SERVICE
	5 TO 10 P.M.		

APPETIZERS

SEA SCALLOPS WITH GREMOLATA AND PROSECCO BUTTER

POLENTA WITH A WILD MUSHROOM AND SUN-DRIED TOMATO RAGU

WOOD-GRILLED PORTOBELLO MUSHROOM OVER BRAISED SPINACH AND GOAT
CHEESE WITH GRILLED BLACK TIGER SHRIMP

CRESPELLE STUFFED WITH SHRIMP AND SPINACH IN GORGONZOLA CREAM
WITH TOASTED PIGNOLI AND ITALIAN PARSLEY

WARM CLAM SALAD WITH GRILLED VEAL SAUSAGE AND WHITE BEANS

ARUGULA IN A PANCETTA VINAIGRETTE WITH SHAVED FENNEL AND ORANGES

ENTREES

COD IN HORSERADISH CRUST WITH WHIPPED POTATOES, RED PEPPER OIL AND
CRISPY LEEKS

PAN-SEARED DOVER SOLE WITH SAUTÉ OF BABY ARTICHOKES, SUN-DRIED
TOMATOES AND FINGERLING POTATOES

PROSCIUTTO WRAPPED SALMON OVER SPRING BEAN RAGU

DOUBLE-THICK BONELESS PORK CHOP AND RED ONION GORGONZOLA BUTTER
OVER WILTED SPINACH WITH FRESH HERB RISOTTO CAKE, MERLOT SAUCE
AND RED CABBAGE ARGO

PROVIMI VEAL CHOP WITH WILD MUSHROOM AND PORT WINE SAUCE, MASHED
RED POTATOES AND SPRING VEGETABLES

GRILLED PRIME DELMONICO STEAK WITH WILD MUSHROOMS IN A BOURBON
DEMIGLACE, MASHED RED POTATOES AND ASPARAGUS

SUCOFINDO WITH CAPELLINI
MARINARA SAUCE WITH CAPELLINI

Serves 4

3/4 cup sliced fresh garlic cloves
1/2 cup olive oil
1 cup basil, cut into thin strips
1 (28-ounce) can peeled Italian plum tomatoes
Kosher salt and fresh ground black pepper, to taste
1 pound capellini, cooked

Place garlic cloves with olive oil in a 3-quart sauce pan. Over medium heat, allow the garlic to brown to a deep rich cocoa color. Discard the garlic and allow the olive oil to cool for about 5 minutes. Add the basil and heat gently, being careful not to burn it.

Add the tomatoes which have been crushed by hand. Add salt and pepper; simmer for about 20 minutes. Toss into a bowl of cooked capellini and serve at once.

This recipe, which doubles nicely and freezes well, comes from Rozann's paternal grandmother, who was born in Bari, Italy, at the turn of the last century. This sauce is made daily at L'Epicureo.

L.J.'s Barbecue

EAT IT AND BEAT IT

Don't go calling Bernie Watson a chef. He's a pitmaster and proud of it. Along with his wife Linda, he owns L.J.'s Barbecue, one of the most fun BYOB (bring your own beer) restaurants in the state. Located in the northern end of Providence, L.J.'s is especially popular with local restaurant chefs, and that says a lot when it comes to what's good in town. Offering authentic Southern-style barbecue, L.J.'s smokes its dry-rubbed meats up to 12 hours over a blend of apple and hickory hardwoods. The side dishes are worth a mention, especially the "ooey-gooey" macaroni and cheese. Pure comfort food.

PINEAPPLE UPSIDE DOWN CAKE

Serves 8

1 stick butter
1 cup brown sugar
1 can unseetened pineapple slices
1 small jar maraschino cherries, no stems
Pecan halves, as needed
1 yellow pudding-style cake mix

Melt butter in iron skillet. Remove from heat and press brown sugar into pan.

Arrange fruit in decorative pattern and dot with nuts.

Make cake according to mix, substituting 3 tablespoons juice from pineapple for water. Pour batter into iron skillet. Bake at 350 degrees for 1 hour. Let cool 5 minutes, then invert onto serving platter.

INSIDE SCOOP

CHEF	BERNIE WATSON, PITMASTER
OWNERS	BERNIE AND LINDA WATSON
OPEN SINCE	2001
CUISINE	SOUTHERN-STYLE BARBECUE
SPECIALTY	AUTHENTIC CAJUN RED BEANS AND RICE
	KANSAS CITY-STYLE TOMATO-BASED BARBECUE SAUCE
PRICE RANGE	ENTREES $5 TO $19
CREDIT CARDS	NOT ACCEPTED, CASH ONLY
RESERVATIONS	RECOMMENDED
HOURS	TUESDAY THROUGH SUNDAY FOR LUNCH AND DINNER SATURDAY/SUNDAY BRUNCH
LIQUOR	BYOB
SMOKING	NO
SERVICES	HANDICAPPED ACCESSIBLE WITH THE EXCEPTION OF THE BATHROOM
	TAKE-OUT ORDERS AVAILABLE
	CATERING
DRESS CODE	CASUAL
PARKING	AVAILABLE ON THE PREMISES

MENU

RED BEANS AND RICE
CHILI, WITH CHEESE AND/OR ONIONS
PULLED PORK BBQ
BBQ CHICKEN
BBQ BEEF BRISKET
BBQ BEEF RIBS
DRY-RUBBED BBQ PORK RIBS
POTATO SALAD, MACARONI SALAD, BBQ BAKED BEANS, COLE SLAW
MACARONI AND CHEESE
CANDIED YAMS AND COLLARD GREENS
CORNBREAD
HOME-STYLE CAKES, PIES AND COBBLERS

Luigi's

AN OFFER YOU CAN'T REFUSE

Rhode Island seems to have more than its share of wonderful, old-fashioned Italian restaurants. Luigi's is one of them. The lunch menu offers more than 70 items priced at $5.95 or less. On Tuesday through Friday, dinner for two is just $24.95, and that includes 23 different entrees and a bottle of wine. The Battista family does it right, offering big portions of traditional Italian food at very reasonable prices for the past 25 years. We especially like creating our own pasta dishes at Luigi's, with seven pastas and a dozen sauces to mix and match. Yumola!

GRAPEVINE GEM: Our accountant, Joe Russolino, turned us on to Luigi's, and he has sophisticated culinary tastes. He raves about this place and its consistently perfect chicken dishes.

INSIDE SCOOP

CHEF	RALPH BATTISTA	LIQUOR	FULL LIQUOR
OWNER	THE BATTISTA FAMILY	SMOKING	PERMITTED
OPEN SINCE	MORE THAN 30 YEARS	SERVICES	BANQUET FACILITIES
CUISINE	ITALIAN		CHILDREN'S MENU
SPECIALTY	CHICKEN CAPRI		HEALTHY/LOW-FAT MENU ITEMS
PRICE RANGE	APPETIZERS $4 TO $8		VEGETARIAN MENU ITEMS
	ENTREES $7 TO $17		HANDICAPPED ACCESSIBLE
CREDIT CARDS	MAJOR CREDIT CARDS ACCEPTED		TAKE-OUT ORDERS AVAILABLE
RESERVATIONS	PARTIES OF SIX OR MORE		CATERING
HOURS	OPEN SEVEN DAYS A WEEK		PRIVATE DINING ROOM
	FOR LUNCH AND DINNER		SATURDAY/SUNDAY BRUNCH
	SUNDAY THROUGH THURSDAY,	DRESS CODE	CASUAL
	11:30 A.M. TO 11 P.M.	PARKING	AVAILABLE ON THE PREMISES
	FRIDAY AND SATURDAY,		AND THROUGH THE VALET SERVICE
	11:30 A.M. TO 1 A.M.		

APPETIZERS

SPINACH AND FETA STUFFED MUSHROOMS WITH SUN-DRIED TOMATO,
   MOZZARELLA AND GARLIC
BREADED EGGPLANT STUFFED WITH MOZZARELLA AND PROSCIUTTO WITH
   A MARINARA SAUCE
MUSSELS MARINARA
GORGONZOLA AND MOZZARELLA BRUSCHETTA WITH TOMATO AND
   FRESH BASIL

ENTREES

PASTA WITH PINK VODKA SAUCE
PASTA WITH RED OR WHITE TUNA SAUCE
SHRIMP SCAMPI WITH BROCCOLI, ARTICHOKE HEARTS, ROASTED PEPPERS AND
   SUN-DRIED TOMATOES OVER LINGUINE
GRILLED SAUSAGES OVER BALSAMIC ROASTED VEGETABLES
CHICKEN SAUTÉED IN A GARLIC BUTTER SAUCE WITH ARTICHOKE HEARTS,
   ROASTED PEPPERS AND MUSHROOMS
VEAL MARSALA
FILET MIGNON FINISHED WITH HOT CHERRY PEPPERS, MUSHROOMS AND
   BLACK OLIVES IN GARLIC BUTTER SAUCE

CHICKEN CAPRI

Serves 4

2 pounds boneless chicken breasts
3 tablespoons olive oil
1/2 cup flour, for dredging
1 pinch kosher salt
1 pinch freshly ground black pepper
2 cups sliced white mushrooms
1 cup pale dry sherry
1 cup chicken broth
6 artichoke hearts, sliced or quartered
1 cup roasted red peppers, cut into strips
1/2 cup garlic butter
1 teaspoon freshly chopped flat leaf parsley

Preheat a skillet that will be large enough to hold all of the chicken and the sauce; add the olive oil.

Season the flour with some salt and pepper to taste. Dredge the chicken cutlets in the flour and shake off any excess flour so that it won't burn in the pan. Sauté the chicken on medium-high heat for approximately 2 minutes on each side, depending on the thickness.

Remove the cooked chicken from the pan and add the mushrooms. The mushrooms may absorb all of the oil in the pan at first, but will give it back when they start to cook. Lower the heat and stir constantly to prevent burning. You may have to drizzle in a little more oil, but be careful not to add too much.

Once the mushrooms have cooked, return the heat to high and add the sherry. Allow the sherry to reduce by half, then add the chicken broth and the remaining ingredients. Simmer the sauce and let it reduce by about one quarter.

Return the chicken to the pan and simmer another 3 to 5 minutes. Arrange the cutlets on a platter and ladle the sauce over the top. Serve immediately.

Summer salad

Mamma Luisa

673 Thames Street, Newport | 401-848-5257 | www.mammaluisa.com

JUST ASK TONY SOPRANO

When our Italian jazz musician friend comes up from NYC, the only restaurant he ever wants to go to is Mamma Luisa's in Newport. Maybe it's because it feels like you're eating in someone's home, or maybe it's the service, which is friendly, but never intrusive. Maybe it's the great wine list, but porbably it is the food. The owners are from Bologna, second-generation restaurant people, and their food is as fresh and authentic as it gets. Totally reliable, always a pleasure, Mamma Luisa is a great place to stop by on a winter night (James Gandolfini, aka Tony Soprano, did just that this past January), but in the summer you better reserve well in advance.

INSIDE SCOOP

CHEF	ALESANDRO ANCARANI	HOURS	OPEN SEVEN DAYS A WEEK
OWNERS	ALESANDRO ANCARANI		FOR DINNER
	AND MARCO TRAZZI	LIQUOR	FULL LIQUOR
OPEN SINCE	1992	SMOKING	PERMITTED
CUISINE	SIMPLE, TRADITIONAL ITALIAN	SERVICES	HEALTHY/LOW-FAT MENU ITEMS
SPECIALTY	VEAL OSSOBUCO		VEGETARIAN MENU ITEMS
PRICE RANGE	APPETIZERS $5 TO $8		TAKE-OUT ORDERS AVAILABLE
	ENTREES $13 TO $24		PRIVATE DINING ROOM
CREDIT CARDS	MAJOR CREDIT CARDS ACCEPTED	DRESS CODE	BUSINESS/CASUAL
RESERVATIONS	RECOMMENDED	PARKING	AVAILABLE ON THE STREET

APPETIZERS

RADICCHIO, ARUGULA, DATES, WALNUTS, GOAT CHEESE AND GRAPES
  IN A HONEY MUSTARD VINAIGRETTE
BRUSCHETTA WITH FAVA BEANS AND SHAVED PECORINO AND
  PROSCIUTTO
CARPACCIO (BEEF TENDERLOIN WITH PARMIGIANO, FRESH
  MUSHROOMS, CAPERS, ARUGULA AND GRILLED ARTICHOKES)
CANTALOUPE WITH PROSCIUTTO, MOZZARELLA AND OLIVES

ENTREES

HOMEMADE RICOTTA AND SPINACH GNOCCHI WITH MARINARA SAUCE
  AND ARUGULA
TAGLIATELLE WITH SAUTÉED SHRIMP AND SEA SCALLOPS WITH EXTRA
  VIRGIN OLIVE OIL, GARLIC AND BASIL
SPAGHETTI CARBONARA
VEAL SCALOPPINE WITH ARTICHOKES, CAPERS, FRESH LEMON JUICE
  AND WHITE WINE
BAKED PORK LOIN STUFFED WITH PROSCIUTTO AND PARMESAN,
  SERVED WITH MUSHROOMS AND SPINACH CREAM SAUCE

Mediterraneo

HEY, ISN'T THAT BILLY JOEL?

If you've never been to Mediterraneo, get yourself over there as soon as possible. As we go to press with this book, Mediterraneo is the only restaurant in the state to win the coveted AAA Four Diamond Award for its food, service and atmosphere. This is one of those very rare and special restaurants that does everything right. The menu offers authentic Italian cuisine with a modern twist. The wine list is simply stellar. The service is friendly yet professional. And then there's the ambiance – sexy and sophisticated, casual and cosmopolitan. Don't be surprised if you see a celebrity or two at Mediterraneo. That's where those in the know head when they come to town.

GRAPEVINE GEM: Late on Saturday nights, after the kitchen closes at Mediterraneo, the upper level turns into a very upscale Latin dance club where couples samba the night away.

INSIDE SCOOP

CHEFS	MICHELE CALISE AND GIANFRANCO CAMPANELLA	LIQUOR	FULL LIQUOR
OWNER	GIANFRANCO MARROCCO, GAETANO MARROCCO AND DR. FABIO POTENTI	SMOKING	PERMITTED AT THE BAR AND IN THE SIDEWALK CAFE
		SERVICES	BANQUET FACILITIES
OPENING	1997		VEGETARIAN MENU ITEMS
CUISINE	ITALIAN		HANDICAPPED ACCESSIBLE
SPECIALTY	SURF AND TURF, FILET MIGNON		PRIVATE DINING ROOM
PRICE RANGE	APPETIZERS $9 TO $22	DRESS CODE	SMART, CASUAL, STYLISH
	ENTREES $14 TO $31	PARKING	AVAILABLE ON THE STREET AND THROUGH THE VALET SERVICE
CREDIT CARDS	MAJOR CREDIT CARDS ACCEPTED		
RESERVATIONS	RECOMMENDED		
HOURS	LUNCH: MONDAY THROUGH FRIDAY, 11:30 A.M. TO 3 P.M. DINNER: MONDAY THROUGH FRIDAY 3 TO 10 P.M. SATURDAY, 4 TO 11 P.M. SUNDAY, 4 TO 10 P.M.		

APPETIZERS

ANTIPASTO – IMPORTED PARMA PROSCIUTTO, ROASTED CIPOLLINE, AURICCHIO
PROVOLONE, EGGPLANT CAPONATA, CANNELLINI BEAN SALAD, POTATO
CROQUETTES, SICILIAN RICE BALLS, FRITTATA, ROASTED RED AND YELLOW
PEPPERS, IMPORTED OLIVES AND PICKLED MUSHROOMS

GRILLED TUSCAN BREAD TOPPED WITH GRILLED PORTOBELLO MUSHROOM AND
PAN-SEARED TENDERLOIN TIPS IN A MADEIRA WINE AND FRESH THYME
CREAM SAUCE

NATIVE LITTLENECK CLAMS SAUTÉED IN OLIVE OIL, GARLIC, WINE AND PLUM
TOMATO SAUCE WITH A DASH OF RED PEPPER AND GRILLED TUSCAN BREAD

PAPER -THIN SLICES OF SUSHI-GRADE TUNA, ARUGULA, FRESH LEMON JUICE,
EXTRA VIRGIN OLIVE OIL AND A MEDITERRANEAN SALMORIGLIO – FINELY
DICED RED AND YELLOW PEPPERS, SCALLIONS, TOMATO, CAPERS, CITRUS
JUICE AND EXTRA VIRGIN OLIVE OIL

ENTREES

GNOCCHI ALLA SORRENTINA

OVERSIZED LOBSTER RAVIOLI FINISHED IN A LIGHT MASCARPONE CREAM
SAUCE

RISOTTO WITH LITTLENECK CLAMS, SHRIMP, MUSSELS, CALAMARI AND CHUNKS
OF FRESH FISH IN A LIGHT PLUM TOMATO SAUCE

OVEN-ROASTED BREADED PORK TENDERLOIN MARINATED IN A HONEY
MUSTARD SAUCE WITH APPLE BRANDY CREAM SAUCE

BAKED SEAFOOD MEDLEY – JUMBO SHRIMP, LOBSTER, SCALLOPS AND FILET OF
SOLE, ALL WITH A STONE CRAB STUFFING

SPAGHETTI ALLA PUTTANESCA

Serves 4

6 tablespoons olive oil
3 garlic cloves, sliced
1 red chili pepper, chopped
1 pound plum tomatoes, peeled
3 canned anchovy filets
1 pound spaghetti
3 tablespoons capers
1/3 cup small pitted black olives (calamata or gaeta)
Salt and pepper, to taste
1/2 bunch fresh Italian parsley, chopped

In a large saucepan, heat the olive oil. Add the garlic and chili pepper, stirring constantly. Stir in the tomatoes and anchovies. Simmer for 15 minutes uncovered.

In a large pot, bring 4 quarts of salted water to a boil. Cook the spaghetti until al dente.

Stir the capers and olives into the sauce. Season with salt and pepper.

Drain the spaghetti and fold immediately into the sauce. Sprinkle with parsley. Serve with freshly grated Parmesan cheese, if desired.

THE BOLD AND THE BEAUTIFUL

The Providence restaurant scene was rocked when Mill's Tavern opened in March 2002, and overnight it became the city's new hot spot. The most positive reviews imaginable started to roll in, and nearly everyone fell in love with this big and bold, warm and vibrant restaurant, owned by the visionary team of Jaime D'Oliveira and Ken Cusson. Overseeing the kitchen is Chef Jules Ramos who lets the soul of the food come out in each and every dish. This is honest food we're talking about, the kind that raises your level of expectation. Our favorite dish: the house sandwich, foie gras and duck confit on a black currant biscuit with tea-braised figs on the side. Oh my......

GRAPEVINE GEM: It simply does not get any better than this. Even the bathrooms are exquisitely appointed.

INSIDE SCOOP

CHEF	JULES RAMOS	LIQUOR	FULL LIQUOR WITH 160 PLUS WINE
OWNERS	PROVIDENCE HOSPITALITY GROUP		SELECTIONS, PLUS AN ASSORTMENT
	(KEN CUSSON AND JAIME D'OLIVEIRA)		OF HALF-BOTTLES
OPEN SINCE	2002	SMOKING	ALLOWED IN THE BAR AREA
CUISINE	NEW AMERICAN CUISINE	SERVICES	HEALTHY/LOW-FAT MENU ITEMS
SPECIALTY	WOOD-FIRED COOKING		VEGETARIAN
PRICE RANGE	APPETIZERS $6 TO $14		HANDICAPPED ACCESSIBLE
	ENTREES $17 TO $29		PRIVATE DINING ROOM
CREDIT CARDS	MAJOR CREDIT CARDS ACCEPTED	DRESS CODE	BUSINESS/SMART CASUAL
RESERVATIONS	RECOMMENDED, ESPECIALLY	PARKING	AVAILABLE ON THE STREET, IN
	ON WEEKENDS		NEARBY LOTS, AND THROUGH
HOURS	SUNDAY THROUGH THURSDAY,		THE VALET SERVICE
	5 TO 10 P.M.		
	FRIDAY AND SATURDAY,		
	5 TO 11 P.M.		
	LATE-NIGHT MENU		
	AVAILABLE ON WEEKNIGHTS,		
	10:30 P.M. TO 12:30 A.M., AND ON		
	WEEKENDS, 11:30 P.M. TO 1:30 A.M.		

APPETIZERS

CRAB CLAWS WITH SPICY MUSTARD SAUCE

SEAFOOD SALD WITH CITRUS AND CHIVE DRESSING

GRAND SHELLFISH PLATTER

MILL'S SANDWICH — BLACK CURRANT BUTTERMILK BISCUIT, SEAARED FOIE GRAS
AND TEA-BRAISED FIGS

SMOKED DUCK BREAST WITH ROASTED GARLIC POLENTA CROUTONS AND
STRAWBERRY-RHUBARB CHUTNEY

OPEN-FACED RABBIT RAVIOLI WITH WILD MUSHROOMS, SAGE AND TRUFFLE
ESSENCE

BRAISED LITTLENECKS IN SPICY TOMATO AND SAGRES BEER BROTH WITH
GRILLED CHORIZO AND SWEET ONIONS

ENTREES

BAROLO-BRAISED BEEF SHORTRIBS WITH MASHED POTATOES

ROASTED COD WITH SPICY CRAB AND SPRING SUCCOTASH OF PEAS, ASPARAGUS
AND CORN

POMMERY MUSTARD AND HORSERADISH-CRUSTED RACK OF LAMB WITH GOAT
CHEESE MASHED POTATOES AND ROSEMARY JUS

BUTTERMILK AND ROSEMARY MARINATED WOOD ROTISSERIE CHICKEN WITH
FINGERLING POTATOES, ROASTED SHALLOTS AND PAN JUS

THE STEAK HOUSE PRIME 14-OUNCE NEW YORK STRIP SIRLOIN

GRILLED VENISON CHOPS WITH JUNIPER AND BLACK PEPPER OIL

CRISPY SALMON AND FRENCH LENTILS WITH TOMATO CITRUS JAM

ROTISSERIE PORK LOIN WITH CARROT-SWEET POTATO MASH, GRILLED ENDIVE
AND GRAPE CONSERVE

CRISPY SALMON
WITH FRENCH LENTILS AND TOMATO CITRUS JAM
Serves 2

For the Lentils:	2 bay leaves
3 strips bacon, finely diced	4 cups chicken stock or broth
1 cup finely chopped onions	2 cups French green lentils
1/2 cup finely diced carrots	Salt and pepper, to taste
1/2 cup finely diced celery	

In a heavy-bottomed pan, over low heat, render bacon for about 5 minutes. Add onions, carrots and celery. Increase heat to medium-high and cook vegetables until translucent. Add bay leaves and stock; bring to a boil. Add lentils. When liquid comes back to a boil, lower heat and simmer, stirring occasionally, for 45 minutes to 1 hour. Check lentils for doneness. Season with salt and pepper at the end, so the salt does not toughen the lentils.

For the Tomato-Citrus Jam:	1/4 cup balsamic vinegar
1 pound ripe Roma tomatoes	1/4 cup extra virgin olive oil
1 cup fresh squeezed orange juice	Zest from 2 oranges

Core the tomatoes, and on the opposite end, cut shallow criss-cross. Plunge tomatoes into hot boiling water for 30 to 40 seconds. Remove and immediately plunge into ice water. Allow to cool, then peel, cut in half, seed and dice into 1/4-inch pieces.

In a saucepan, combine tomatoes, orange juice, balsamic vinegar and olive oil. Bring to a boil. Lower heat to a simmer and reduce, cooking for 1 to 1 and 1/2 hours, or until nice and thick. Cool completely. Stir in zest. Serve at room temperature over seared salmon.

For the Crispy Salmon:
2 (6-ounce) salmon filets, boned and skinned
Salt and pepper, to taste
2 tablespoons extra virgin olive oil

Heat a sauté pan on medium-high heat. Season the filets with salt and pepper. Add oil to pan. Sear fish on both sides; reduce heat and cook to medium rare, approximately 5 minutes per side.

The Mooring

SITTIN' ON THE DOCK OF THE BAY

For more than 20 years, The Mooring has been specializing in traditional New England seafood in a waterfront setting quite popular with local yachtsmen. Award-winning Chef Chris Ferris changes his menu three times a year and offers daily specials. He's especially fond of his versatile Chunky Lobster Sauce. Highly recommended is the creamy Scallop Chowder with its touch of white wine and fresh dill. The calamari is so good, it's sold by the pound rather than the plate. The Mooring is especially known for its lobster roll, perhaps the best in the state. For landlubbers, the menu also offers a half-dozen chicken and beef dishes.

GRAPEVINE GEM: If it's your birthday, you can have lunch or dinner for free at The Mooring. Come in with your friends and family, bring along some proof of your birth date, and before you know it, they'll be singing "Happy Birthday" to you.

INSIDE SCOOP

CHEF	CHRIS FERRIS	SERVICES	BANQUET FACILITIES
OWNER	NEWPORT HARBOR CORPORATION		CHILDREN'S MENU
OPEN SINCE	1981		VEGETARIAN MENU ITEMS
CUISINE	SEAFOOD		HANDICAPPED ACCESSIBLE
SPECIALTY	CHUNKY LOBSTER SAUCE		TAKE-OUT ORDERS AVAILABLE
PRICE RANGE	APPETIZERS $3 TO $14		PRIVATE DINING ROOM
	ENTREES $9 TO $28		FIREPLACE
CREDIT CARDS	MAJOR CREDIT CARDS ACCEPTED	DRESS CODE	CASUAL
RESERVATIONS	RECOMMENDED	PARKING	VALIDATED IN THE FALL,
HOURS	OPEN DAILY, EXCEPT CHRISTMAS.		WINTER AND SPRING IN
	HOURS VARY BY SEASON		PARKING LOT ON THE PREMISES
LIQUOR	FULL LIQUOR		
SMOKING	PERMITTED AT THE		
	BAR AND OUTSIDE		

APPETIZERS

SCALLOP CHOWDER (SEA SCALLOPS IN A CREAM STOCK WITH WHITE WINE
   AND DILL)

PORTUGUESE MUSSELS STEAMED WITH TOMATO, GARLIC, CHORIZO, PEPPERS
   AND ONIONS

MAINE SNOW CRAB AND ROCK CRAB CHILLED AND SERVED WITH TWO ROCK
   CRAB CLAWS AND COCKTAIL SAUCE

WARM BRIE AND ITALIAN BREAD WITH HONEY MUSTARD SAUCE, GRAPES
   AND PINE NUTS

ENTREES

GRILLED YELLOWFIN TUNA WITH A FRESH VEGETABLE SALSA

PORTUGUESE SHELLFISH STEW (CLAMS, MUSSELS, SCALLOPS AND SHRIMP IN A
   TOMATO SEAFOOD STOCK WITH CHORIZO AND ONIONS)

BAKED LOBSTER STUFFED WITH SCALLOPS AND CRAB MEAT

LOIN LAMB CHOPS GRILLED WITH GARLIC AND FRESH ROSEMARY, SERVED
   WITH A BAKED STUFFED TOMATO

SLICED GRILLED CHICKEN BREAST OVER A STUFFED PORTABELLO MUSHROOM
   WITH SMOKED MOZZARELLA, TOMATOES AND ARTICHOKE HEARTS

PRIME RIBEYE STEAK WITH HORSERADISH SOUR CREAM SAUCE

BEEF TENDERLOINN WITH LEMON TARRAGON BUTTER AND GRILLED
   ASPARAGUS

CHUNKY LOBSTER SAUCE

4 lobster culls	1/2 gallon white wine
Butter and oil, as needed	Salt and pepper, to taste
8 large carrots, chopped	1 pinch thyme
3 stalks celery, chopped	1 pinch chopped parsley
5 large shallots	2 quarts heavy cream
1 cup brandy	2 tablespoons tarragon

Split lobsters in half; save juice and tamale. Sauté lobsters in butter and oil in a heavy stock pot. Add carrots and celery; cook until lobsters start to turn red. Add brandy. Cook off the alcohol; add the wine, salt, pepper, thyme and parsley. Reduce almost completely.

Remove lobster; allow to cool. Add heavy cream; reduce to three-quarters. In a blender, puree the tamale, tarragon and any juice left from splitting the lobster. When pureed, whip slowly in saucepan. Remove lobster meat from lobster, cut up into bite-size pieces, and add to sauce.

This sauce goes well with veal, chicken and seafood. You can even use it as a soup or bisque.

A summer night on Federal Hill

Naissance

GOING GLOBAL

Still considered the new kid on the Federal Hill block, Naissance is different from the rest, offering intercontinental fusion cuisine and specializing in fondues. The food is quite exciting and adventuresome, with the flavors of the Southwest, Asia and Italy dancing on your plate. The surroundings are sophisticated yet comfortable, thanks to the vision of owners Rick Simone and John Velez, two of the movers and shakers in this renaissance city. This is one restaurant where you can count on the kitchen being open late at night, which is especially appealing to the under-30 crowd.

INSIDE SCOOP

CHEF	VINCENT C. COSTABLE	LIQUOR	FULL LIQUOR
OWNERS	JOHN VELEZ AND RICK SIMONE	SMOKING	PERMITTED AT BAR ONLY
OPEN SINCE	2000	SERVICES	BANQUET FACILITIES
CUISINE	INTERCONTINENTAL FUSION		HEALTHY/LOW-FAT MENU ITEMS
SPECIALTY	FONDUES		VEGETARIAN MENU ITEMS
PRICE RANGE	APPETIZERS $8 TO $9		HANDICAPPED ACCESSIBLE
	ENTREES $20 TO $24		TAKE-OUT ORDERS AVAILABLE
CREDIT CARDS	MAJOR CREDIT CARDS ACCEPTED		CATERING
RESERVATIONS	RECOMMENDED		PRIVATE DINING ROOM
HOURS	OPEN SEVEN NIGHTS A WEEK	DRESS CODE	CASUAL
	FOR DINNER	PARKING	AVAILABLE ON THE STREET AND
	SUNDAY BRUNCH		THROUGH THE VALET SERVICE

APPETIZERS

SOUTHWESTERN BLUE CRAB AND TIGER SHRIMP TIMBALE

GREEN-LIP MUSSELS WITH WHITE WINE, GARLIC, TOMATOES, BUTTER
AND CREAM ON A BAGUETTE

THAI-STYLE STEAK SKEWERS WITH GINGER, GARLIC AND SPICES IN A
SPICY PLUM-GINGER SAUCE WITH CRISP WONTONS

GRILLED PIZZA WITH GRILLED SHRIMP AND GOAT CHEESE

ENTREES

ASIAN-STYLE PLUM-GINGER FONDUE WITH FRESH VEGETABLE
TEMPURA, PETITE CHICKEN TENDERLOINS, SHRIMP SPRING ROLLS
AND WONTON WAFERS

SPINACH AND ARTICHOKE FONDUE WITH TOASTED GARLIC, IMPORTED
PARMESAN, FRESH CREAM, TOASTED PITA CHIPS, ROASTED POTATO
WEDGES AND GRILLED SQUASH

GRILLED VEAL T-BONE WITH MASHED POTATOES, TOASTED GARLIC
RAPINI AND ZINFANDEL DEMIGLACE

GRILLED TIGER SHRIMP AND GRILLED LEMON-GARLIC DIVER SCALLOPS
WITH PEPPER-CRUSTED FILET MIGNON, RICE PILAF, FRESH
ASPARAGUS AND ZINFANDEL DEMIGLACE

CIOPPINO WITH MUSSELS, ROCK SHRIMP, CALAMARI AND FRESH FISH
IN A WHITE WINE TOMATO BROTH OVER CAPELLINI

CALIFORNIA DREAMIN'

Napa Valley Grille is undoubtedly the jewel in the crown of restaurants at Providence Place mall. Yet it doesn't seem like it's in the mall, at all. Chef Stuart Cameron's "wine country" cuisine is extraordinary, served graciously in casually elegant surroundings. A large fresco in an autumnal hue graces one wall of the large restaurant. The innovative menu changes with the seasons, and game items such as ostrich are regularly featured. The cocktail lounge is the perfect spot to meet friends for a bit of wine sampling after work, or for tourists to relax in handsome surroundings. The restaurant's massive wine list is recognized as one of the best in the country by *Wine Spectator* magazine.

GRAPEVINE GEM: In addition to the warm and inviting main dining room and patio, Napa Valley Grille offers two private areas for entertaining – the Vintner's Room, which accommodates 32 guests, and the Wine Country Estate, which can comfortably seat 75.

INSIDE SCOOP

CHEF:	STUART CAMERON	LIQUOR:	FULL LIQUOR
OWNER:	CONSTELLATION CONCEPTS	SMOKING:	PERMITTED
OPEN SINCE:	1999	SERVICES:	BANQUET FACILITIES
CUISINE:	WINE COUNTRY CASUAL		CHILDREN'S MENU
SPECIALTY:	SEASONAL RISOTTO		HEALTHY/LOW-FAT MENU ITEMS
PRICE RANGE:	APPETIZERS $5 TO $13		VEGETARIAN MENU ITEMS
	ENTREES $14 TO $30		HANDICAPPED ACCESSIBLE
CREDIT CARDS:	MAJOR CREDIT CARDS ACCEPTED		TAKE-OUT ORDERS AVAILABLE
RESERVATIONS:	RECOMMENDED		CATERING
HOURS:	LUNCH:		PRIVATE DINING ROOM
	MONDAY THROUGH SATURDAY,		SUNDAY BRUNCH
	11:30 A.M. TO 4 P.M.	DRESS CODE:	CASUAL
	DINNER:	PARKING:	PROVIDENCE PLACE GARAGE
	EVERY DAY OF THE WEEK, 5 TO 10:30 P.M.		
	BRUNCH ON SUNDAY, 11:30 A.M. TO 3 P.M.		

APPETIZERS

CRISPY MIX OF CALAMARI, LEMON, POTATO FRITES

SWEET ROASTED GARLIC WITH WARM BRIE CHEESE, TOMATO CHUTNEY AND
  CROSTINI

ARTISAN CHEESE PLATE WITH FRUITS, CANDIED WALNUTS, AND BAGUETTE

DUCK LIVER PATE WITH BRANDIED CHERRY COMPOTE, WHOLE GRAIN MUSTARD-
  PORT WINE REDUCTION

BABY ARUGULA AND FRESH FIGS WITH PROSCIUTTO, GOAT CHEESE, FIELD
  GREENS AND HONEY BALSAMIC VINAIGRETTE

CHOPPED COBB SALAD WITH SHRIMP, CHICKEN, BACON, AVOCADO,
  ARTICHOKES, BLUE CHEESE AND A SHALLOT DRESSING

ENTREES

GRILLED PORK LOIN WITH ROASTED PLUMS, WILD RICE, HAZELNUTS, AND PORT
  WINE JUS

SLOW-ROASTED LEG OF LAMB, POTATOES BOULANGÈRE AND GREEN BEANS
  PROVENCAL

GRILLED FLAT IRON STEAK WITH WATERCRESS, BROILED TOMATO, BISTRO
  POTATOES AND BLUE CHEESE BEARNAISE BUTTER

CRISPY SKIN SALMON WITH LITTLENECK CLAMS, TARRAGON CREAM AND
  FINGERLING POTATOES

GRILLED SWORDFISH WITH AVOCADO-OLIVE RELISH, SOFT POLENTA AND WARM
  TOMATO VINAIGRETTE

BACON WILTED SPINACH

Serves 4

6 slices bacon
1 small onion, diced
2 bags spinach, rinsed
2 tablespoons red wine vinegar
Salt and pepper, to taste

Microwave or pan fry bacon until crispy. Save fat.

Heat large sauté pan until hot. Add bacon fat and onion. Sauté onion until wilted. Add spinach to pan, in batches if necessary, and all of the vinegar.

Remove spinach from heat as soon as it is wilted; season with salt and pepper. Serve immediately.

Neath's

EAST MEETS WEST

Neath's is so good, it would definitely be in our top ten list of restaurants. Chef-owner Neath Pal was born in Cambodia, raised in the United States, and learned to be a chef in Paris. So it's no surprise that his waterview restaurant offers an eclectic blend of French and Asian cuisine, often utilizing classic New England ingredients. Neath, as he is known to all, has cooked at some of the finest restaurants in Providence, including Al Forno and L'Epicureo. He considers his best dish to be the Braised New England Lobster in red curry with coconut milk and chowfoon noodles. His coconut bruschetta is like all his food – so different, so good. Neath's is an excellent spot to dine on a night when WaterFire is scheduled.

Chef Neath Pal's specialties include Chocolate Wontons served with ginger ice cream. Here is the recipe for that unusual ice cream:

GINGER ICE CREAM
Makes 1 quart ice cream

2 cups milk
1 cup heavy cream
1 cup sugar, divided

3 tablespoons fresh ginger, chopped and peeled
7 egg yolks

In a saucepan, bring milk, cream and 1/2 cup sugar just to a boil. Reserve the other 1/2 cup sugar. Remove from heat and add the ginger. Steep for 15 minutes.

In a large bowl, whisk egg yolks with remaining 1/2 cup sugar. Drizzle milk mixture into egg mixture, whisking constantly, then pour back into saucepan and cook over moderate heat for 3 to 4 minutes, until slightly thickened. Do not boil; stir constantly with a wooden spoon to avoid curdling. Strain and cool completely.

Freeze mixture in ice cream machine according to directions.

INSIDE SCOOP

CHEF-OWNER	NEATH PAL	HOURS	OPEN TUESDAY THROUGH
OPEN SINCE	1998		SATURDAY FOR DINNER
CUISINE	SOUTHEAST ASIAN	LIQUOR	FULL LIQUOR
	FUSED WITH AMERICAN	SMOKING	PERMITTED IN THE LOUNGE
SPECIALTY	BRAISED NEW ENGLAND	SERVICES	HEALTHY/LOW-FAT MENU ITEMS
	LOBSTER IN RED CURRY		VEGETARIAN MENU ITEMS
	WITH COCONUT MILK AND		HANDICAPPED ACCESSIBLE
	CHOWFOON NOODLES		TAKE-OUT ORDERS AVAILABLE
PRICE RANGE	APPETIZERS $7 TO $17	DRESS CODE	CASUAL
	ENTREES $21 TO $27	PARKING	AVAILABLE ON THE STREET AND IN
CREDIT CARDS	MAJOR CREDIT CARDS ACCEPTED		AN ADJACENT PARKING LOT
RESERVATIONS	RECOMMENDED		

APPETIZERS

WOOD-GRILLED BAGUETTE WITH COCONUT MILK AND SCALLION
    DIPPING SAUCE
ROASTED JUMBO OYSTERS WITH LIME AND BLACK PEPPER MIGNONETTE
PAN-SEARED FOIE GRAS, CARAMELIZED MANGO AND STRAWBERRY
    WITH PORT AND BALSAMIC GLAZE
CAMBODIAN SPRING ROLL WITH SHRIMP, BEAN SPROUTS AND THAI
    BASIL WITH A PEANUT DIPPING SAUCE

ENTREES

ROASTED CHILEAN SEA BASS WITH A CHINESE BLACK BEAN MARINADE
WOOD-GRILLED CHICKEN BREAST WITH LEMON GRASS RUB OVER
    GREEN PAPAYA AND THAI BASIL SALAD
GRILLED YELLOWFIN TUNA WITH A SOY GINGER GLAZE OVER SOBA
    NOODLE GALETTE AND GRILLED BABY BOK CHOY
PAN-ROASTED DUCK BREAST AND DUCK CONFIT WITH A GINGER
    GLAZE, WILTED SPINACH AND SWEET POTATO GRATIN
LOBSTER BRAISED IN RED CURRY AND COCONUT MILK WITH SNOW
    PEAS AND SHIITAKE OVER GARLICKY CHOWFOON NOODLES

New England Fish Factory

FISHING FOR COMPLIMENTS

Outstanding fresh seafood – as well as many delicious items for landlubbers – can be found at this modern and immaculate Pawtucket restaurant. We recommend starting with ice-cold selections from the raw bar or the piping hot clam chowder. The Seafood Platter will give you a taste of almost everything on a single visit to the New England Fish Factory, where the whole family can be satisfied. The overstuffed sandwiches are mighty tempting, and the creative salads will leave you feeling healthy and full. Save room for dessert, especially in the summer when the ice cream parlor caters to warm-weather cravings.

INSIDE SCOOP

CHEF	GREG MURPHY	SMOKING	NO
OWNER	GREG AND ELLEN MURPHY	SERVICES	BANQUET FACILITIES
OPEN SINCE	2001		CHILDREN'S MENU
CUISINE	NEW ENGLAND SEAFOOD		HEALTHY/LOW-FAT MENU ITEMS
SPECIALTY	FISH AND CHIPS		HANDICAPPED ACCESSIBLE
PRICE RANGE	APPETIZERS $2 TO $8		TAKE-OUT ORDERS AVAILABLE
	ENTREES $5 TO $15		CATERING
CREDIT CARDS	MAJOR CREDIT CARDS ACCEPTED		PRIVATE DINING ROOM
RESERVATIONS	NOT NECESSARY		FIREPLACE
HOURS	OPEN SEVEN DAYS A WEEK	DRESS CODE	CASUAL
	FOR LUNCH AND DINNER	PARKING	AVAILABLE ON THE PREMISES
LIQUOR	FULL LIQUOR		

APPETIZERS

MAINE CRAB CAKE WITH DIPPING SAUCE
BUFFALO CHICKEN TENDERS WITH BLUE CHEESE DRESSING
LOBSTER BISQUE
CRISPY FRIED ONION STRINGS WITH DIPPING SAUCE
RAW BAR

ENTREES

FISH AND CHIPS
SALMON WITH FRIES AND SALAD
BOILED LOBSTER
SEAFOOD PLATTER – CLAMS, SCALLOPS, SHRIMP AND FISH
CRABMEAT-STUFFED SOLE
BAKED STUFFED SHRIMP CASSEROLE

WASABI RUSH

A precious gem of a restaurant, New Japan is quite near Trinity Repertory Theater, making it a great spot for a pre-show dinner. With only 30 seats, it's wise to get there early. Chef-owner Yukio Hiyama was trained in Tokyo and has operated this authentic Japanese restaurant since 1978 with a very loyal following. It's simply amazing what he and his staff produce in their tiny kitchen – the freshest sushi and sashimi, steamed dumplings, teriyaki and tofu dishes, soups including udon, and our favorite, tempura. You might be surprised to see curry on the menu, but Hiyama tells us it is quite common for restaurants in Japan to offer spicy curry sauce dinners.

GRAPEVINE GEM: Hiyama is an authority on sake and always willing to explain its nuances to interested customers. This alcoholic drink from Japan is usually served hot, but very expensive sakes should be chilled.

INSIDE SCOOP

CHEF-OWNER:	YUKIO HIYAMA	LIQUOR:	WINE, BEER AND SAKE ONLY
OPEN SINCE:	1978	SMOKING:	NO SMOKING ALLOWED
CUISINE:	JAPANESE	SERVICES:	CLOSE TO THEATRES AND ARTS DISTRICT
SPECIALTY:	SUSHI AND SASHIMI		HEALTHY/LOW-FAT MENU ITEMS
PRICE RANGE:	APPETIZERS $2.50 TO $3.50		VEGETARIAN MENU ITEMS
	ENTREES $6 TO $9	DRESS CODE:	CASUAL
CREDIT CARDS:	MAJOR CREDIT CARDS ACCEPTED	PARKING:	AVAILABLE ON THE STREET AND IN NEARBY
RESERVATIONS:	NONE		PARKING LOTS
HOURS:	CLOSED MONDAYS		
	LUNCH TUESDAY THROUGH FRIDAY,		
	11:30 A.M. TO 2:30 P.M.		
	DINNER TUESDAY THROUGH SUNDAY,		
	5 TO 9:30 P.M.		

APPETIZERS

SASHIMI (DELICATELY SLICED ASSORTMENT OF OCEAN-FRESH RAW FISH)

GYOZA (STEAMED DUMPLINGS FILLED WITH FINELY CHOPPED BEEF AND VEGETABLES)

YAKI-TORI (SUCCULENT SKEWERED CHICKEN BREAST BROILED IN TERIYAKI SAUCE)

AGETASHI TOFU (CUBED TOFU FRIED AND TOPPED WITH A GRATED GINGER AND SCALLION SAUCE)

SNOW CRAB AND AVOCADO WITH SOY SAUCE AND WASABI

ENTREES

CURRY DINNERS (VEGETABLE AND/OR MEAT IN A SPICY CURRY SAUCE OVER RICE)

SHRIMP, FISH AND VEGETABLE TEMPURA

SASHIMI DINNER

YAKI DINNER (FISH, CHICKEN, SHRIMP AND VEGETABLES WRAPPED IN FOIL AND SEASONED WITH SOY SAUCE AND BUTTER)

DEEP-FRIED PORK CUTLET WITH DARK AND SPICY SAUCE

BARBECUED FRESH WATER EEL

JAPANESE NOODLES WITH FRESH VEGETABLES, SEA GREENS AND SHIITAKE MUSHROOMS IN A LIGHT FISH BROTH

SALMON TERIYAKI

WAKAME SALAD
SEA GREENS SALAD

Serves 4

1/2 cup Wakame sea greens*
1 cucumber
2 tablespoons rice wine vinegar (high-end brand such as Shiragiku is recommended)
1 tablespoon soy sauce
1 tablespoon mirin (rice wine)
1 teaspoon toasted sesame seeds

Reconstitute Wakame sea greens in a bowl of cold water. Thinly slice cucumber.

Stir together rice wine vinegar, soy sauce and mirin for dressing.

Pour dressing over sea greens. Sprinkle sesame seeds in; stir and serve.

*Wakame sea greens are available at Asian food markets.

SMALL PACKAGE, BIG SURPRISE

One of the very best restaurants in the city of Providence is the oh-so-romantic New Rivers. Precious and intimate well describe this tiny bistro, where New American Cuisine is offered along with global influences and seasonal local produce. It doesn't get much better than that. The constantly changing menu is the creation of chef-owner Bruce Tillinghast, who is one of the very few Rhode Island chefs to be nominated for a prestigious James Beard award. When you dine at New Rivers, whether you're tucked into a cozy booth or seated at the world's smallest bar, you will most certainly be delighted with the creative food and impeccable service. One of our absolute favorites.

GRAPEVINE GEM: A lot of the gracious touches in this restaurant come from Bruce Tillinghast's late wife, Pat. Another legacy of Pat that remains on the menu is her fresh baked cookies – unbeatable.

INSIDE SCOOP

CHEFS	BRUCE TILLINGHAST,	CREDIT CARDS	MAJOR CREDIT CARDS ACCEPTED
	MATTHEW UNDERWOOD,	RESERVATIONS	RECOMMENDED
	BEAU VESTAL	HOURS	MONDAY THROUGH SATURDAY,
OWNER	BRUCE TILLINGHAST		5:30 TO 10 P.M.
OPEN SINCE	1990	LIQUOR	FULL LIQUOR
CUISINE	NEW AMERICAN, USING	SMOKING	NOT PERMITTED
	GLOBAL INFLUENCES AND	SERVICES	HEALTHY/LOW-FAT MENU ITEMS
	SEASONAL AND LOCAL PRODUCE		VEGETARIAN MENU ITEMS
SPECIALTY	LAMB CHOPS (SEASONAL)	DRESS CODE	CASUAL
PRICE RANGE	APPETIZERS $7 TO $12	PARKING	AVAILABLE ON NEARBY STREETS
	ENTREES $16 TO $27		AND PARKING LOTS

APPETIZERS

GREEN OLIVE TAPENADE WITH SUN-DRIED TOMATO CRACKERS AND WHITE
    ANCHOVIES

MIXED SUMMER GREENS WITH CANDIED PISTACHIOS, RASPBERRIES AND
    ALEPPO-LEMON VINAIGRETTE

NIME CHOW WITH LUMP CRABMEAT, SOY SPROUTS, THAI BASIL AND SPICY
    PEANUT SAUCE

CHILLED RARE BEEF TENDERLOIN WITH FIGS, SHAVED FENNEL, PICKLED RED
    ONION AND PORT SYRUP

ENTREES

SEARED POLENTA CAKES WITH ROASTED RED PEPPER SAUCE, SUMMER
    SQUASHES AND SALAD

PORK CHOP WITH SMOKY BLACK BEANS AND CINNAMON-CHIPOTLE BUTTER

ROASTED CHICKEN BREAST WITH CREAMY RED LENTILS, SWISS CHARD AND
    RAITA

GRILLED YELLOWFIN TUNA ON UDON NOODLES WITH THAI BASIL BROTH AND
    DAIKON-CUCUMBER SLAW

GRILLED SUGARCANE-SKEWERED SHRIMP WITH JICAMA, MIZUNA SALAD, AND
    MANGO-LIME NECTAR

FRESH TOMATO SOUP
WITH BASIL AND BASIL OIL

Serves 4 to 6

3 pounds beefsteak tomatoes, ripe and unpeeled
1 teaspoon garlic, minced
1 teaspoon salt
Fresh ground pepper, to taste
1 tablespoon balsamic vinegar or lemon juice
1/4 to 1/3 cup extra virgin olive oil
6 large basil leaves
Basil oil, commercial or homemade
6 small basil tops

Chop the tomatoes; remove and discard the entire core. Toss with garlic, salt, pepper and vinegar or lemon juice. Macerate for 2 hours in the refrigerator.

In a blender, puree the chilled tomato mixture until smooth. With the blender on, add the olive oil in a slow stream. Strain; adjust seasoning with salt, pepper and vinegar or lemon juice, and chill.

To serve, finely chiffonade the basil leaves and stir into the soup. Pour into chilled bowls; drizzle with basil oil and garnish with basil tops and cracked black pepper.

Note: If available, peppery nasturtium leaves and colorful nasturtium flower petals can be used with or in place of the basil.

Nicks On Broadway

IN THE NICK OF TIME

Derek Wagner has been wowwing local foodies for years, first at the Agora restaurant in the Westin Hotel and now at Nicks on Broadway, a tiny café that's open for breakfast and lunch only. Nicks is also available for private dinner parties where you can have Chef Wagner and his staff all to yourself. In addition to typical diner fare, their menu also offers highly innovative dishes such as pan-seared yellowfin tuna with black olives, roasted peppers and goat cheese. They have an original concept – any of the lunch preparations can be served as a sandwich, wrap or salad. Nicks is a real neighborhood restaurant where people become acquainted with one another while they dine on Wagner's creative cuisine. Best bet: any of the wonderful soups on the seasonal menu, and the American burger is outstanding.

GRAPEVINE GEM: If you like Derek Wagner's food at Nicks on Broadway, you'll love his catering menu.

STEAMED COD
WITH FRESH TOMATOES AND LEMON-FENNEL BROTH
Serves 2

8 ounces cod (halibut, flounder, scallops
  or shrimp also work well)
1 tablespoon olive oil (extra virgin is
  recommended for more flavor)
1 teaspoon chopped fennel tops (the dark
  green tips) or scallions
Salt and pepper, to taste (sea salt and fresh
  cracked pepper are recommended)
1/4 cup diced onions

1/4 cup diced fennel
1 tablespoon minced fresh garlic
1/4 cup chopped tomatoes
1/4 cup Chardonnay (or any white wine)
2 cups chicken stock or water
1 teaspoon lemon juice
1 teaspoon lemon zest
1 tablespoon softened butter

Cut fish into 2-ounce pieces and rub them with some of the olive oil, the fennel tops, salt and pepper. In a deep sauté pan over high heat, add remaining olive oil, just enough to coat bottom of pan. Add the fish to the pan; brown on both sides. Add the diced onions and fennel. Allow the combination to cook for a few moments, gently stirring the onions and fennel.

Add the garlic, tomatoes and white wine. Simmer until the wine is reduced by half. Add the chicken stock, bring to a boil, and reduce to a light simmer. Add the lemon juice, zest and any left-over chopped fennel tops. Simmer for 3 to 4 minutes. Gently whisk in the soft butter; season with salt and pepper.

Serve in an oversized bowl with some warm toasted or grilled French bread.

INSIDE SCOOP

CHEF-OWNERS	DEREK WAGNER AND	LIQUOR	BYOB
	STEPHEN DOYLE	SMOKING	NO
OPEN SINCE	2002	SERVICES	CHILDREN'S MENU
CUISINE	FRESH AMERICAN		HEALTHY/LOW-FAT MENU ITEMS
SPECIALTY	WONDERFUL INGREDIENTS		VEGETARIAN MENU ITEMS
	THAT CAN BE SERVED AS A		HANDICAPPED ACCESSIBLE
	SANDWICH, SALAD OR ENTRÉE		TAKE-OUT ORDERS AVAILABLE
PRICE RANGE	APPETIZERS $3.50 TO $5		CATERING
	ENTREES $5.25 TO $8.95	DRESS CODE	CASUAL
CREDIT CARDS	MAJOR CREDIT CARDS ACCEPTED	PARKING	AVAILABLE ON THE STREET
RESERVATIONS	NO		
HOURS	WEDNESDAY THROUGH SATURDAY		
	FOR BREAKFAST AND LUNCH		
	SUNDAY BRUNCH ALL DAY		

APPETIZERS

FRESH COLD TOMATO SOUP WITH CAPERS AND BASIL WITH A SLICE OF
  GRILLED BAGUETTE
CREAM OF MUSHROOM SOUP
ARUGULA AND SPINACH SALAD WITH MANGO, GOAT CHEESE, TOASTED
  MACADAMIA NUTS AND STRAWBERRY-BALSAMIC VINAIGRETTE

ENTREES

(ALL INGREDIENTS MAY BE ORDERED AS A SANDWICH, WRAP OR
  SALAD)
ROASTED TURKEY WITH SUN-DRIED TOMATOES, ARTICHOKES AND
  HAVARTI
GRILLED CHICKEN WITH LEMON-THYME PEPPER, TOMATO, FRESH
  MOZZARELLA AND ARUGULA
HEREFORD BEEF STEAK WITH CARAMELIZED ONIONS, MUSHROOMS
  AND PEPPER JACK CHEESE
MAPLE-GLAZED PORK WITH HONEY BARBECUE, SMOKED GOUDA AND
  CARAMELIZED ONIONS
PAN-SEARED YELLOWFIN TUNA WITH GINGERED CARROTS, CUCUMBER,
  SESAME AND SOY

Norey's Star

TWINKLE, TWINKLE

Norey's Star is a converted diner that now serves casual, yet elegant fare. The stainless steel counter and stools remain, but the walls are sponge-painted a golden yellow. Mirrors, recessed lighting, and fresh flowers complete the picture. Everything on the American bistro menu is made from scratch, just like chef-owner Norey Cullen's mother used to make. *The New York Times* declared Norey's Star to be the best new restaurant in Newport in May 2002. Aren't we lucky – Norey's Star is open for breakfast, lunch and dinner. They even have hot Maypo on the menu. Highly recommended: the Vegetable Quesadilla, and the fresh-cut fries with rock salt.

CHOCOLATE BREAD PUDDING

Serves 8

Butter, as needed
1 loaf cinnamon raisin bread
2 cups chocolate chips
1 quart heavy cream
2 teaspoons vanilla
Dash of salt

4 eggs

Butter an 8x11-inch pan. Slice bread into cubes and arrange in pan.

Heat chocolate until melted; add cream, vanilla and salt. Beat in the eggs. Pour over bread. Let sit for 1 hour.

Bake at 350 degrees for 45 minutes or until done.

Test with a knife for doneness. Serve with whipped cream or vanilla ice cream.

INSIDE SCOOP

CHEFS	NOREY CULLEN, ALAN SANDERS AND WAYNE BOTTETO	LIQUOR	WINE AND BEER ONLY
		SMOKING	NO
OWNER	NOREY CULLEN	SERVICES	HEALTHY/LOW-FAT MENU ITEMS
OPEN SINCE	2000		VEGETARIAN MENU ITEMS
CUISINE	AMERICAN BISTRO WHERE EVERYTHING IS HOMEMADE, LIKE MOM'S COOKING		HANDICAPPED ACCESSIBLE
			TAKE-OUT ORDERS AVAILABLE
			CATERING
			SUNDAY BRUNCH
SPECIALTY	COBB SALAD	DRESS CODE	CASUAL
PRICE RANGE	APPETIZERS $7 TO $9 ENTREES $4 TO $20	PARKING	AVAILABLE ON THE STREET
CREDIT CARDS	MAJOR CREDIT CARDS ACCEPTED		
RESERVATIONS	RECOMMENDED		
HOURS	TUESDAY THROUGH SUNDAY FOR BREAKFAST AND LUNCH OPEN WEDNESDAY THROUGH SATURDAY FOR DINNER		

APPETIZERS

BAY SCALLOPS PAN-SEARED WITH LEMON BUTTER
AHI TUNA WITH ROASTED RED PEPPERS AND SOY GINGER SAUCE
FOUR-CHEESE RAVIOLI WITH A SUN-DRIED TOMATO AND FRESH BASIL CREAM SAUCE
FRIED DUMPLINGS WITH DIPPING SAUCE
ROASTED TOMATO SALAD WITH CAPERS, BASIL, GOAT CHEESE AND BALSAMIC VINAIGRETTE

ENTREES

VEGETABLE QUESADILLA WITH HOMEMADE SALSA AND SOUR CREAM
LEMON CHICKEN
NEW ZEALAND RACK OF LAMB WITH DOTTERER'S PEPPER JELLY
CHICKEN AND BROCCOLI ALFREDO
TENDERLOIN BEEF TIPS
LOBSTER AND SHRIMP RAVIOLI
SHRIMP AND SCALLOPS ON ANGEL-HAIR PASTA WITH PESTO
PORK TENDERLOIN WITH HOMEMADE APPLESAUCE

Olga's Cup and Saucer

FEELING GROOVY

On that first spring day that's warm enough for outdoor dining, there's no place we'd rather be than Olga's Cup and Saucer with its whimsical sun-dappled patio and outrageously good food. It's a lovely, quiet spot in the middle of a busy city where you can sit in the sun and read the newspaper at breakfast, or meet friends for steaming cups of afternoon coffee. The Corn, Tomato and Pesto Pizza is one of our favorites, so delicious we hate to share it with anyone. In colder weather, the wonderful soups help chase away the chill in the air. And the baked good, especially the breads, are superb.

INSIDE SCOOP

CHEF	LINDA EDMUNDSON	LIQUOR	FULL LIQUOR
OWNER	OLGA BRAVO	SMOKING	NO
OPEN SINCE	1997	SERVICES	CHILDREN WELCOME
CUISINE	FRESHLY BAKED GOODS,		HEALTHY/LOW-FAT MENU ITEMS
	SOUPS AND SALADS		VEGETARIAN MENU ITEMS
SPECIALTY	BREADS		HANDICAPPED ACCESSIBLE
PRICE RANGE	APPETIZERS $4 TO $7		TAKE-OUT ORDERS AVAILABLE
	ENTREES $6 TO $10		PATIO DINING IN SEASON
CREDIT CARDS	MAJOR CREDIT CARDS ACCEPTED	DRESS CODE	CASUAL
RESERVATIONS	NO	PARKING	AVAILABLE ON THE STREET
HOURS	MONDAY THROUGH SATURDAY,		
	7 A.M. TO 4 P.M.		

MENU

SPINACH AND GOAT CHEESE CALZONE

CORN, TOMATO AND BASIL PESTO PIZZA

PROSCIUTTO, APPLE AND GORGONZOLA MOUSSE PANINI

UDON NOODLES WITH THAI-SPICED CHICKEN OR SHRIMP IN A PEANUT
CHILI SAUCE WITH SUGAR SNAP PEAS, CUCUMBERS, CARROTS AND
CILANTRO

SMOKED TURKEY COBB SALAD

PAN-SEARED SALMON SALAD

MUFFALETTA — SWEET CAPOCOLLO, SOPRESSATA AND PROVOLONE
WITH OLIVE RELISH ON A POTATO-ROSEMARY ROLL

HEIRLOOM TOMATO SALAD WITH MOZZARELLA AND BASIL OVER
ARUGULA WITH BALSAMIC GLAZE

Olympia Tea Room

DAYS OF SPARKLING WINE AND BEACH ROSES

Step back in time with a visit to the Olympia Tea Room in quaint Watch Hill. In nice weather, you can sit outside to watch and be watched. Inside, the soda fountain has been converted into a bar where sun-kissed customers sip champagne in the summer. Pink walls, dark brown wooden booths, and bizarre decor, including a very strange chandelier, give this seaside restaurant a funky old-fashioned feel. The food is extraordinary, but it ain't cheap (fish and chips, $17). The Rhode Island clam chowder is swimming with chopped clams, and there's plenty of real crab meat in the crab cakes. The briny Point Judith clams and Watch Hill oysters go well with some of that champagne. By the way, kids are welcome, but baby strollers are a no-no.

GRAPEVINE GEM: Make sure someone at your table orders the Avondale Swan for dessert – puff pastry in the graceful shape of a swan, filled with vanilla ice cream and swimming in a pool of dark chocolate.

INSIDE SCOOP

CHEF	KEVIN MOSHER	LIQUOR	FULL LIQUOR, WITH AN
OWNERS	JACK AND MARCIA FELBER		EXTENSIVE WINE LIST
OPEN SINCE	1916	SMOKING	NO
CUISINE	NEW AMERICAN	SERVICES	HEALTHY/LOW-FAT MENU ITEMS
SPECIALTY	SEAFOOD AND PASTA		VEGETARIAN MENU ITEMS
PRICE RANGE	APPETIZERS $7 TO $12		HANDICAPPED ACCESSIBLE
	ENTREES $16 TO $25	DRESS CODE	CASUAL
CREDIT CARDS	MAJOR CREDIT CARDS ACCEPTED	PARKING	AVAILABLE ON THE STREET
RESERVATIONS	RECOMMENDED FOR		
	PARTIES OF 6 OR MORE		
HOURS	SUMMER: OPEN SEVEN DAYS A		
	WEEK FOR LUNCH AND DINNER		
	SHOULDER SEASON:		
	CALL FOR HOURS		
	WINTER: CLOSED		

APPETIZERS

NEW ENGLAND CLAM CHOWDER
POINT JUDITH CLAMS ON THE HALF SHELL
BRUSCHETTA PARADISO – THICK TUSCAN BREAD WITH OLIVES,
    ROASTED TOMATOES AND PEPPERS, GRILLED ARTICHOKES, ROASTED
    GARLIC, FONTINA CHEESE, FAVA BEANS, BASIL AND OLIVE OIL
FRIED OYSTERS ON WILTED SPINACH WITH SWEET ONION MARMALADE
FIG SALAD WITH APPLES, WALNUTS AND GORGONZOLA TOSSED WITH
    FIELD GREENS AND BALSAMIC VINAGRETTE

ENTREES

LITTLENECK CLAMS AND SAUSAGES SIMMERED IN MARINARA SAUCE
SPINACH PASTA ROLLS STUFFED WITH BABY SPINACH AND THREE
    CHEESES, BAKED IN MARINARA UNDER FRESH MOZZARELLA
PAN-SEARED SCALLOPS WITH PICKLED GINGER AND SPICY CITRUS SOY
GRILLED LAMB CHOPS WITH MUSHROOM-RED WINE GLAZE
GRILLED PRESSED CHICKEN AND ROASTED VEGETABLES

Pane e Vino

A LOAF OF BREAD, A JUG OF WINE, AND THOU

Pane e Vino is one of the newest restaurants on Federal Hill, but its Old World atmosphere makes you think it's been in business for years. Warm and cozy, this Italian wine bar serves hearty peasant-style food in a rustic Mediterranean setting. Pane e Vino, which means "bread and wine," focuses on the simple basic things in life. The cuisine from Chef Kevin DiLibero is regional Italian, with an emphasis on the Campagna region near Naples. His reasonably priced menu features authentic dishes which may be new to your palate. The wine list is exclusively Italian, with more than 20 wines available by the glass. The decor at Pane e Vino is just gorgeous and so appealing, from the earthy colors to the miniature Tiffany lamps to the handsome mural that hangs behind the chef's table.

GRAPEVINE GEM: The best tables, especially on cold wintry nights, are near the brick fireplace at the back of the restaurant.

INSIDE SCOOP

CHEFS	KEVIN DILIBERO AND ERIN ARMOUR	LIQUOR	FULL LIQUOR
OWNER	JOSEPH DEQUATTRO	SMOKING	PERMITTED AT THE WINE BAR
OPEN SINCE	2002	SERVICES	BANQUET FACILITIES
CUISINE	ITALIAN REGIONAL, WITH AN		CHILDREN'S MENU
	EMPHASIS ON THE CAMPAGNA		HEALTHY/LOW-FAT MENU ITEMS
	REGION, SPECIFICALLY NAPLES		VEGETARIAN MENU ITEMS
SPECIALTY	HEARTY PEASANT-STYLE CUISINE		HANDICAPPED ACCESSIBLE
	IN A RUSTIC MEDITERRANEAN SETTING		TAKE-OUT ORDERS AVAILABLE
PRICE RANGE	APPETIZERS $8 TO $17		CATERING
	ENTREES $14 TO $27		PRIVATE DINING ROOM
CREDIT CARDS	MAJOR CREDIT CARDS ACCEPTED		FIREPLACE
RESERVATIONS	RECOMMENDED	DRESS CODE	CASUAL
HOURS	OPEN SEVEN NIGHTS A WEEK	PARKING	AVAILABLE ON THE STREET AND
	FOR DINNER		THROUGH THE VALET SERVICE
	MONDAY THROUGH SATURDAY,		
	BEGINNING AT 5 P.M.		
	SUNDAY, BEGINNING AT 4 P.M.		

APPETIZERS

ANTIPASTO FRUITTI DI MARE/ALLA MONTANARO
CALAMARI ALLA GRIGLIA/FRITTI
INSALATA CAPRESE

ENTREES

LINGUINE ALLA PUTTANESCA
GNOCCHI ALLA SORRENTINA
RISOTTO ALLA PESCATORE
COSTOLETTA ALLA MILANESE (BREADED VEAL CHOP)
FILETTO DI MANZO (GRILLED BEEF TENDERLOIN)

GATTO DI PATATE

Serves 8

5 pounds Yukon Gold potatoes, peeled
1 cup whole milk, heated (more may be needed if potatoes are starchy)
1 cup Parmigiano-Reggiano cheese
1 tablespoon chopped parsley
1/2 teaspoon kosher salt
3 ounces unsalted butter (3/4 stick)
Breadcrumbs, unflavored, for dusting pan and finishing

Cut potatoes in half, and place in large pot. Cover potatoes with water and bring to a boil. Lower heat to a simmer so as not to boil all the starch out of the potatoes. Simmer until tender and drain. Place potatoes in a large bowl; mash until smooth, incorporating the milk into the potatoes. Add cheese, parsley and salt.

Butter the bottom and sides of a large, deep baking dish. Coat pan with breadcrumbs and shake off excess. Spoon potatoes into prepared pan, and smooth to an even layer. Cut cubes of butter and dot surface, pressing into the potatoes. Sprinkle top of potatoes with breadcrumbs.

Bake in a preheated 350-oven for approximately 25 to 35 minutes until lightly browned and set in the center. Cut into squares to serve.

This will keep for several days wrapped tightly in plastic wrap and refrigerated (does not freeze well).

BEFORE OR AFTER THE SHOW

On the way to almost everywhere in the state of Rhode Island, the new Paragon Café offers a sophisticated ambiance and down-to-earth food. Just off Route 95 next to the cinema complex in Warwick, Paragon is a big, handsome restaurant. The style is an enhanced version of its sister operation, Café Paragon on Thayer Street on Providence's East Side. So you can count on all the basics, like steaks and burgers, to be first-rate. But the new Paragon also has kicked it up a notch with a raw bar, many more menu options, plenty of fresh fish, great weekly specials and entrees that include rack of lamb and surf and turf. You don't have to go far, and you can't go wrong.

GRAPEVINE GEM: This is one of the state's best examples of great food and quality ingredients at fair prices.

INSIDE SCOOP

OWNER	ANDREW MITRELIS AND MARIO PANAGOS	LIQUOR	FULL LIQUOR
		SMOKING	PERMITTED IN BAR AND SMOKING SECTION
OPEN SINCE	2003		
CUISINE	AMERICAN CONTEMPORARY WITH ATTITUDE	SERVICES	BANQUET FACILITIES
			HEALTHY/LOW-FAT MENU ITEMS
SPECIALTY	FRESH SEAFOOD AND WOOD-COOKING		VEGETARIAN MENU ITEMS
			HANDICAPPED ACCESSIBLE
PRICE RANGE	APPETIZERS $7 TO $9 ENTREES $14 TO $22		TAKE-OUT ORDERS AVAILABLE
			PRIVATE DINING ROOM
CREDIT CARDS	MAJOR CREDIT CARDS ACCEPTED	DRESS CODE	TASTEFUL
RESERVATIONS	RECOMMENDED FOR PARTIES OF 8 OR MORE AND FOR SPECIAL OCCASIONS	PARKING	PLENTY OF FREE PARKING IS AVAILABLE ON THE PREMISES
HOURS	OPEN SEVEN DAYS A WEEK LUNCH AND DINNER 11:30 A.M. TO 1 A.M.		

APPETIZERS

RAW BAR

SMOKED SALMON OVER CROSTINI WITH RED ONIONS, CHOPPED HARD
 BOILED EGGS, DILL MAYONNAISE, CAPERS AND LEMON

PARAGON PLATTER (COUNTRY OLIVES, AGED PROVOLONE, GRILLED
 MARINATED ARTICHOKES, VINE-RIPE TOMATOES, GENOA SALAMI,
 PROSCUITTO, SERVED WITH GRILLED FOCACCIA AND EXTRA VIRGIN
 OLIVE OIL)

SESAME CHICKEN SKEWERS WITH AN ASIAN SLAW AND PONZU
 DIPPING SAUCE

CRAB AND LOBSTER CAKES WITH A DILL CAPER MAYONNAISE

SALADS

GREEK SALAD, WITH TOMATOES, CUCUMBERS, KALAMATA OLIVES, RED
 ONIONS, SCALLIONS, CAPERS, FETA CHEESE AND GREEN PEPPERS

BEEFSTEAK TOMATOES OVER A BED OF SPINACH AND BLUE CHEESE

ENTREES

CHILEAN SEA BASS BROILED WITH SEASONED PANKO CRUMBS IN A
 LOBSTER REDUCTION SAUCE

HERB GARLIC RUBBED GRILLED RACK OF LAMB

GRILLED SALMON WITH CITRUS HERB BUTTER

PRIME RIB OF BEEF AU JUS WITH CRISPY FRIED ONIONS

LOBSTER RAVIOLI WITH SHRIMP AND SWORDFISH IN A PINOT GRIGIO
 PINK SAUCE

SEAFOOD RISOTTO WITH SHRIMP, SCALLOPS, TOMATOES AND ASPARAGUS
 AND A SAFFRON SEASONING

BAKED RIGATONI WITH SPINACH AND FOUR CHEESES IN A TOMATO
 CREAM SAUCE

BURGERS WITH A CHOICE OF CHEESES (BLUE, CHEDDAR, BOURSIN, SWISS)

LOBSTER AND CRAB CAKES

Makes 12 small cakes

12 ounces lobster meat from tail, knuckle and clam
1 pound snow crab
3 whole eggs
3/4 cup breadcrumbs
1/2 cup mayonnaise
Salt and white pepper, to taste
1/4 cup Old Bay seasoning
1 red pepper, minced
1 bunch scallions, minced

Mince lobster meat; combine with crab meat and all other ingredients. Shape into 3-ounce portions; dip in flour and pan fry in olive oil until golden brown on both sides.

Chef's note: Add more bread crumbs, if desired.

Parkside Rotisserie & Bar

VROOM, VROOM

Like Cheers, the friendly pub made famous on television, Parkside Rotisserie & Bar is the kind of place where everyone soon knows your name. Go once to this handsome Manhattan-style bistro, and you'll find yourself going back again and again for a great lunch and dinner, especially on a WaterFire night. With fair prices and a nice staff, Parkside is reliable and comfortable. It's just a great place to hang out. Our favorite dish: the Tenderloin and Portobello Salad. When he isn't manning the imported-from-France rotisserie at Parkside, Chef-owner Steve Davenport relaxes by riding his Harley Davidson on the highways and byways of Rhode Island.

GRAPEVINE GEM: Parkside may have a warm feeling because there's family all around you, Deanna, Donna, and Davenport himself.

INSIDE SCOOP

CHEF-OWNER:	STEVE DAVENPORT	LIQUOR:	FULL LIQUOR
OPEN SINCE:	1996	SMOKING:	PERMITTED AT BAR AREA ONLY
CUISINE:	NEW AMERICAN CUISINE	SERVICES:	VEGETARIAN MENU ITEMS
SPECIALTY:	ROTISSERIE DUCK WITH		HANDICAPPED ACCESSIBLE
	ORANGE AND ESPRESSO GLAZE		PRIVATE DINING ROOM
PRICE RANGE:	APPETIZERS $3 TO $10	DRESS CODE:	SMART CASUAL/BUSINESS ATTIRE
	ENTREES $11 TO $24	PARKING:	ON THE STREET AND
CREDIT CARDS:	MAJOR CREDIT CARDS ACCEPTED		THROUGH THE VALET SERVICE
RESERVATIONS:	RECOMMENDED		
HOURS:	LUNCH, MONDAY THROUGH FRIDAY		
	11 A.M. TO 4 P.M.		
	DINNER, MONDAY THROUGH THURSDAY		
	4 TO 10 P.M.		
	FRIDAY, 4 TO 11 P.M.		
	SATURDAY, 5 TO 11 P.M.		
	SUNDAY, 4 TO 9 P.M.		

APPETIZERS

GRILLED MARGARITA PIZZA

SPICY CRAB CAKES WITH LOUISIANA SPICES, SWEET RED PEPPERS AND ROASTED
   CORN, DUSTED WITH CORNMEAL, SERVED WITH A LEMON AND RED PEPPER
   SAUCE

MUSHROOM BRUSCHETTA (PORTOBELLO, SHIITAKE AND WHITE MUSHROOMS
   IN A SAGE CREAM SAUCE)

FRIED THAI DUMPLINGS STUFFED WITH LEAN PORK, SCALLIONS, THAI CHILI
   PASTE, TAMARI, SESAME AND GINGER WITH TWO DIPPING SAUCES

CLAM AND MUSSEL CASSOULET WITH LITTLENECKS, TUSCAN SAUSAGE, WHITE
   NORTHERN BEANS AND PLUM TOMATOES STEWED IN A FRESH FENNEL
   BROTH

ENTREES

CENTER-CUT 14-OUNCE SIRLOIN STEAK WITH A CHIPOTLE PEPPER DEMIGLACE,
   SERVED WITH MASCARPONE AND GORGONZOLA CROSTINI

LONG ISLAND DUCK COOKED ON THE ROTISSERIE, BRUSHED WITH AN
   ORANGE ESPRESSO GLAZE AND GARNISHED WITH A CREPE STUFFED WITH
   JULIENNE ASIAN STIR-FRIED VEGETABLES

ROASTED HALF CHICKEN MARINATED IN OLIVE OIL, BALSAMIC VINEGAR AND
   FRESH HERBS, SERVED WITH GREEN HERB SAUCE

HERB-ENCRUSTED SALMON, PAN ROASTED AND TOPPED WITH A SUN-DRIED
   CHERRY AND CITRUS BUTTER

VEAL AND SAGE AGNOLOTTI TOSSED WITH SWEET PEAS, TUSCAN SAUSAGE AND
   OYSTER MUSHROOMS IN A ROASTED PLUM TOMATO AND VEAL REDUCTION
   FINISHED WITH ARUGULA MASCARPONE PESTO

ORANGE ESPRESSO GLAZED DUCK

Serves 2

Brine:
4 cups water
1/2 cups soy sauce
2 cups maple syrup
1 cup espresso, brewed or instant

1/2 cup sugar
1 whole white onion, sliced
5 garlic cloves
2 whole oranges, sliced in half
1 rosemary sprig

1 duck, fresh or frozen

Place all brine ingredients in a saucepot and simmer for 30 minutes; chill.
Reserve 2 cups of liquid for later to deglaze pan,

Truss a duck and place in brine to marinate for 24 hours; remove duck from brine and
place in roasting pan with a rack if possible and mirepoix of carrots, leeks and oranges.
Bake for 1 1/2 hours or until crispy and tender (if possible, use an outdoor rotisserie).

When duck is done, remove from pan and pour out excess fat. Place on stove top over
low to medium heat, and add reserved brine to deglaze roasting pan. Cook for 10 to 15
minutes and strain; set aside.

For the finished plate:
Cut duck in half using scissors or poultry shears and remove bones from breast cavity.
Place sauce on each plate and place duck on top. Serve with stir-fried vegetables.

Pizzico

MOONSTRUCK

For more than a decade, Pizzico has been pleasing people who truly appreciate authentic regional Italian food. Where else can you order Strozzapreti, "priest stranglers" with grilled spicy lamb sausage? Co-owner Steve Harris trained under the legendary Normand Leclair at the Red Rooster Tavern, His co-chef, Warley Araujo, insists on using only the freshest ingredients. Their intriguing menu changes with the seasons. This Italian ristorante, which has a superb award-winning wine list, has become a landmark on the East Side of Providence. Tiny white lights and a greenhouse atmosphere beckon people to come in for lunch and dinner.

GRAPEVINE GEM: Pizzico offers entree salads, featuring chicken, veal, duck, salmon and pasta as toppings, which are wonderful when you want to eat light.

PROSCIUTTO AND ASPARAGUS DI STEFANO

Serves 4

16 medium-size asparagus spears
1/4 pound prosciutto, sliced thin (8 slices)
3 to 4 black olives, sliced
1/2 teaspoon black pepper
1/2 teaspoon Parmesan cheese

Olive oil, as needed
1 garlic clove, chopped
2 cups cooked cannellini beans
1 tablespoon olive oil
6 fresh basil leaves, chopped

Blanch asparagus in boiling water until spears appear dark in color, approximately 2 to 3 minutes. Let cool.

Lay prosciutto slices flat and place the olives, black pepper and Parmesan cheese on top. Place 2 spears of asparagus on slice and wrap prosciutto and toppings around.

Coat bottom of a small sheet pan with olive oil and sprinkle with chopped garlic. Lay prosciutto wraps on pan. Cook at 400 degrees for about 8 to 10 minutes.

Toss cannellini beans with olive oil and fresh basil; chill 20 minutes prior to serving. Serve prosciutto wraps over bed of cannellini beans.

INSIDE SCOOP

CHEFS	WARLEY ARAUJO AND STEVE HARRIS	LIQUOR	FULL LIQUOR
		SMOKING	NO
OWNERS	CHERYL BOYLE, STEVE AND JIM HARRIS	SERVICES	HEALTHY/LOW-FAT MENU ITEMS
OPEN SINCE	1991		VEGETARIAN MENU ITEMS
CUISINE	AUTHENTIC REGIONAL ITALIAN		HANDICAPPED ACCESSIBLE
SPECIALTY	VITELLO ARAUJO GRILLED LOBSTER TAILS WITH SAFFRON RISOTTO		TAKE-OUT ORDERS AVAILABLE
			CATERING
			PRIVATE DINING ROOM
		DRESS CODE	CASUAL
PRICE RANGE	APPETIZERS $5 TO $8 ENTREES $12 TO $24	PARKING	AVAILABLE ON THE STREET
CREDIT CARDS	MAJOR CREDIT CARDS ACCEPTED		
RESERVATIONS	RECOMMENDED		
HOURS	MONDAY THROUGH SATURDAY FOR LUNCH AND DINNER SUNDAY – DINNER ONLY		

APPETIZERS

PASTA E FAGIOLI — SOUTHERN ITALIAN-SYLE PASTA AND BEAN SOUP
RUCHETTA — ROASTED PEPPERS AND BALSAMIC VINEGAR OVER ARUGULA
GRILLED SALMON OVER A BED OF GREENS WITH ASPARAGUS AND SLICED TOMATO WITH LEMON VINAIGRETTE
WARM PASTA TOSSED WITH MIXED GREENS, WALNUTS, BLUE CHEESE, CAPERS AND CHOPPED FRESH TOMATOES IN A BALSAMIC DRESSING

ENTREES

STROZZAPRETI — PRIEST STRANGLER PASTA SAUTÉED WITH GRILLED SPICY LAMB
SAUSAGE, GARLIC, HERBS, TOMATO SAUCE AND PARMIGIANO CHEESE
PAPPARDELLE WITH PANCETTA AND DUCK MEAT RAGU SAUCE AND GRATED PECORINO CHEESE
RISOTTO WITH SHRIMP, SEA SCALLOPS, CALAMARI AND CLAMS IN A GARLIC, LEMON, TOMATO AND WHITE WINE SAUCE
ROASTED RACK OF WILD BOAR, SERVED IN A RED WINE REDUCTION, WITH CRANBERRY AND HOMEMADE APPLE PUREE
GRILLED T-BONE STEAK WITH A BLACK PEPPERCORN, ROASTED SHALLOT, WHISKEY SAUCE WITH ROASTED POTATOES

Plaza Grille

WORTH THE WAIT

The Plaza Grille on DePasquale Plaza honestly surprised us at lunch one beautiful summer day. Ravenous, we stopped there for a bite and were served an exquisite lunch, made with the freshest ingredients imaginable. Chef-owner Fran Whiting obviously takes a great deal of pride in her little storefront restaurant, which offers al fresco dining in warm weather. All the food is prepared to order, so be prepared to wait just a bit for your lunch or dinner. It's BYOB, so plan on bringing a cold bottle of Prosecco to celebrate your good fortune in dining at the Plaza Grille.

INSIDE SCOOP

CHEF-OWNER	FRAN WHITING	LIQUOR	BYOB
OPEN SINCE	1990	SMOKING	NO
CUISINE	AMERICAN	SERVICES	WILL CATER TO SPECIAL DIETS
SPECIALTY	FRESH, PREPARED TO ORDER		WITH NOTICE
PRICE RANGE	APPETIZERS $8 TO $10		HEALTHY/LOW-FAT MENU ITEMS
	ENTREES $14 TO $20		VEGETARIAN MENU ITEMS
CREDIT CARDS	NOT ACCEPTED,		HANDICAPPED ACCESSIBLE
	CASH OR CHECK ONLY		TAKE-OUT ORDERS AVAILABLE
RESERVATIONS	FOR 8 OR MORE		SEASONAL OUTDOOR SEATING
HOURS	SUMMER: OPEN SEVEN DAYS A	DRESS CODE	CASUAL
	WEEK FOR LUNCH AND DINNER	PARKING	AVAILABLE ON THE STREET
	WINTER: OPEN THURSDAYS AND		
	FRIDAYS FOR LUNCH, WEEKENDS		
	FOR BRUNCH AND DINNER ONLY		

APPETIZERS

SHRIMP RAVIOLI WITH WHITE TRUFFLE BUTTER

BAKED ARTICHOKE BOTTOMS WITH GOAT CHEESE, SHRIMP AND SAUCE BEARNAISE

MESCLUN SALAD WITH GOAT CHEESE, MANGOES, TOASTED PECANS AND MAPLE VINAIGRETTE

ROASTED GARLIC WITH CAMBOZOLA TRIPLE CREAM ROQUEFORT, WHITE TRUFFLE OIL AND ROSEMARY FOCACCIA

ENTREES

LEMON RISOTTO WITH ASPARAGUS, SHRIMP AND ASIAGO

FREE-FORM LASAGNA WITH BROCCOLI RABE, WILD MUSHROOMS, ASIAGO, MASCARPONE AND SHRIMP, SCALLOPS AND LUMP CRABMEAT

ROSEMARY SKEWERED NEW ZEALAND LAMB RACK WITH PORT WINE DEMIGLACE AND MORELS

HALIBUT FILET ON A BED OF WILTED SPINACH WITH CITRUS BUERRE BLANC AND PARMA CRACKLINGS

Portofino

AND THE OSCAR GOES TO...

When Academy Award-winning actor Anthony Hopkins was in Rhode Island to shoot the film Meet Joe Black, he happened upon Portofino in Warwick and ate there almost every night. Something about the fava beans with a nice Chianti? Seriously, this cozy, romantic and friendly restaurant would appeal to anyone who enjoys upscale Italian food, sometimes with unexpected Asian and Indian influences. Located in an unassuming strip mall, the often-crowded restaurant also offers daily specials. Chef Kyle Alves, who learned the restaurant business from his parents, lists the Chilean Sea Bass, Crab Cakes, and Veal Marsala as his favorite dishes.

CHICKEN YUCATAN

Serves 2

1/4 cup oil
1 pound boneless chicken, pounded thin
1/2 cup flour
2 eggs, beaten
1/2 cup white wine
1/4 cup fresh lemon juice
2 tablespoons butter, cold
2 tablespoons chopped parsley
1 tablespoon capers

Heat sauté pan with oil until very hot. Dip chicken first in flour and then in egg. Place in hot sauté pan and turn once, cooking altogether for approximately 5 to 7 minutes.

Drain oil from pan. Place pan back on heat and add the white wine. Cook off alcohol and then add lemon juice, butter, parsley and capers.

Heat thoroughly and serve at once.

INSIDE SCOOP

CHEF	KYLE ALVES	SMOKING	PERMITTED AT THE BAR
OWNER	BRENDA ALVES	SERVICES	BANQUET FACILITIES
OPEN SINCE	1986		UP TO 30 PEOPLE
CUISINE	ITALIAN WITH ASIAN INFLUENCES		HEALTHY/LOW-FAT MENU ITEMS
SPECIALTY	CHILEAN SEA BASS,		VEGETARIAN MENU ITEMS
	CRAB CAKES, VEAL MARSALA		HANDICAPPED ACCESSIBLE
PRICE RANGE	APPETIZERS $6 TO $11		TAKE-OUT ORDERS AVAILABLE
	ENTREES $14 TO $24		EVERY NIGHT BUT SATURDAYS
CREDIT CARDS	MAJOR CREDIT CARDS ACCEPTED		PRIVATE DINING ROOM
RESERVATIONS	RECOMMENDED	DRESS CODE	CASUAL
HOURS	MONDAY THROUGH SATURDAY	PARKING	AVAILABLE ON THE PREMISES AND
	FOR DINNER		THROUGH THE VALET SERVICE
LIQUOR	FULL LIQUOR		

APPETIZERS

SHRIMP IN GARLIC WINE SAUCE
CLAMS ZUPPA
STUFFED MUSHROOMS WITH SEAFOOD TOPPING
ASIAN SWEET-GLAZED CHICKEN WINGS

ENTREES

LINGUINE WITH VEAL SAUSAGE
BONELESS CHICKEN SAUTÉED WITH MUSHROOMS, ARTICHOKE
 HEARTS, ROASTED RED PEPPERS, TOPPED WITH MOZZARELLA
VEAL STEAK WITH MUSHROOM SHERRY SAUCE
BISTECCA ALL PIZZAIOLA WITH BLACK OLIVES IN A MARINARA SAUCE
RACK OF LAMB WITH MINT JELLY
BATTER-DIPPED SOLE WITH BUTTER, LEMON, CAPERS AND WINE

Post Office Cafe

11 Main Street, East Greenwich | 401-885-4444 | www.postofficecafé.com

SPECIAL DELIVERY

Walking up the canopied front steps into this former post office, you start to get the feeling this is a special restaurant. Once inside, all it takes is a glance at the handsome bar, and you become certain you are in for a serious dining experience. Soaring ceilings, towering draped windows, and a dimly lit dining room set a romantic mood. The service is friendly and extremely attentive. The extensive menu offers classic Italian cuisine with creative twists and upscale flair. Our recommendation: the Pesto Grilled Salmon, served with a sun-dried tomato fondue. Delicioso!

GRAPEVINE GEM: If you like the Post Office Cafe, you might want to check out the other Rhode Island restaurants in the Pinelli-Marra Restaurant Group. They include Grille on Main, Quattro Italian Grille, Pinelli's Cucina, Pinelli's Gourmet Deli and Cafe at Night, and Pinelli's North End Cafe.

INSIDE SCOOP

OWNERS	WILLIAM PINELLI AND STEPHEN MARRA	SMOKING	PERMITTED
OPEN SINCE	1995	SERVICES	BANQUET FACILITIES
CUISINE	CLASSIC ITALIAN CUISINE WITH CREATIVE TWISTS AND UPSCALE FLAIR		CHILDREN'S MENU ON REQUEST HEALTHY/LOW-FAT MENU ITEMS VEGETARIAN MENU ITEMS HANDICAPPED ACCESSIBLE
SPECIALTY	VEAL GORGONZOLA AND CHICKEN MARSALA		TAKE-OUT ORDERS AVAILABLE CATERING
PRICE RANGE	APPETIZERS $6 TO $8 ENTREES $9 TO $21	DRESS CODE	PRIVATE DINING ROOM CASUAL
CREDIT CARDS	MAJOR CREDIT CARDS ACCEPTED	PARKING	AVAILABLE IN THE IMMEDIATE AREA AND THROUGH THE VALET SERVICE
RESERVATIONS	RECOMMENDED		
HOURS	OPEN SEVEN NIGHTS A WEEK FOR DINNER		
LIQUOR	FULL LIQUOR		

APPETIZERS

BRUSCHETTA TRIO — WILD MUSHROOM, SPINACH AND OLIVE TOMATO, MOZZARELLA AND BASIL SAUSAGE, CANNELLINI BEANS AND REGGIANO

SNAIL SALAD

CALAMARI WITH ROASTED PEPPERS, FRESH ONIONS IN A CHAMPAGNE GARLIC SAUCE WITH TAMARI GARLIC BUTTER

ENTREES

PINK VODKA CREAM SAUCE WITH CHOICE OF PASTA

GRILLED CHICKEN AND SAUSAGE WITH WHITE BEAN PUREE ON PENNE

GRILLED PORK CHOPS PIZZAIOLA

GRILLED SALMON CARBONARA WITH PANCETTA, PEAS AND ONIONS IN A LIGHT ROMANO CHEESE SAUCE

VEAL SCALOPPINE LAYERED WITH SPINACH AND MUSHROOMS IN A TOMATO SAUCE WITH CRUMBLED GORGONZOLA CHEESE

BAKED COD FISH IN A LIGHT HERB CRUMB TOPPING

Pot au Feu

44 Custom House Street, Providence | 401-273-8953 | www.potaufeu_ri.com

OO-LA-LA

This well-established French restaurant offers fine dining in its upper salon and hearty fare in the lower-level bistro. It's the dark and romantic bistro that won our hearts. This is the kind of rustic place where people fall in love and celebrate the moment with a bottle of really good champage. It's also a fine spot for a business lunch – the Croque Monsieur sandwich is outstanding – or a martini at the bar after work. Owner Bob Burke is usually on the premises, making one and all feel most welcome.

INSIDE SCOOP

CHEF	JOHN B. RICHARDSON	LIQUOR	FULL LIQUOR
OWNERS	ANN AND BOB BURKE	SMOKING	PERMITTED ONLY IN BAR AREA
OPEN SINCE	1972	SERVICES	BANQUET FACILITIES
CUISINE	CLASSIC FRENCH		CHILDREN'S MENU BY REQUEST
SPECIALTY	POT AU FEU, DUCK CONFIT,		HEALTHY/LOW-FAT MENU ITEMS
	RACK OF LAMB		VEGETARIAN MENU ITEMS
PRICE RANGE	APPETIZERS $6 TO $10		PRIVATE DINING ROOM
	ENTREES $19 TO $32	DRESS CODE	CASUAL
CREDIT CARDS	MAJOR CREDIT CARDS ACCEPTED	PARKING	AVAILABLE ON THE STREET
RESERVATIONS	RECOMMENDED		AND IN FREE LOT AFTER 6 P.M.
HOURS	OPEN WEEKDAYS FOR LUNCH		
	MONDAY THROUGH SATURDAY		
	FOR DINNER		

APPETIZERS

LOBSTER BISQUE

ESCARGOTS WITH GARLIC-PARSLEY BUTTER

PATE MAISON

PATE DE FOIE GRAS DE CANARD

TERRINE OF GRILLED VEGETABLES WITH GOAT CHEESE AND BALSAMIC
    REDUCTION

MOONSTONE OYSTERS GRATINEED WITH SOUR CREAM, MUSTARD,
    BACON AND HORSERADISH

ENTREES

GRILLED PEKING DUCK BREAST AND CONFIT DUCK LEG SERVED WITH
    GREEN AND BLACK MADAGASCAR PEPPERCORN SAUCE

PAN-SEARED SEA SCALLOPS AND SHRIMP SAUTÉED WITH WHITE WINE,
    GARLIC, TOMATO CONCASSE AND FRESH BASIL

RACK OF LAMB WITH POMMERY MUSTARD AND HONEY WITH RED WINE
    DEMIGLACE, SHALLOTS, GARLIC, THYME AND BLACK PEPPERCORNS

CHARGRILLED PORK TENDERLOIN IN SWEET PLUM SAUCE WITH SPICED
    RUM FLAVORING

BEEF TENDERLOIN MEDALLIONS WITH SHALLOTS, MUSTARD, BRANDY,
    DEMIGLACE AND CREAM SAUCE

A REAL GEM

Located in the jewelry district, the oh-so-hip Prov has evolved over the years. In its current incarnation, Prov is a bar and cocktail lounge with a wonderful bar menu, an exciting late-night gathering spot for young professionals, and a private function facility, available for private parties, big and small. Groups of 10 to 250 can make reservations for dinner at Prov, where the remarkable Chef Kevin Millonzi and his crack kitchen staff will create cutting-edge global fusion cuisine that will leave you satisfied and, at the same time, eager to come back for more.

GRAPEVINE GEM: Prov is also home to Atomic Catering, the fastest-growing catering company in New England. If you liked dinner, you'll love what Chef Millonzi and his crew can do at your next catered affair. Just ask Bill Clinton. At a private party, the former president loved Kevin's famous house-made potato chips, served with a Gorgonzola dipping sauce.

INSIDE SCOOP

CHEF	KEVIN MILLONZI	HOURS	DINNER ONLY ON FRIDAY
OWNERS	JOHN SKEFFINGTON		AND SATURDAY, STARTING AT 5 P.M.
	PETER SKEFFINGTON	LIQUOR	FULL LIQUOR
	KEVIN MILLONZI	SMOKING	PERMITTED
OPEN SINCE	2000	SERVICES	BANQUET FACILITIES
CUISINE	CUTTING-EDGE SOPHISTICATED		HEALTHY/LOW-FAT MENU ITEMS
	GLOBAL CUISINE		VEGETARIAN MENU ITEMS
SPECIALTY	SHRIMP MILLONZI		TAKE-OUT ORDERS AVAILABLE
PRICE RANGE	APPETIZERS $8 TO $12		PRIVATE DINING ROOM
	ENTREES $12 TO $26	DRESS CODE	CASUAL
CREDIT CARDS	MAJOR CREDIT CARDS ACCEPTED	PARKING	AVAILABLE ON NEARBY STREETS
RESERVATIONS	REQUIRED		AND PARKING LOTS

APPETIZERS

SPRING ROLLS WITH PEKING DUCK, VEGETABLE AND APRICOT DUCK SAUCE

WILD MUSHROOM BRUSCHETTA WITH TOMATO, MOZZARELLA, AND TRUFFLE
BUTTER

LOBSTER RANGOON WITH CREAM CHEESE, HERBS, MUSTARD AIOLI AND SOY
SAKE DIP

BUTTERMILK CHICKEN TENDERLOINS WITH ASIAN BARBECUE SAUCE AND
BLUE CHEESE

GRILLED JUMBO TIGER SHRIMP WITH KIM-CHEE SLAW, CITRUS COCKTAIL
SAUCE, MANGO COULIS CHILI PEPPER EMULSION

SARATOGA POTATO CHIPS WITH GORGONZOLA GRAVY AND SCALLIONS

ENTREES

FETTUCCINE AND LOBSTER WITH CHORIZO, PEAS AND TRUFFLE BUTTER

VEAL PARMESAN WITH RIGATONI PASTA AND TOMATO BASIL CREAM SAUCE

HEREFORD BEEF TENDERLOIN WITH MUSTARD AND HORSERADISH RUB,
SMOKED MUSHROOM DEMIGLACE AND BLANCHED BROCCOLI, SMASHED
POTATOES AND BEER-BATTERED VIDALIA ONION RINGS

PISTACHIO AND POPPY-SEEDED SASHIMI-GRADE TUNA STEAK OVER ROASTED
HERB POTATOES, ASPARAGUS SPEARS AND ROASTED SHALLOT AND
CRANBERRY AU JUS

MARINATED PORTOBELLO MUSHROOM RISOTTO WITH GARLIC FOCACCIA BREAD

CAJUN SWORDFISH PAN-BLACKENED OVER A SPICY CRAB CAKE, WITH SAUTÉED
HARICOTS VERT, TOPPED WITH MANGO LOBSTER SALAD

SHRIMP MILLONZI

Serves 2

1 tablespoon olive oil
12 large shrimp (16 to 20 per pound), peeled and deveined
1/2 cup sun-dried tomato pesto (recipe follows)
1/2 cup white wine
2 cups heavy cream
2 tablespoons whole butter
2 tablespoons fresh basil, chiffonade
2 tablespoons fresh parsley, chopped
Salt and pepper, to taste
1 pound penne pasta, cooked al dente
1 cup grated Asiago cheese

Add the olive oil to a sauté pan. Heat for 1 minute or until oil is hot. Add the shrimp and sun-dried tomato pesto; sauté for 2 minutes. Deglaze the pan with white wine; add the heavy cream and butter. Reduce by half. Finish with fresh herbs; season with salt and pepper. Re-warm pasta in boiling salted water. Drain and add pasta to sauce and reseason. Garnish with grated cheese and a sprinkling of fresh herbs.

SUN-DRIED TOMATO PESTO

4 cups sun-dried tomatoes
1/2 cup minced garlic
4 bunches chopped scallions
2 cups fresh sweet basil
2 bunches fresh parsley
2 tablespoons dry English mustard
Salt and pepper, to taste
4 cups grated Parmesan or Asiago cheese
2 cups olive oil, more or less as needed

Puree the sun-dried tomatoes, garlic, scallions, herbs and seasonings in a food processor. Add the cheese and slowly blend in the olive oil. Mixture should resemble a paste-like mixture. Season to taste.

Providence Oyster Bar

283 Atwells Avenue (Federal Hill), Providence | 401-272-8866 | www.provoyster.com

AW SHUCKS

This is one of those cool restaurants that has a real New York feel to it the minute you walk in. A long bar on the left tempts you, and tables -- stocked with real sea salt -- extend deep into the back. A terrific spot for lunch (make sure to try the grilled tuna sandwich with wasabi mayonnaise), for cocktails after work, and for a leisurely dinner. While seafood is the specialty of the house, the menu also offers plenty of food for landlubbers. But the real reason to go is the oysters. With a glass of very cold white wine, what more could you desire?

INSIDE SCOOP

CHEF	GENO BERNARDO	LIQUOR	FULL LIQUOR
OWNERS	MICHAEL DEGNAN	SMOKING	PERMITTED ONLY IN BAR AREA
	AND FRANK DIBIASE	SERVICES	BANQUET FACILITIES
OPEN SINCE	1999		CHILDREN'S MENU
CUISINE	SEAFOOD		HEALTHY/LOW-FAT MENU ITEMS
SPECIALTY	OYSTERS		VEGETARIAN MENU ITEMS
PRICE RANGE	APPETIZERS $6 TO $14		HANDICAPPED ACCESSIBLE
	ENTREES $17 TO $25		TAKE-OUT ORDERS AVAILABLE
CREDIT CARDS	MAJOR CREDIT CARDS ACCEPTED		CATERING
RESERVATIONS	RECOMMENDED FOR		PRIVATE DINING ROOM
	PARTIES OF EIGHT OR MORE	DRESS CODE	CASUAL
HOURS	OPEN WEEKDAYS FOR LUNCH	PARKING	AVAILABLE ON THE STREET AND
	MONDAY THROUGH SATURDAY		THROUGH THE VALET SERVICE
	FOR DINNER		

APPETIZERS

COCONUT SHRIMP
OYSTERS ROCKEFELLER
BLACKENED AHI TUNA
SEA SCALLOPS WRAPPED WITH APPLE-SMOKED BACON
PACIFIC RIM CAESAR SALAD
CAPRICE SALAD
SHRIMP BISQUE

ENTREES

GRILLED SALMON WITH DILL MAYONNAISE
GRILLED YELLOWFIN TUNA
BAKED STUFFED FLOUNDER
BAKED CHILEAN SEA BASS
LOUISIANA BLACKENED CATFISH
LOBSTER, BOILED, GRILLED OR BAKED STUFFED
LOBSTER RAVIOLI
SEAFOOD BOUILLABAISE

Raphael Bar-Risto

ARTISTS AT WORK

One of the most sophisticated restaurants in Providence, Raphael Bar-Risto offers progressive Italian cuisine in understated minimalist/modern surroundings. You might almost think you are in a Manhattan art gallery when you take in the fluid sculpture at the entrance and the oversized works of art on the walls. The kitchen is big and wide open for all to see. The bar, known as the Tunnel Lounge, is a happening place, especially after business hours. All this is the successful vision of Ralph and Elisa Conte. He's the creative executive chef; she's the bold designer. Together, they've created the perfect city restaurant.

BRAISED PORK CHEEKS
WITH CANNELLINI BEANS AND FRESH THYME
Serves 2

1 pound pork cheeks, quartered (available in large supermarkets and butcher shops)
Salt and pepper, to taste
1/4 cup fresh thyme, picked and chopped fine
1/2 cup olive oil
1 cup diced celery
1 cup diced onions

1 cup diced carrots
1 cup orange juice
1 cup red wine
2 cups demiglace (available in gourmet shops)
1 bay leaf
1/4 cup cannellini beans, cooked

Preheat oven to 325 degrees. Season pork cheeks with salt, pepper and half of the chopped thyme. Heat olive oil in a heavy-bottomed roasting pan. Lay pork cheeks in hot oil; cook on one side until deep brown in color. Turn cheeks over and cook until deep brown. Remove from pan and place on a plate.

Add celery, onions and carrots to pan, and sauté until they are dark brown. Add pork cheeks, orange juice, red wine, demiglace and bay leaf. Bring to a simmer. Cover pan tightly with aluminum foil and place in oven for approximately 2 1/2 to 3 hours or until pork cheeks nearly fall apart when pricked with a fork. Remove cheeks from braising liquid and place on a plate until needed.

Transfer pan containing braising liquid to stovetop over medium high heat. Simmer for approximately 1 hour until liquid just coats back of a wooden spoon. Puree vegetable/sauce mixture. Add cheeks to mixture and keep warm until needed.

On a small plate, place the cooked cannellini beans near the center of the plate. Divide pork cheeks over cannellini beans. Sprinkle all with the remaining thyme and garnish with a sprig of fresh thyme.

INSIDE SCOOP

CHEF	JOHN YODER	LIQUOR	FULL LIQUOR
OWNERS	RALPH AND ELISA CONTE	SMOKING	PERMITTED AT THE BAR
OPEN SINCE	1998	SERVICES	HEALTHY/LOW-FAT MENU ITEMS
CUISINE	PROGRESSIVE ITALIAN		VEGETARIAN MENU ITEMS
SPECIALTY	LOBSTER FRA DIAVOLO		HANDICAPPED ACCESSIBLE
PRICE RANGE	APPETIZERS $6 TO $14		TAKE-OUT ORDERS AVAILABLE
	ENTREES $12 TO $29		CATERING
CREDIT CARDS	MAJOR CREDIT CARDS ACCEPTED		PRIVATE DINING ROOM
RESERVATIONS	RECOMMENDED	DRESS CODE	BUSINESS/CASUAL
HOURS	OPEN SEVEN NIGHTS A WEEK	PARKING	AVAILABLE IN AN ADJACENT
	FOR DINNER		PARKING LOT

APPETIZERS

PIZZA OF THE DAY
PASTA E FAGIOLE
BROCCOLI DI RABE WITH GRILLED SWEET SAUSAGE
BLACK SESAME CREPES WITH DUCK RAGU, CITRUS-GINGER LETTUCES, ASIAGO CHEESE AND SPICY PEACH PUREE
TUNA AND SALMON WITH CUCUMBER, AVOCADO AND HORSERADISH
PAN-SEARED BLUE CRAB CAKES WITH LOBSTER SCALLION SALAD AND LEMON CAPER CREAM

ENTREES

EGGPLANT RAVIOLI PRIMAVERA WITH WILTED BABY GREENS AND TRUFFLE OIL
LOBSTER TORTELLI WITH WHITE TRUFFLE CREAM, SAUTÉED LOBSTER MEAT AND PAN-FLASHED SPINACH
ROASTED CHICKEN BREAST WITH PORTABELLO, SAGE, FONTINA, GARLIC DEMIGLACE AND GORGONZOLA POLENTA
POTATO-WRAPPED SEA BASS WITH PANCETTA, ARTICHOKES AND TOMATO-PINOT NOIR SAUCE
BALSAMIC GLAZED BONELESS DUCK WITH STEWED WHITE BEANS, GRILLED RADICCHIO AND ENDIVE

Red Fez

WHERE'S THE MONKEY?

The Red Fez is an inconspicuous little place with old stained glass windows that make you think you will need to know the password to gain entrance. With only six booths and a smattering of tables, you'd be wise to go early or late for dinner. Chef Edward Reposa and co-owner Sara Kilguss might hold the record for the smallest bar in town, a mere four seats, decorated year-round with Christmas lights. "Super casual, friendly, unforced hip" is how they describe the Red Fez. The food is as funky as the surroundings, yet clean and simple, a curious mix of cuisines. Late at night, the upstairs lounge is popular with the 20-something crowd.

GRAPEVINE GEM: The Red Fez makes the best grilled cheese sandwich on earth, and we have had some great grilled cheese sandwiches over the years. Extra-thick slices of bread (from Olga's Cup and Saucer) are used to sandwich the melted cheddar cheese and slices of plum tomato, and it's all served with top-notch French fries.

THAI CINNAMON AND GINGER BEEF BOWL

Serves 10

10 quarter-size slices ginger	5 pieces star anise
1 pound scallions, cut into 1/2-inch pieces and lightly smashed	5 pounds stewing beef, cut into large chunks
10 garlic cloves, lightly smashed	Kosher salt and freshly ground pepper, to taste
2 tablespoons canola oil	3 pounds wide wheat noodles, cooked and drained*
1 tablespoon Sambal Olek chili paste*	2 pounds spinach
5 quarts water	Fried shallots*
1 cup soy sauce	Chili oil, to taste*
5 sticks cinnamon	

In a deep, heavy stock pot, sauté ginger, scallions and garlic in canola oil for 1 minute. Add chili paste. Sauté another 15 seconds. Add water, soy sauce, cinnamon and star anise. Season beef with salt and pepper; add beef to the pot.

Bring to a rolling boil, then turn down the heat and allow to simmer, periodically skimming away impurities, for 1 1/2 hours or until the beef is falling apart tender.

To serve, pour over cooked and drained wide wheat noodles and a handful of raw spinach. Top with fried shallots and chili oil to taste.

*Available at most Asian markets

INSIDE SCOOP

CHEF	ED REPOSA	LIQUOR	FULL LIQUOR
OWNERS	ED REPOSA AND SARA KILGUSS	SMOKING	PERMITTED IN UPSTAIRS LOUNGE ONLY
OPEN SINCE	2001		
CUISINE	WORLD CUISINE	SERVICES	HEALTHY/LOW-FAT MENU ITEMS
SPECIALTY	MEXICAN, INDIAN AND THAI DISHES		VEGETARIAN MENU ITEMS
			HANDICAPPED ACCESSIBLE FIRST FLOOR
PRICE RANGE	APPETIZERS $4 TO $7		
	ENTREES $8 TO $14		TAKE-OUT ORDERS AVAILABLE
CREDIT CARDS	MAJOR CREDIT CARDS ACCEPTED	DRESS CODE	SUPER CASUAL, UNFORCED HIP
RESERVATIONS	RECOMMENDED FOR PARTIES OF 6 OR MORE	PARKING	AVAILABLE IN PARKING LOT NEXT DOOR
HOURS	TUESDAY THROUGH SATURDAY FOR DINNER		

APPETIZERS

GREEN APPLE AND GORGONZOLA SALAD WITH WALNUT VINAIGRETTE

MADE-TO-ORDER WHITE FLOUR TORTILLA CHIPS WITH FRESH FRUIT SALSA AND SOUR CREAM

SWEET PEA AND POTATO SAMOSAS WITH CILANTRO CHUTNEY

NOODLE BOWL WITH GINGER, CHILES AND VEGETABLES

ENTREES

GRILLED CORIANDER-CARDOMOM CHICKEN THIGHS WITH A TOMATO-MINT SALAD OVER COUSCOUS

GRILLED HARISSA SALMON WITH COCONUT RICE, GREEN CURRY SAUCE AND SESAME SPINACH

JAMAICAN JERK CHICKEN SANDWICH

GRILLED CHILE LIME MARINATED HEREFORD FLANK STEAK WITH GORGONZOLA MASHED POTATOES, TOMATO-POBLANO SALSA AND GRILLED BALSAMIC BUTTER ASPARAGUS

Redlefsen's

SOME ENCHANTED EVENING

 One of the most unique restaurants in the state, Redlefsen's whisks you away from your everyday life with its European hospitality and unusual menu offerings. You will feel like you are seated in a charming German beer hall, with twinkling white lights high above and exquisite stained glass windows hanging behind the very long, very inviting bar. If you're lucky, you can dine right by the roaring double-sided fireplace. Where else in Rhode Island can you get authentic Wiener Schnitzel? The menu also offers many classic New England dishes, making Redlefsen's a real crowd pleaser.

PECAN-ENCRUSTED PORK TENDERLOIN
Serves 4

2 pork tenderloins, about 1 pound each
1/2 pound sheeled pecans
3/4 cup dried breadcrumbs
2 tablespoons all-purpose flour
6 eggs, beaten

For the sauce:
1 and 1/2 cups extra heavy cream
1/2 cup pure maple syrup
1 cup margarine, melted

Cut pork into 12 (2-inch) pieces (allowing 3 pieces per serving).

Pulse the pecans in a food processor until coarse and combine with breadcrumbs.

Flatten pork to 1/8-inch thickness and dredge first in the flour, then in the beaten eggs, and then in the pecan-breadcrumb mixture. Pat firmly.

In a separate saucepan, combine the cream and maple syrup. Bring to a boil. Thicken with a cornstarch slurry until sauce coats the back of a spoon.

In a 12-inch sauté pan over medium-high heat, add 1/4 cup melted margarine. Add 3 pork medallions and cook until golden brown on both sides. Repeat steps with remaining pork. Transfer to baking sheet and place in preheated 350-oven for 5 to 8 minutes. Serve with sauce and sweet mashed potatoes.

INSIDE SCOOP

CHEF	DAVID RENIERE	LIQUOR	FULL LIQUOR
OWNERS	WALTER AND SALLY GUERTLER	SMOKING	PERMITTED IN
OPEN SINCE	1989		DESIGNATED AREAS
CUISINE	ECLECTIC BISTRO FARE	SERVICES	CHILDREN'S MENU
SPECIALTY	WIENER SCHNITZEL		HEALTHY/LOW-FAT MENU ITEMS
PRICE RANGE	APPETIZERS $4 TO $11		VEGETARIAN MENU ITEMS
	ENTREES $7 TO $24		HANDICAPPED ACCESSIBLE
CREDIT CARDS	MAJOR CREDIT CARDS ACCEPTED		TAKE-OUT ORDERS AVAILABLE
RESERVATIONS	RECOMMENDED	DRESS CODE	CASUAL
HOURS	TUESDAY THROUGH SUNDAY	PARKING	AVAILABLE ON THE STREET
	FOR DINNER		

APPETIZERS

GRILLED GRAVLAX IN A SWEET MUSTARD DILL SAUCE
LITTLENECKS STEAMED WITH LAGER BEER, CHORIZO, ONION AND KALE
VEGETABLE SPRING ROLLS WITH MANGO CHUTNEY AND PICKLED GINGER
CRABCAKES ON A MESCLUN SALAD WITH BAVARIAN SWEET AND SPICY MAYONNAISE
BAKED BRIE WRAPPED IN PUFF PASTRY
NEW ENGLAND CLAM CHOWDER

ENTREES

SEA SCALLOPS AND FETTUCCINE WITH SHIITAKE MUSHROOMS, RED AND YELLOW CHERRY TOMATOES, IN AN ORANGE-GINGER SAUCE
LOBSTER POT PIE
SAUTÉED CHICKEN BREAST IN SUN-DRIED TOMATO AND GARLIC CREAM SAUCE WITH GORGONZOLA CHEESE
MEDALLIONS OF PORK LOIN RUBBED WITH HICKORY AND MOLASSES WITH SMOKED BACON AND CORN RELISH
GRILLED BAUERWURST AND BRATWURST

Red Rooster Tavern

RISE AND SHINE

The venerable Red Rooster Tavern has been satisfying hearty New England appetites since 1969. These days the popular restaurant offers casual upscale dining with a great cocktail lounge. The current owner is Jeffrey Cooke, who has spent the past quarter century working in some of Rhode Island's best restaurants. He shares chef duties with Christian Corcoran, and together they continue to offer the traditional New England fare for which the Red Rooster is so well known, while incorporating foods and tastes from all parts of the globe. The menu changes seasonally. One of its most famous dishes is the Fisherman-Style Lobster stuffed with scallops and shrimp.

GOUGÈRES

1 cup water	1 cup all-purpose flour
1/4 cup butter	1 cup Gruyere cheese
1/2 teaspoon salt	4 whole eggs
1/4 teaspoon pepper	1 egg white (save yolk for egg wash by adding 1
Dash nutmeg	tablespoon water)

In a small saucepan, bring to a boil the water, butter, salt, pepper and nutmeg. Add flour and stir with a wooden spoon until it pulls away from the sides. Remove the saucepan from the heat and add half the cheese; then add the whole eggs and egg white, blending until smooth.

Scoop mixture (about 1 tablespoon in size) onto a greased baking pan. Brush with eggwash and sprinkle remaining cheese on top. Bake at 400 degrees for 15 minutes, then 10 minutes at 300 degrees or until brown and somewhat dry.

These can be made up ahead and refrigerated or even frozen. Also these "puffs" could be filled with salad mixtures such as crab, duck, smoked salmon or even vegetables. These are great for hors d'ouevres to accompany wine.

Chef's tip: Egg wash is made by mixing an egg yolk with water, then brushed on dough to aid in browning.

INSIDE SCOOP

CHEFS	JEFFREY COOKE AND CHRISTIAN CORCORAN	LIQUOR	FULL LIQUOR
		SMOKING	PERMITTED
OWNER	JEFFREY COOKE	SERVICES	BANQUET FACILITIES
OPEN SINCE	1969		CHILDREN'S MENU
CUISINE	TRADITIONAL NEW ENGLAND		HEALTHY/LOW-FAT MENU ITEMS
	FARE INCORPORATED WITH TASTES		VEGETARIAN MENU ITEMS
	FROM ALL OVER THE WORLD		HANDICAPPED ACCESSIBLE
SPECIALTY	BAKED STUFFED LOBSTER		TAKE-OUT ORDERS AVAILABLE
PRICE RANGE	APPETIZERS $6 TO $10		PRIVATE DINING ROOM
	ENTREES $11 TO $20		FIREPLACE
CREDIT CARDS	MAJOR CREDIT CARDS ACCEPTED	DRESS CODE	CASUAL TO DRESSY
RESERVATIONS	RECOMMENDED	PARKING	AVAILABLE ON THE PREMISES
HOURS	TUESDAY THROUGH SATURDAY		
	FOR DINNER		
	SUNDAY 1 TO 10 P.M.		

APPETIZERS

GRILLED SHRIMP BRUSHED WITH CHIPOTLE-HONEY GLAZE OVER MIXED GREENS

ROASTED GARLIC AND CAMBOZOLA CHEESE WITH TOMATO-FRUIT CHUTNEY

BRIE EN CROUTE WITH CRACKERS AND WARM FRUIT SAUCE

GOOSE PATE DRIZZLED WITH TRUFFLE OIL

BAKED ONION SOUP GRATINEE

SMOKED SALMON WITH CAPERS, DICED ONION AND DILL SAUCE

ENTREES

ROASTED GLAZED HALF DUCKLING

ASIAN DUCK BREAST OVER A BED OF ASIAN NOODLE SALAD WITH A SOY BALSAMIC REDUCTION

GRILLED PORK TENDERLOIN WITH A CHIPOTLE-HONEY SAUCE, CARAMELIZED ONIONS AND SWEET POTATO MASHED

FILET AU POIVRE WITH BRANDY, DEMIGLACE AND CREAM

SALMON FILET GLAZED WITH ORANGE-RASPBERRY MARMALADE WITH A RASPBERRY MELBA SAUCE

SEA SCALLOPS WITH A WASABI-BACON BUTTER, SHALLOTS AND SCALLIONS

LOBSTER AND ARTICHOKE TURNOVER WITH DILL MASCARPONE CHEESE

Restaurant Bouchard

HAUGHTY BUT NICE

Considered by those-in-the-know as one of the very best restaurants in the state, Restaurant Bouchard promises you a distinctly elegant dining experience, so make sure you dress accordingly. Located in a quaint historical building on Thames Street in busy Newport, this very French restaurant offers a quiet respite, superb service, and classic dishes with a modern twist – for example, the creative chef's tower of foie gras. Exquisitely appointed, Restaurant Bouchard is a delight to all the senses and is especially romantic during Christmas holidays. The intimate bar is quite inviting.

OYSTERS VIVAROIS

Serves 12 to 16

48 oysters
1/2 cup white wine
3 tablespoons finely chopped shallots
1 teaspoons finely chopped garlic
2 teaspoons curry powder (madras is
   recommended)
Juice from 1 lemon
2 cups fish stock reduced to 1/2

2 cups heavy cream
1 teaspoon cornstarch and 1 tablespoon water,
   combined
Salt and pepper, to taste
1 cup cooked spinach
1 cup grated Gruyere cheese (or Swiss cheese, if
   preferred)

Ask your fish man to open your oysters, then place them in a covered roasting or baking pan in the refrigerator.

In a sauce pan, combine wine, shallots, garlic, curry powder and lemon juice; bring to a boil. Add fish stock and cream, then add the corn starch-water mixture. Return to a boil; season with salt and pepper. Set aside to cool.

With the oysters lying open on a sheet pan, place an equal amount of spinach and then curry sauce on each. Sprinkle with grated cheese. Bake at 400 degrees for about 12 minutes or until the cheese has browned. Serve immediately.

Chef's tip: Cornstarch and water combine to form what is called a slurry.

INSIDE SCOOP

CHEF	ALBERT BOUCHARD	LIQUOR	FULL LIQUOR
OWNERS	SARAH AND ALBERT BOUCHARD	SMOKING	NO
OPEN SINCE	1995	SERVICES	HEALTHY/LOW-FAT MENU ITEMS
CUISINE	CREATIVE CLASSIC FRENCH		VEGETARIAN MENU ITEMS
SPECIALTY	OYSTERS VIVAROIS		CATERING
PRICE RANGE	APPETIZERS $8 TO $18		PRIVATE DINING ROOM
	ENTREES $23 TO $28		FIREPLACE
CREDIT CARDS	MAJOR CREDIT CARDS ACCEPTED	DRESS CODE	TASTEFUL
RESERVATIONS	RECOMMENDED	PARKING	AVAILABLE ON THE STREET
HOURS	WEDNESDAY THROUGH MONDAY		
	FOR DINNER		

APPETIZERS

LOBSTER BISQUE WITH BASIL AND GARLIC
FOIE GRAS WITH PETITE SALAD WITH RASPBERRY VINAIGRETTE
ASPARAGUS AND LOBSTER IN PUFF PASTRY, LEMON BEURRE BLANC
ARTICHOKE MOUSSE WITH TOMATO-GARLIC BEURRE BLANC
SMOKED SALMON WRAPPED AROUND GOAT CHEESE WITH CRACKED
   PEPPERCORNS WITH TWO SAUCES
HOUSE PATE

ENTREES

DOVER SOLE WITH SOREL SAUCE
SALMON WITH SPICY THAI CRUST AND LEMON GRASS SAUCE
PORK TENDERLOIN WITH ROASTED RED PEPPERS, SPINACH, GOAT
   CHEESE AND ROASTED GARLIC SAUCE
LOBSTER, SCALLOPS AND SHRIMP WITH VEGETABLES IN BROWNED
   GRUYERE AND BOURSIN CHEESE SAUCE
DUCK BREAST WITH COFFEE CRUST IN BRANDY BALSAMIC GLAZE
SLICED LAMB WITH HERB-RED WINE SAUCE WITH A HINT OF CURRY

Riverwalk Cafe

DOWN BY THE RIVERSIDE

In one of the city's most promising locations, the Riverwalk Cafe is making its mark with exciting food and a high-energy atmosphere. As you enter this café, an inviting bar and lounge area makes you want to linger. A few steps above is the main dining room with an open kitchen where the creative chef and his staff perform nightly. The menu has it all, from Asian to Italian, and is especially strong in the area of seafood. This is a happening place – great for drinks right after work, dinner with friends, or late-night grazing.

INSIDE SCOOP

CHEF	BRIAN TORTORELLA	LIQUOR	FULL LIQUOR
OWNERS	PETER AND KEVIN GAUDREAU	SMOKING	PERMITTED AT THE BAR
OPEN SINCE	2002	SERVICES	HEALTHY/LOWFAT MENU ITEMS
CUISINE	CREATIVE AMERICAN WITH		VEGETARIAN MENU ITEMS
	ASIAN AND FRENCH INFLUENCES		HANDICAPPED ACCESSIBLE
SPECIALTY	CHILEAN SEA BASS		TAKE-OUT ORDERS AVAILABLE
PRICE RANGE	APPETIZERS $4 TO $12		CATERING
	ENTREES $15 TO $25		PRIVATE DINING ROOM
CREDIT CARDS	MAJOR CREDIT CARDS ACCEPTED	DRESS CODE	BUSINESS/CASUAL
RESERVATIONS	RECOMMENDED	PARKING	AVAILABLE ON THE
HOURS	OPEN SEVEN NIGHTS A WEEK		STREET AND IN AN
	FOR DINNER		ADJACENT PARKING LOT

APPETIZERS

PEPPERED AHI TUNA WITH FENNEL SLAW, PORT WINE SYRUP AND
   TOMATO TARTARE
CHICKEN SPRING ROLLS WITH CITRUS SOY SAUCE AND SWEET PEPPER
   GLAZE
SUSHI MEDLEY
SATAY SAMPLER
VEGETABLE RISOTTO
CRISPY SHRIMP WITH LOBSTER MASHED POTATOES

ENTREES

LOBSTER RAVIOLI WITH SHELLFISH AND TARRAGON TOMATO CREAM
   SAUCE
ROASTED DUCK BREAST WITH MISSION FIGS, FINGERLING POTATOES
   AND CALVADOS JUS
BARBECUE MAHI MAHI WITH ROASTED LOBSTER AND CORN RAGOUT,
   CRISPY ONIONS AND CITRUS GINGER JUS
BLACKENED SWORDFISH WITH BROCCOLI RABE, CANDIED YAMS AND
   MANGO RELISH
SLICED HEREFORD STEAK WITH LOBSTER BEARNAISE, CHIVE WHIPPED
   POTATOES AND ASPARAGUS

Rue de l'Espoir

STREET SMART

American bistro cooking, with French, Italian and Asian influences, is what Rue de L'Espoir is all about. The Rue, as it is lovingly called by regulars, does it all by being open for breakfast, brunch, lunch and dinner. Deborah Norman is the owner, and Michael Koussa is the very talented chef. Thanks to their creative juices, the Rue has been written up in *Food & Wine, Gourmet, Bon Appetit* and many other national publications since the restaurant opened in 1976. Some of the most popular dishes at the Rue include the Lemon Ricotta Cheese Griddle Cakes, Lobster Madeira, and Pistachio-Orange Crusted Salmon.

ROSEMARY SHRIMP MARINADE

Serves 6 to 8

Marinade:
1/4 cup balsamic vinegar
1 1/2 cups olive oil
1/8 cup tamari (or soy sauce)
2 tablespoons chopped garlic
1/8 cup fresh rosemary, destemmed

24 extra-large shrimp
Lemon wedges, for garnish

Add all marinade ingredients, except rosemary, to blender. Mix well, then add rosemary. Pour over shrimp and marinate for 2 hours. Put on skewers and grill for approximately 1 minute on each side.

Arrange on platter with remoulade in the center. Garnish with lemon wedges.

SHRIMP REMOULADE SAUCE

3 egg yolks
1 tablespoon Dijon mustard
1 cup vegetable oil
1/2 cup lemon juice

1/2 celery stalk, chopped
1 green onion, chopped
1/2 teaspoon cayenne pepper
Salt, to taste

Blend yolks and mustard in food processor. Add oil in steady stream. Add lemon juice. Add remaining ingredients; mix until blended well.

INSIDE SCOOP

CHEF	MICHAEL KOUSSA	LIQUOR	FULL LIQUOR
OWNER	DEBORAH NORMAN	SMOKING	NO
OPEN SINCE	1976	SERVICES	HEALTHY/LOW-FAT MENU ITEMS
CUISINE	AMERICAN BISTRO WITH STYLES		VEGETARIAN MENU ITEMS
	FROM FRANCE, ITALY AND ASIA		HANDICAPPED ACCESSIBLE
SPECIALTY	BREAKFAST: EGGS BENEDICT,		TAKE-OUT ORDERS AVAILABLE
	BREAKFAST ENCHILADA		CATERING
	LUNCH: CHOPPED SALAD,		PRIVATE DINING ROOM
	SANDWICH DU JOUR OR	DRESS CODE	CASUAL
	GRILLED EGGPLANT SANDWICH	PARKING	AVAILABLE ON THE PREMISES
	DINNER: GRILLED CHICKEN		
	OVER HOMEMADE RAVIOLI,		
	LOBSTER FRICASSE		
PRICE RANGE	APPETIZERS $7 TO $11		
	ENTREES $17 TO $28		
CREDIT CARDS	MAJOR CREDIT CARDS ACCEPTED		
RESERVATIONS	RECOMMENDED		
HOURS	TUESDAY THROUGH SUNDAY FOR		
	BREAKFAST, LUNCH AND DINNER		
	SATURDAY/SUNDAY BRUNCH		

APPETIZERS

ASPARAGUS AND PORTABELLO MUSHROOM SPRING ROLLS WITH
    GREEN CABBAGE, CARROTS, SESAME, FRESH GINGER IN PEACH,
    PASSION FRUIT SAUCE
ROASTED DUCK SALAD ON SPRING GREENS WITH MANGO SALSA AND
    RASPBERRY VINAIGRETTE
SESAME CHICKEN IN A HONEY MUSTARD DIPPING SAUCE

ENTREES

GRILLED FILET MIGNON DUSTED WITH ESPRESSO, CINNAMON AND
    CORIANDER, SERVED WITH A RED WINE JUS
BABY RACK OF LAMB, RUBBED WITH PORCINI MUSHROOMS AND DIJON
    MUSTARD IN A MADEIRA WINE AND SHALLOT DEMIGLACE
LOBSTER FRICASSE SERVED WITH BRAISED ROOT VEGETABLES, RISOTTO
    CAKE AND LOBSTER AND SHRIMP BUERRE BLANC
CHAMPAGNE-BATTERED COD AND MASHED POTATO CHIPS

Salvation Cafe

149 Broadway, Newport | 401-847-2620 | www.salvationcafé.com

CHANGES IN LATITUDE

This has got to be the wackiest restaurant in the state, from the tiki bar in the rear to the Asian pagoda-style dining room in the middle, to the cool retro cocktail lounge at the front entrance. The global cuisine on the Salvation Cafe's well-worn menu is just as adventuresome, offering dishes from exotic ports of call. Jamaica, Cuba, Mexico and Thailand, to name just some of the stops we have made on our visits there. If you're in need of a vacation but can't get away, just check into the Salvation Cafe for a couple of hours – it reminds us of that other wacky spot on earth, Key West.

INSIDE SCOOP

CHEF	ALEX HART NIBBRIG	SMOKING	PERMITTED IN DESIGNATED AREAS
OWNER	SUE LAMOND	SERVICES	BANQUET FACILITIES
OPEN SINCE	1992		CHILDREN'S MENU
CUISINE	ECLECTIC WORLD CUISINE		HEALTHY/LOW-FAT MENU ITEMS
SPECIALTY	PAD THAI		VEGETARIAN MENU ITEMS
PRICE RANGE	APPETIZERS $4.50 TO $11		HANDICAPPED ACCESSIBLE
	ENTREES $12 TO 23		TAKE-OUT ORDERS AVAILABLE
CREDIT CARDS	MAJOR CREDIT CARDS ACCEPTED		CATERING
RESERVATIONS	NO RESERVATION POLICY		PRIVATE DINING ROOM
HOURS	OPEN SEVEN NIGHTS A WEEK	DRESS CODE	CASUAL
	FOR DINNER	PARKING	AVAILABLE IN AN ADJACENT
	SUNDAY BRUNCH		PARKING LOT AND ON
LIQUOR	FULL LIQUOR		THE STREET

APPETIZERS

SHRIMP NIME CHOW

EDAMAME - SOYBEANS TOSSED IN SEA SALT

VEGETABLE DUMPLINGS

LOBSTER PIZZA

BARBECUED CHICKEN QUESADILLA WITH BASIL-SCENTED ROASTED
    GARLIC AND CORN SALSA

ASIAN TUNA CARPACCIO

ENTREES

JAMAICAN JERK PORK CHOP WITH JICAMA SLAW AND BANANA CURRY
    KETCHUP

CUBAN MARINATED TUNA WITH SPANISH RISOTTO

CODFISH WRAPPED IN RICE PAPER WITH GINGER AND SCALLIONS AND
    CILANTRO

CHILE-CRUSTED SIRLOIN WITH HORSERADISH-LIME CRÈME FRAICHE
    AND CILANTRO MASHED

MANGO-GLAZED DUCK BREAST OVER SPICED SWEET POTATOES AND
    SESAME SPINACH

Sardella's

30 Memorial Boulevard, Newport | 401-849-6312 | www.sardellas.com

SCENES FROM AN ITALIAN RESTAURANT

It's a beautiful summer night, and you're sitting on the patio at Sardella's, sipping a glass of Pinot Grigio. Six months later, it's snowing but you're cozy and warm by the fire in the Fireplace Dining Room. No matter what time of year it is, Sardella's is an appealing, family-style restaurant, a year-round favorite with local residents and popular as well with visitors to trendy Newport. Generous portions of Italian food are offered in a relaxed atmosphere by a friendly wait staff, who treat everyone like "regular" customers. Bring on the lasagna.

INSIDE SCOOP

CHEF	KEVIN FITZGERALD
OWNERS	RICHARD SARDELLA
	AND PATRICK FITZGERALD
OPEN SINCE	1983
CUISINE	CLASSIC ITALIAN
SPECIALTY	VEAL LORETTA
PRICE RANGE	APPETIZERS $4.75 TO $11
	ENTREES $10 TO $22
CREDIT CARDS	MAJOR CREDIT CARDS ACCEPTED
RESERVATIONS	RECOMMENDED
HOURS	OPEN SEVEN DAYS A WEEK
	FOR DINNER
LIQUOR	FULL LIQUOR
SMOKING	PERMITTED

SERVICES	BANQUET FACILITIES
	CHILDREN'S MENU
	HEALTHY/LOW-FAT MENU ITEMS
	VEGETARIAN MENU ITEMS
	HANDICAPPED ACCESSIBLE
	TAKE-OUT ORDERS AVAILABLE
	CATERING
	PRIVATE DINING ROOM
	FIREPLACE
	GARDEN AND PATIO DINING
DRESS CODE	PROPER
PARKING	AVAILABLE ON THE STREET AND
	THROUGH THE VALET SERVICE

APPETIZERS

MUSSELS STEAMED IN OLIVE OIL, CLAM BROTH, WHITE WINE, ONIONS
  AND GARLIC
ESCARGOTS SAUTÉED WITH ARTICHOKE HEARTS AND GARLIC BUTTER
GORGONZOLA ON CROSTINI
CALAMARI FRIED WITH CHERRY PEPPERS AND LEMON OLIVE OIL
WARM GOAT CHEESE SALAD WITH SUN-DRIED TOMATO

ENTREES

CLASSIC LASAGNA
CHEESE RAVIOLI BAKED WITH SPINACH, FRESH TOMATO AND
  MOZZARELLA
SHRIMP, SCALLOPS AND ONIONS IN A SPICY PLUM TOMATO SAUCE
EGGPLANT PARMIGIANA
VEAL MEDALLIONS SAUTÉED WITH PANCETTA, MUSHROOMS, ONIONS,
  BRANDY AND VEAL STOCK
GRILLED SIRLOIN WITH ROASTED GARLIC BUTTER

Sea Shai

SHE SELLS SEA SHELLS

Sushi chef and owner Jung Lee has been quietly pleasing customers at the award-winning Sea Shai in Middletown since 1987. Japanese and Korean cuisine is offered in this serene restaurant, with its clean Asian decor. Paper lanterns in shades of red, pink and yellow hang over the very long, 14-seat sushi bar. A wild assortment of impeccably fresh sushi, sashimi and maki is served in beautiful wooden boats. Our favorites? The delicious Beef Mondoo dumplings from Korea, the lacy vegetable tempura, and the delectable panko-crusted soft shell crab.

GRAPEVINE GEM: Especially appealing is the attractive waitstaff attired in gorgeous geisha kimonos.

INSIDE SCOOP

CHEF-OWNER	JUNG LEE	LIQUOR	FULL LIQUOR
OPEN SINCE	1987	SMOKING	PERMITTED
CUISINE	JAPANESE AND KOREAN	SERVICES	BANQUET FACILITIES
SPECIALTY	SUSHI		HEALTHY/LOW-FAT MENU ITEMS
PRICE RANGE	APPETIZERS $2 TO $13		VEGETARIAN MENU ITEMS
	ENTREES $10 TO $19		HANDICAPPED ACCESSIBLE
CREDIT CARDS	MAJOR CREDIT CARDS ACCEPTED		TAKE-OUT ORDERS AVAILABLE
RESERVATIONS	RECOMMENDED		CATERING
HOURS	LUNCH:	DRESS CODE	CASUAL
	MONDAY THROUGH FRIDAY,	PARKING	PLENTY OF FREE PARKING
	11:30 A.M. TO 2:30 P.M.		AVAILABLE ON THE PREMISES
	DINNER:		
	SEVEN DAYS A WEEK, 5 TO 10 P.M.		

APPETIZERS

SUSHI, SASHIMI, MAKI AND TEMAKE
GRILLED KUSHI-YAKI (SQUID, CHICKEN, BEEF, VEGETABLE OR SEAFOOD)
DUMPLINGS, PAN-FRIED OR STEAMED
TEMPURA

ENTREES

THINLY SLICED BEEF MARINATED IN BARBECUE SAUCE
SLICED LOIN OF PORK MARINATED IN A HOT SPICY SAUCE
CHICKEN MARINATED IN KOREAN GINGER SAUCE
SQUID SAUTÉED WITH VEGETABLES IN HOT PEPPER SAUCE
CLAM, SQUID, SCALLOPS, SHRIMP AND VEGETABLES IN SPECIAL SAUCE
BATTERED BEEF AND VEGETABLES TOPPED WITH A SWEET AND SOUR SAUCE
PEPPER AND SCALLION SHRIMP PANCAKE
VERMICELLI AND SHREDDED VEGETABLES SAUTÉED IN SAUCE
BENTO (COMPLETE JAPANESE TRADITIONAL DINNER WITH MISO SOUP, RICE
    AND SHRIMP TEMPURA AND TERIYAKI BEEF, CHICKEN, SEAFOOD OR
    VEGETABLE)
SUKI YAKI (BEEF, CHICKEN OR SEAFOOD WITH VEGETABLES, NOODLES AND
    TOFU IN BROTH)

PA-JUN
SCALLION PANCAKES

Serves 4

1 bunch scallions

1 cup Korean pancake mix
OR
1/2 cup flour
2 tablespoons sweet rice powder
1/2 teaspoon salt
2 eggs
2 tablespoons vegetable oil

1/4 cup soy sauce
2 tablespoons vinegar
1 teaspoon sesame seeds

Cut scallions into 2-inch pieces. Combine pancake mix with 2 cups water.

In hot frying pan, add 1 tablespoon oil and spread the scallions. Then add pancake batter in the pan. Cook slightly until golden brown on both sides.

Combine soy sauce, vinegar and sesame seeds to make a dipping sauce to be served with pancakes.

Chef's tip: Add meat, seafood or fresh hot pepper to the pancake batter, if desired.

RECIPE FOR SUCCESS

Ah, Spain. It seems as if this restaurant is always crowded. What's the big attraction? It's a combination of the handsome architecture, the beautiful flower-filled courtyard with its outdoor fireplace, the attractive wait staff, and the consistently satisfying, affordable food. We love the Artichoke Hearts, stuffed with smoked ham, spinach and fresh herbs, and the paella dishes overflowing with lobster, clams, mussels, shrimp and scallops. The charbroiled Filet Mignon with a red wine-mushroom sauce is as good as it gets. (We are big fans of the Spain restaurant in Narragansett; the original Spain is located in Cranston.)

INSIDE SCOOP

CHEF-OWNER	SALVADOR GOMES	LIQUOR	FULL LIQUOR
OPEN SINCE	1987	SMOKING	PERMITTED IN BAR ONLY
CUISINE	SPANISH AND AMERICAN	SERVICES	BANQUET FACILITIES
SPECIALTY	PAELLA VALENCIANA FOR TWO		CHILDREN WELCOME
PRICE RANGE	APPETIZERS $7.95		HEALTHY/LOW-FAT MENU ITEMS
	ENTREES $11 TO $15		VEGETARIAN MENU ITEMS
CREDIT CARDS	MAJOR CREDIT CARDS ACCEPTED		HANDICAPPED ACCESSIBLE
RESERVATIONS	RECOMMENDED FOR		TAKE-OUT ORDERS AVAILABLE
	PARTIES OF 6 OR MORE		PRIVATE DINING ROOM
HOURS	TUESDAY THROUGH SATURDAY		OUTSIDE DINING IN SEASON
	FOR DNNER	DRESS CODE	CASUAL
	SUNDAYS – 1 TO 9 P.M.	PARKING	AVAILABLE ON THE PREMISES

APPETIZERS

CLAMS CASINO

GRILLED SMOKED SPANISH SAUSAGE

ARTICHOKE HEARTS STUFFED WITH SMOKED HAM, SPINACH AND
    FRESH HERBS

CALAMARI WITH MILD AND HOT PEPPERS

MUSHROOM CAPS WITH SHRIMP, SCALLOPS AND CRABMEAT

ENTREES

VEAL SAUTÉED WITH ASPARAGUS, SPINACH, IMPORTED PROSCIUTTO
    AND PROVOLONE IN A LIGHT SHERRY SAUCE

BREAST OF CHICKEN STUFFED WITH PINE NUTS, DICED SMOKED
    HAM, SPINACH, CHEESE AND TOPPED WITH FRESH CILANTRO AND
    TOMATO SAUCE

CHARCOAL-BROILED SIRLOIN TOPPED WITH ROASTED GARLIC AND
    LEMON SAUCE

LOBSTER, CLAMS, MUSSELS, SHRIMP AND SCALLOPS IN A TOMATO,
    SPINACH, BRANDY AND SHERRY SAUCE

PAELLA MARINERA

Sunflower Cafe

THERE'S NO PLACE LIKE HOME

This modest restaurant is located in a Cape-style house in a residential neighborhood, the perfect location for dining on food like Mama used to make. The Sunflower Cafe opened in 1994, and current owner Ezio Gentile is devoted to making every guest feel welcome and satisfied while Chef Steven DiSano is busy turning out excellent regional Italian dishes. DiSano understands the secret to really good Italian food – simplicity. His Veal Valdostano, flavored with prosciutto, fontina cheese and sage in a Barolo wine sauce, is definitely worth the trip to Cranston. Who says you can't go home again?

FARFALLE GIRASOLE

Serves 4

1 pound farfalle pasta
2 tablespoons butter
1/2 cup chopped prosciutto
1 1/2 cups chopped portabello mushrooms
1/2 cup chopped leeks
1/2 cup Marsala wine
1 1/2 cups of heavy cream
Grated pecorino cheese, as needed

Boil farfalle pasta 7 to 10 minutes. Drain and set aside.

In a large sauté pan, melt the butter. Add the prosciutto, portabello mushrooms and leeks; sauté for 3 to 5 minutes. Add the Marsala wine and cream; reduce by half. Toss with the cooked farfalle and pecorino cheese.

INSIDE SCOOP

CHEF	STEVEN DI SANO	LIQUOR	FULL LIQUOR
OWNER	EZIO GENTILE	SMOKING	NO
OPEN SINCE	1994	SERVICES	HEALTHY/LOW-FAT MENU ITEMS
CUISINE	UPSCALE ITALIAN REGIONAL		VEGETARIAN MENU ITEMS
SPECIALTY	VEAL VALDOSTANO,		HANDICAPPED ACCESSIBLE
	LINGUINE PESCATORE		TAKE-OUT ORDERS AVAILABLE
PRICE RANGE	APPETIZERS $6 TO $7		CATERING
	ENTREES $12 TO $17		PRIVATE DINING ROOM
CREDIT CARDS	MAJOR CREDIT CARDS ACCEPTED	DRESS CODE	CASUAL
RESERVATIONS	RECOMMENDED	PARKING	AVAILABLE ON THE PREMISES
HOURS	OPEN WEEKDAYS FOR LUNCH		
	MONDAY THROUGH SATURDAY		
	FOR DINNER		

APPETIZERS

PASTA FAGIOLI
MESCLUN SALAD WITH ROASTED PEPPERS, ARTICHOKE HEARTS AND GORGONZOLA CHEESE
PORTABELLO MUSHROOM WITH SPINACH, ROASTED PEPPERS AND MOZZARELLA
SHRIMP WITH LEMON, GARLIC, WHITE WINE AND CANNELLINI BEANS
ROSEMARY FOCACCIA WITH ROASTED PEPPERS, PROSCIUTTO AND FONTINA CHEESE

ENTREES

PENNE WITH ONION, PANCETTA, TOMATO AND RED WINE
CHICKEN WITH EGGPLANT AND MOZZARELLA CHEESE WITH PENNE
VEAL VALDOSTANO WITH PROSCIUTTO, FONTINA AND SAGE IN A BAROLO WINE SAUCE
TERRINE OF PORK MEDALLIONS WITH MUSHROOMS, ARBORIO RICE AND A BREADED PARMESAN CRUST
SIRLOIN STEAK WITH SAUTÉED SHIITAKE MUSHROOMS AND ROASTED PEPPERS IN A BLACK PEPPERCORN WHISKEY SAUCE

Ten Prime Steak & Sushi

PRIME TIME

Outrageous...exciting...high-energy...all that and more describes Ten Prime Steak & Sushi, a Providence restaurant owned by the highly creative team of John Elkhay, Rick and Cheryl Bready (who also brought you XO Cafe). Nicholas Rabar is the impressive young chef in the kitchen at Ten, which has been described as a 21st-century steakhouse that also offers fresh sushi. Rabar says he offers "a twist of the typical steakhouse menu, focusing on New American Cuisine with a classic French attitude." His best dish? The Steak au Poivre with Port-Stilton Sauce. It never fails to make the customers rave.

GRAPEVINE GEM: The bathrooms at Ten Prime Steak & Sushi have actually won an award for their bizarre sound effects, everything from a clickety-clack roller coaster to nighttime in the jungle. Best loo in town.

INSIDE SCOOP

CHEF	NICHOLAS RABAR	LIQUOR	FULL LIQUOR
OWNER	JOHN ELKHAY	SMOKING	PERMITTED AT THE BAR
	RICK AND CHERYL BREADY	SERVICES	BANQUET FACILITIES
OPENING	2001		HEALTHY/LOW-FAT MENU ITEMS
CUISINE	STEAKHOUSE FOCUSING ON		VEGETARIAN MENU ITEMS
	NEW AMERICAN CUISINE WITH		TAKE-OUT ORDERS AVAILABLE
	A CLASSIC FRENCH ATTITUDE,		CATERING
	WITH THE INCLUSION OF FRESH SUSHI		PRIVATE DINING ROOM
SPECIALTY	STEAK AU POIVRE WITH	DRESS CODE	UPSCALE CASUAL
	A PORT STILTON SAUCE	PARKING	AVAILABLE ON THE STREET, IN
PRICE RANGE	APPETIZERS $9 TO $11		NEARBY PARKING LOTS AND
	ENTREES $16 TO $26		GARAGES, AND THROUGH
CREDIT CARDS	MAJOR CREDIT CARDS ACCEPTED		THE VALET SERVICE
RESERVATIONS	RECOMMENDED		
HOURS	MONDAY THROUGH THURSDAY,		
	11:30 A.M. TO 10 P.M.		
	(WITH SUSHI AVAILABLE UNTIL 11 P.M.)		
	FRIDAY, 11:30 A.M. TO 11 P.M.		
	(SUSHI UNTIL MIDNIGHT)		
	SATURDAY, 5 TO 11 P.M.		
	(SUSHI UNTIL MIDNIGHT)		
	CLOSED SUNDAY		

APPETIZERS

GRILLED SALMON SKIN MAKI - SMOKED SALMON SKIN, BONINO FLAKES,
   BURDOCK ROOT

TUNA CEVICHE, LEMON GRASS, CILANTRO AND GINGER JUICE IN COCONUT
   SHELL

SKEWERED GINGER BEEF, PEANUT LIME CHICKEN, COCONUT SHRIMP AND
   DIPPING SAUCES

SEAWEED SALAD WITH SESAME DRESSING

EGG-FREE CAESAR SALAD

ENTREES

MAINE LOBSTERS - 3 POUNDS AND UP

GRILLED MEATLOAF FROM OUR BEST GROUND SIRLOIN, THREE-ONION
   DEMIGLACE, GARLIC SMASHED POTATOES AND ONION STRINGS

OSSOBUCO OVER GARLIC SMASHED POTATOES

WICKED STEAK - FIERY SPICED FLAT-IRON STEAK

VEAL CHOP TUSCAN STYLE, GRILLED PORTABELLO MUSHROOM, ARUGULA,
   SHAVED PARMESAN AND TRUFFLE OIL

24-OUNCE PORTERHOUSE STEAK

BONE-IN GRILLED PRIME RIB

PRIME SIRLOIN AU POIVRE
Serves 4

For the sirloin:
4 (14-ounce) Prime sirloin steaks
Salt and coarsely ground pepper, to taste

For the garlic mashed potatoes:
1 1/2 pound red bliss potatoes
5 cloves garlic, minced
1/2 cup butter
1/2 cup heavy cream
1 teaspoon salt
1/2 teaspoon pepper

For the asparagus:
24 thin asparagus
2 tablespoons extra virgin olive oil
Salt and pepper, to taste

For the sauce:
1 cup port wine
1 pint veal stock
1/2 cup Stilton bleu cheese
1 tablespoon butter
Salt and pepper, to taste

For the sirloin:
Coat one side of each steak with coarsely ground pepper, and season both sides with salt. For medium-rare steaks, grill on each side for about 6 minutes.

For the potatoes:
Begin by boiling the potatoes in 3 to 4 quarts salted water. Make sure potatoes are covered with an inch or two of water. Add garlic. Boil until potatoes are fork tender, which takes about 20 to 25 minutes. Drain and mash the potatoes and garlic with the butter and cream. Season with salt and pepper. Set aside in a warm area.

For the asparagus:
Rub asparagus with extra virgin olive oil and season with salt and pepper. Grill for approximately 4 minutes.

For the sauce:
In a 2-quart pot, reduce port wine by half. Add stock and reduce by half again. Fold in bleu cheese and butter at the end. Season and set aside.

For the final dish:
Plate the steak with mashed potatoes in the middle of the plate, sauce around the potatoes, and the grilled asparagus on the mashed potatoes, tips up. Serve with a full-bodied Cabernet or Syrah wine.

DO YOU BELIEVE IN MAGIC?

Ever since Trattoria Simpatico opened, it has been charming its guests with a romantic setting by the sea and delectable food to match. Just driving by this indoor/outdoor restaurant, with all its twinkling white lights, will make you want to stop in for a glass of wine, an appetizer or two, or perhaps even brunch. The folks here know how to have fun -- what other restaurant around has a Frostbite Night to mark the end of the summer season? And then they decorate this quaint establishment for the holidays. A wonderful place to dine and drink, any time of the year.

GRAPEVINE GEM: The outside garden would be a lovely place to hold a small wedding.

INSIDE SCOOP

CHEF	KEVIN GAUDREAU	LIQUOR	FULL LIQUOR
OWNER	PHYLLIS BEDARD	SMOKING	PERMITTED IN BAR
OPEN SINCE	1993		AND GARDEN AREAS
CUISINE	CREATIVE AMERICAN	SERVICES	HEALTHY/LOW-FAT MENU ITEMS
SPECIALTY	SEAFOOD		VEGETARIAN MENU ITEMS
PRICE RANGE	APPETIZERS $6 TO $12		HANDICAPPED ACCESSIBLE
	ENTREES $12 TO $25		TAKE-OUT ORDERS AVAILABLE
CREDIT CARDS	MAJOR CREDIT CARDS ACCEPTED		CATERING
RESERVATIONS	RECOMMENDED		PRIVATE DINING ROOM
HOURS	OPEN SEVEN DAYS A WEEK	DRESS CODE	CASUAL
	FOR DINNER FROM 5 TO 9:30 P.M.,	PARKING	AVAILABLE ON THE PREMISES
	SUNDAYS, OPEN AT 4 P.M.,		AND ON THE STREET
	IN THE SUMMER, LUNCH IS		
	SERVED MONDAY THROUGH FRIDAY		
	BEGINNING AT 11:30 A.M.		
	BRUNCH, SATURDAY, 11 A.M. TO 2:30 P.M.,		
	AND SUNDAY 11:30 A.M. TO 4 P.M.		
	WITH LIVE JAZZ MUSIC		

APPETIZERS

ROASTED LITTLENECKS WITH PANCETTA, SWEET CORN CREAM SAUCE AND
    ROASTED PEPPERS

FRIED CALAMARI WITH HOT PEPPERS, SPICY AIOLI, TENDER GREENS, SWEET
    AND TANGY DIPPING SAUCE

GARLIC-RUBBED BRUSCHETTA WITH SMOKED TOMATO-JALAPENO JAM, BLACK
    OLIVES, ROASTED RED PEPPERS, SPINACH AND GOAT CHEESE

VEGETABLE TIMBALE WITH CHEVRE, RED PEPPER COULIS AND BASIL PESTO

CRISPY SHRIMP WITH LOBSTER MASHED AND MICRO GREENS SALAD

GRILLED CHICKEN SAUSAGE WITH BALSAMIC POACHED BLACK FIGS, BROCCOLI
    RABE AND RED ONION CONFIT

ENTREES

SEARED AHI TUNA WITH HUDSON VALLEY FOIE GRAS, SAUTÉED ARUGULA,
    CARAMELIZED RED ONION AND POTATO ROSTI, WITH A FOREST MUSHROOM
    DEMIGLACE

LAMB CHOPS WITH CHICKPEA CAKES, STEAMED BROCCOLINI AND BALSAMIC
    MERLOT REDUCTION

PORK TENDERLOIN WITH MAPLE WHIPPED SWEET POTATO, BROCCOLI RABE,
    WHOLE GRAIN MUSTARD BORDELAISE AND APPLE CHUTNEY

VEAL CHOP WITH PORCINI RISOTTO, SAUTÉED BABY SPINACH AND HERBED
    PORT DEMIGLACE

GRILLED SWORDFISH MEDALLIONS WITH PERUVIAN BLUE POTATO, BEAN AND
    PEPPER SALAD, WITH A WARM CHARRED TOMATO VINAIGRETTE

CRISPY SHRIMP

serves 4

8 large shrimp (16 to 20 per pound), cleaned
Salt and pepper, to taste
1 cup egg wash
6 ounces shredded phyllo dough

3/4 cup mashed potatoes
1/3 cup chopped lobster meat
2 tablespoons chopped fresh herbs

Oil, as needed, for frying
1 cup mixed baby greens
1/4 cup red pepper coulis
1/4 cup basil oil

Season shrimp with salt and pepper and then dip into the egg wash. Divide the phyllo dough into 8 equal strands. Stretch the phyllo dough out completely and then, starting at one end, roll the shrimp up in the phyllo dough. Set aside.

Mixed the mashed potatoes, lobster meat and chopped fresh herbs together. Keep warm.

In a deep fryer set at 350 degrees, place the shrimp in the oil and cook for 4 minutes, or until shrimp begin to float. Remove from oil, drain on paper towels, and season with salt.

On 4 plates, place equal portions of baby greens in the center. On top of greens, add some mashed potatoes and then place 2 shrimp on top. (The potatoes will act like a glue to hold the shrimp in place.) Garnish with red pepper coulis and basil oil.

Trieste

INNER BEAUTY

Trieste of Bonnet Shores is an intimate café that offers excellent Northern Italian cuisine. It may not look like much from the outside, but it's what's on the inside that counts. The minute you enter Trieste, you are made to feel welcome, almost as if you are having dinner at someone's home. And then the food is so creative, you'll want to go back again and again to try everything on the seasonal menu. Trieste is a BYOB establishment, so make sure to bring a great bottle of wine to go with your delicious dinner. This is fine dining at very affordable prices.

MUSSELS ZUPPA

Serves 4

2 tablespoons olive oil
1 medium Vidalia onion, chopped
2 tablespoons chopped garlic
15 to 20 kalamata olives, pitted
1 tablespoon capers
2 pounds fresh mussels, with beards removed
1/4 cup white wine
4 tablespoons unsalted butter
1/4 cup fresh basil, chopped
Salt and pepper, to taste

Heat olive oil in large skillet. Add onion, garlic, olives and capers. When onions begin to brown, add mussels. Toss mussels with hot ingredients.

Add wine, butter, fresh basil, salt and pepper. Cover. Simmer for 2 to 3 minutes or until mussels just begin to open.

Serve immediately in bowls with broth. Serve with crusty Italian bread for dipping.

INSIDE SCOOP

CHEF-OWNER	GENE ALLSWORTH	LIQUOR	BYOB
OPEN SINCE	1999	SMOKING	NO
CUISINE	RUSTIC ITALIAN	SERVICES	HEALTHY/LOW-FAT MENU ITEMS
SPECIALTY	RABBIT CONFIT WITH		VEGETARIAN MENU ITEMS
	BABY FAVA BEANS		TAKE-OUT ORDERS AVAILABLE
PRICE RANGE	APPETIZERS $5 TO $9		CATERING
	ENTREES $13 TO $23	DRESS CODE	CASUAL
CREDIT CARDS	MAJOR CREDIT CARDS ACCEPTED	PARKING	AVAILABLE ON THE PREMISES
RESERVATIONS	RECOMMENDED		
HOURS	WEDNESDAY THROUGH SUNDAY		
	FOR DINNER		
	(EXPANDED HOURS IN SUMMER)		

APPETIZERS

SHRIMP BRUSCHETTA WITH OVEN-DRIED TOMATOES AND KALAMATA OLIVES IN WHITE WINE AND GARLIC BUTTER SAUCE

PORCINI TORTELLONI PASTA TOSSED WITH BRAISED RADICCHIO AND PANCETTA IN A SAGE BUTTER SAUCE

GRILLED VEGETABLES WITH WARM GOAT CHEESECAKE AND PESTO VINAIGRETTE

SPRING ASPARAGUS SAUTÉED WITH MIXED WILD MUSHROOMS, RED AND YELLOW PEAR TOMATOES, GARLIC AND FRESH BASIL

SPINACH SALAD TOSSED WITH GORGONZOLA, ALMONDS AND STRAWBERRIES WITH BALSAMIC SYRUP

ENTREES

GARLIC MASCARPONE RISOTTO WITH GRILLED VEGETABLE RATATOUILLE, RADICCHIO AND SPINACH

GNOCCHI WITH STEWED VEAL AND SAUSAGE IN A TOMATO-BAROLO WINE SAUCE

OVEN-ROASTED SEA BASS WITH LIGHT HERB CRUMB TOPPING IN A LOBSTER TOMATO BROTH WITH FENNEL AND POTATOES

GRILLED PORK TENDERLOIN WITH BAROLO WINE DEMIGLACE, POLENTA AND BROCCOLI RABE

BREADED EGGPLANT CUTLETS STUFFED WITH SPINACH AND RICOTTA AND SERVED WITH CAPPELLINI PASTA IN A ROASTED TOMATO-BASIL SAUCE

Tucker's Bistro

CROSSING OVER

Its deep red walls are covered with closely spaced mirrors and original works of art (some better than others). Tucker's Bistro gives new meaning to the word decadent. It is so dimly lit that you're handed a little pen light to read the multicultural menu. Gossamer-like chandeliers twinkle, and the tables are set with odd little lamps and a hodge-podge of china and silverware. The ornate beaded bread basket alone is worth the trip to this intimate 1920s French-style bistro. Just when you think it's time for a spooky seance to begin, the food – glorious food – arrives, often served by owner Tucker Harris himself.

RASPBERRY-WHITE CHOCOLATE CHEESECAKE

Serves 10

2 pounds cream cheese
1 pound white chocolate
6 to 8 tablespoons butter
1/2 box vanilla wafers (Nilla brand is
   recommended)
1/2 teaspoon cinnamon

1/2 teaspoon nutmeg
4 eggs
1/4 cup sugar
1 teaspoon vanilla extract
3/4 cup raspberry puree

Preheat oven to 350 degrees.

In the top of a double boiler, soften the cream cheese and white chocolate. In a separate pan, melt the butter. In a food processor, pulse the vanilla wafers until crumbled finely. Add cinnamon, nutmeg and melted butter to mixture in the food processor.

Line the bottom of an 8-inch springform pan with parchment paper and spray with non-stick cooking spray. Press wafer mixture to cover the bottom of pan.

When chocolate and cream cheese are soft, add eggs, sugar, vanilla and raspberry puree. Mix well. Pour mixture on top of crumb base in springform pan.

Bake for approximately 1 hour. The top of cake should be a light golden brown color when removed from oven. The center of the cheesecake will appear underdone. Refrigerate until firm and then serve.

INSIDE SCOOP

CHEF	SUE ZINNO-DEEN
OWNER	TUCKER HARRIS
OPEN SINCE	1995
CUISINE	MULTICULTURAL
SPECIALTY	THAI SHRIMP NACHOS
	VEGETARIAN WELLINGTON
PRICE RANGE	APPETIZERS $5 TO $10
	ENTREES $16 TO $27
CREDIT CARDS	MAJOR CREDIT CARDS ACCEPTED
RESERVATIONS	RECOMMENDED
HOURS	OPEN SEVEN NIGHTS A WEEK
	FOR DINNER
	SUNDAY BRUNCH
LIQUOR	FULL LIQUOR
SMOKING	PERMITTED AT THE BAR
SERVICES	HEALTHY/LOW-FAT MENU ITEMS
	VEGETARIAN MENU ITEMS
	TAKE-OUT ORDERS AVAILABLE
	PRIVATE DINING ROOM
DRESS CODE	CASUAL
PARKING	AVAILABLE ON THE STREET

APPETIZERS

WARM GOAT CHEESE WITH MESCLUN SALAD AND SESAME VINAIGRETTE

STEAMED MUSSELS WITH GARLIC, SHALLOTS, BASIL AND TOMATOES IN A WHITE WINE BROTH

THAI SHRIMP NACHOS WITH SCALLIONS, SWEET RED PEPPERS AND LEEKS IN A COCONUT THAI RED CURRY BROTH

ASIAN-STYLE CALAMARI SAUTÉED IN SESAME OIL, GARLIC, GINGER, TOSSED WITH RED PEPPERS, SCALLIONS AND THAI SEVEN SPICE

SLICED FRIED ARTICHOKES WITH CAPERS, WATER CHESTNUTS AND SPICY RED PEPPER REMOULADE

ENTREES

CARAMELIZED GINGER-SCENTED SEA SCALLOPS IN A BROWN SUGAR AND SAKE SAUCE WITH COCONUT CREAM RISOTTO, SNOW PEAS AND CARROTS

HOT JAMAICAN JERK SHRIMP WITH A BLACK BEAN-CORN SALSA AND JASMINE RICE

ORIENTAL DUCK BREAST WITH SESAME SOBA NOODLES, CUCUMBER SALAD AND MANDARIN ORANGE VINAIGRETTE, GARNISHED WITH MACADAMIA NUTS AND FLAKED COCONUT

CHIPOTLE-GLAZED PORK LOIN CHOP WITH WARM VEGETABLE COUSCOUS AND TOMATILLO SALAD

Turtle Soup

COME OUT OF YOUR SHELL

Whether you are in the city or down by the shore, there's a Turtle Soup waiting for you to explore. In either location, Providence or Narragansett, the lively bar area is a great place to unwind after work. The food is eclectic with Asian and Italian influences, from potstickers with Thai peanut sauce to pesto pizza. The salads are creative, and the burgers are huge. The seasonal menu, which seems to have the proverbial "something for everyone," offers plenty of pasta and seafood to tempt your taste buds. Not to be missed is the Pistachio-Crusted Catfish with Pineapple Salsa. Can't you just feel that summer breeze?

APPETIZERS

ROCKED CRAB CAKES WITH JALAPENO REMOULADE

PESTO PIZZA WITH GRILLED PORTABELLO, TOMATOES AND MOZZARELLA

CHINESE POTSTICKERS, PAN FRIED, ON RED LEAF CABBAGE AND CARROT SHOOTS, WITH A THAI PEANUT SAUCE

MUSSELS SIMMERED IN A CLASSIC RED SAUCE WITH EXTRA VIRGIN OLIVE OIL AND FRESH HERBS

ENTREES

LEMON GRASS CHICKEN PICCATA WITH FARFALLE AND FRESH BASIL

ANGEL HAIR PASTA WITH JUMBO SHRIMP, LITTLENECKS AND SCALLOPS IN A GARLIC HERB BUTTER SAUCE

LOBSTER RAVIOLI IN A VODKA CREAM SAUCE

PISTACHIO-CRUSTED CATFISH WITH A CARIBBEAN PINEAPPLE SALSA

HONEY SOY COD WITH COCONUT COUSCOUS AND WATERCRESS SALAD

GRILLED BEEF OR CHICKEN WITH SEASONAL VEGETABLES AND POTATOES

NARRAGANSETT LOCATION

LOCATION	113 OCEAN ROAD NARRAGANSETT	HOURS	TUESDAY THROUGH SATURDAY FOR DINNER
CHEF	CHRISTOPHER GAUVIN	LIQUOR	FULL LIQUOR
OWNERS	AMY STREETER AND LINDA J. CINCO	SMOKING	IN BAR AREA ONLY
		SERVICES	HEALTHY/LOW-FAT MENU ITEMS
OPEN SINCE	1999		VEGETARIAN MENU ITEMS
CUISINE	AMERICAN ECLECTIC		HANDICAPPED ACCESSIBLE
SPECIALTY	SHELLFISH		TAKE-OUT ORDERS AVAILABLE
PRICE RANGE	APPETIZERS $5 TO $8		LATE-NIGHT MENU
	ENTREES $11 TO $20		CHILDREN FRIENDLY
CREDIT CARDS	MAJOR CREDIT CARDS ACCEPTED	DRESS CODE	CASUAL
RESERVATIONS	NO	PARKING	AVAILABLE ON THE PREMISES

PROVIDENCE LOCATION

LOCATION	166 BROADWAY PROVIDENCE	LIQUOR	FULL LIQUOR
		SMOKING	PERMITTED
CHEF	CARISA DIXON	SERVICES	HEALTHY/LOW-FAT MENU ITEMS
OWNERS	AMY STREETER AND LINDA J. CINCO		VEGETARIAN MENU ITEMS
OPEN SINCE	2002		HANDICAPPED ACCESSIBLE
CUISINE	AMERICAN		TAKE-OUT ORDERS AVAILABLE
SPECIALTY	BLACKENED TUNA WITH AVACADO BUTTER		CATERING
			FIREPLACE
PRICE RANGE	APPETIZERS $5 TO $8		
	ENTREES $11 TO $20	DRESS CODE	CASUAL
CREDIT CARDS	MAJOR CREDIT CARDS ACCEPTED	PARKING	AVAILABLE ON THE STREET
RESERVATIONS	ONLY FOR SPECIAL OCCASIONS		
HOURS	OPEN TUESDAY THROUGH SUNDAY FOR DINNER SUNDAY BRUNCH		

1200 Ocean Grill

LESS IS MORE

In a modern minimalist setting, Chef-owner Steve Siravo serves up the freshest seafood imaginable in straightforward, effective presentations. The crowd is buzzing, there is usually a waiting line, and the atmosphere is easy and relaxed. For non-seafood eaters, there are several great choices, and no one will be disappointed. You'll feel like you are at the seashore, and indeed, it is only a stone's throw from the parking lot. This restaurant delivers a perfect summer supper, but the place is full all winter long, mainly because of its reliably delicious food.

ROASTED GARLIC

6 garlic heads
Corn oil, as needed

Expose the tops of all the garlic cloves by slicing across the pointed end of each head down about 3/4 of an inch. Place the garlic heads in a 9x9-inch pan. Pour in 1/2 inch of corn oil. Roll and coat the garlic heads in the oil, and then arrange them with cut ends facing up. Cover with foil and bake in 400-degree oven for 30 to 40 minutes until the exposed cloves caramelize. Cool slightly and scoop out the roasted garlic to spread on crusty bread.

INSIDE SCOOP

CHEF-OWNER	STEVEN SIRAVO	LIQUOR	WINE AND BEER ONLY
OPEN SINCE	1998	SMOKING	NO
CUISINE	ITALIAN/SEAFOOD	SERVICES	HEALTHY/LOW-FAT MENU ITEMS
SPECIALTY	FRESH NATIVE FISH		VEGETARIAN MENU ITEMS
PRICE RANGE	APPETIZERS $2.95 TO $8.95		HANDICAPPED ACCESSIBLE
	ENTREES $9.95 TO $18.95		TAKE-OUT ORDERS AVAILABLE
CREDIT CARDS	MAJOR CREDIT CARDS ACCEPTED		CATERING
RESERVATIONS	NOT REQUIRED BUT	DRESS CODE	CASUAL
	RECOMMENDED FOR	PARKING	AVAILABLE ON THE PREMISES
	PARTIES OF 8 OR MORE		
HOURS	OPEN SEVEN NIGHTS A WEEK		
	FOR DINNER IN SUMMER		
	CALL FOR WINTER HOURS		

APPETIZERS

FRENCH ONION SOUP WITH SWISS CHEESE TOAST
CRISPY FRIED CALAMARI WITH HOT PEPPERS AND MARINARA
SPICY PAN-FRIED CRAB CAKES WITH ORANGE-CHIPOTLE MAYO
1200 SALAD – GREENS WITH PEARS, WALNUTS, PANCETTA AND BLUE CHEESE
BRUSCHETTA WITH SAUTÉED ESCAROLE, WHITE BEANS AND PANCETTA

ENTREES

GNOCCHI WITH WILTED RADICCHIO IN GORGONZOLA-GARLIC CREAM SAUCE
PAPPARDELLE PASTA WITH BRAISED PORK SHOULDER, ESCAROLE AND OLIVES
SOLE FRANCESE WITH LEMON-WHITE WINE SAUCE
HONEY CORNMEAL-CRUSTED FLOUNDER WITH A LEMON BEURRE BLANC
ROASTED GARLIC CHICKEN IN WHITE WINE SAUCE WITH ROSEMARY
ROASTED HALF DUCKLING WITH BLACK CURRANTS, DUCK GLACE AND WILD RICE

ON THE WATERFRONT

Classic steakhouse cuisine is offered at 22 Bowen's Wine Bar & Grille, located on picturesque Bowen's Wharf in Newport. Prime steaks and fresh seafood are on tap at this crisp, clean and classic restaurant. Considered by many to be the state's premiere surf-and-turf destination, 22 Bowen's is downright handsome with its teak bar and gracious dining rooms that offer fabulous views of Newport Harbor and its many yachts. The restaurant draws an eclectic clientele from around the world. In winter, mostly locals. In summer, jet-setters, the nautical crowd, and tourists. The steaks are prime, the seafood impeccably fresh, and the service is superb. (Check out the gorgeous rest rooms.)

GRAPEVINE GEM: Location, location, location. If tourists have time for only one Newport restaurant, this is it – handsome 22 Bowen's has been carefully designed right down to the last masculine detail. And the view of all the nearby yachts is breathtaking.

INSIDE SCOOP

CHEF	BRIAN MANSFIELD	LIQUOR	FULL LIQUOR
	AND GARY JEFFERDS	SMOKING	NOT PERMITTED
OWNER	NEWPORT HARBOR CORPORATION	SERVICES	PRIVATE DINING ROOM
OPEN SINCE	2001		BANQUET FACILITIES
CUISINE	CLASSIC STEAKHOUSE CUISINE		SEASONAL OUTDOOR PATIO DINING
SPECIALTY	PRIME STEAKS AND FRESH SEAFOOD		CHILDREN'S MENU
PRICE RANGE	APPETIZERS $7 TO $14		VEGETARIAN MENU ITEMS
	ENTREES $22 TO $37		HANDICAPPED ACCESSIBLE
CREDIT CARDS	MAJOR CREDIT CARDS ACCEPTED		TAKE-OUT ORDERS AVAILABLE
RESERVATIONS	RECOMMENDED		CATERING
HOURS	OPEN SEVEN DAYS A WEEK	DRESS CODE	CASUAL
	FOR LUNCH AND DINNER	PARKING	AVAILABLE ON THE STREET
	SUNDAY THROUGH THURSDAY,		AND IN NEARBY LOTS
	11:30 A.M. TO 10 P.M.		
	FRIDAY AND SATURDAY,		
	11:30 A.M. TO 11 P.M.		

RAW BAR

CHILLED POACHED SHRIMP

LITTLENECKS ON THE HALF SHELL

OYSTERS ON THE HALF SHELL WITH VARIOUS SAUCES

COLD BABY LOBSTER WITH LEMON TARRAGON MAYONNAISE

CHILLED NEW ENGLAND SHELLFISH SAMPLER

CAVIAR – SEVRUGA, OSETRA AND BELUGA

APPETIZERS

TUNA TARTARE

SMOKED SALMON TART WITH STOLICHNAYA CREME FRAICHE

STEAMED LITTLENECKS WITH TOMATO, FENNEL, WHITE WINE AND CHORIZO

LOBSTER FRITTERS WITH SWEET PEPPER REMOULADE

FRIED BLACK BEAN RAVIOLI WITH SALSA AND SPIKED CREAM

SPINACH SALAD WITH CRIMINI MUSHROOMS, SWEET ONIONS, CHOPPED EGGS
    AND A WARM PANCETTA AND SHERRY DRESSING

22'S LOBSTER BISQUE

NEW ENGLAND CLAM CHOWDER

ENTREES

ALL CUTS ARE USDA PRIME BEEF

GRILLED TUNA STEAK

GRILLED LAMB CHOPS

BROILED OR STEAMED LOBSTER

BAKED STUFFED LOBSTER WITH SEAFOOD STUFFING

PORK TENDERLOIN
WITH APRICOT-SAUSAGE STUFFING AND ROSEMARY GARLIC JUS
Serves 2

Stuffing:

1 tablespoon olive oil

1/4 cup minced red onion

1/4 pound mild sausage, crumbled

1 large garlic clove, peeled and minced

1 cup chicken stock

1/2 cup dried apricots, minced

1/4 teaspoon kosher salt

1/4 teaspoon black pepper

1 cup plain bread crumbs

Rosemary garlic jus:

1 tablespoon extra virgin olive oil

2 large garlic cloves, roasted and minced

1 teaspoon rosemary, finely chopped

1 cup chicken stock

1/4 cup apricot preserves

1/4 cup white wine

1/4 teaspoon kosher salt

1/4 teaspoon black pepper

Pork:

1 whole pork tenderloin, approximately 1 pound

Seasoned salt, to taste

For the stuffing:

Preheat oven to 350 degrees. In a heavy-bottomed pan, heat olive oil. Add onion and sauté until translucent. Add the sausage and garlic, and brown well. Add chicken stock, minced apricots, salt and pepper. Bring to a boil, reduce heat, and simmer 5 minutes. Add breadcrumbs. Transfer stuffing to oven-proof container. Heat stuffing as needed in 350-degree oven.

For the rosemary garlic jus:

In a saucepan, over medium-high flame, heat olive oil with roasted garlic. Add white wine, bring to a boil, and reduce by half. Add chicken stock, apricot preserves and rosemary. Add salt and pepper. Simmer 10 minutes.

For the pork:

Preheat grill. Season tenderloin on both sides. Grill to desired temperature. Allow meat to rest 5 minutes.

For the final dish:

Cut pork on bias into 1-inch slices. Arrange 1 cup of heated stuffing in center of each dinner plate. Fan pork slices over stuffing. Drizzle with rosemary garlic jus.

Twin Oaks

A RHODE ISLAND INSTITUTION

Every state seems to have a restaurant like Twin Oaks. It's big, been around forever, and always filled to the brim even though it's far off the beaten path. Everything about Twin Oaks is huge – the parking lot, the restaurant itself (with 650 seats), the menu, and the portions. Even the cocktails are rather large. People have been known to wait for hours for a table on a Saturday night. If you're lucky, you'll get a table with a waterview. Take a look around when you visit – you'll be surrounded by people with hearty appetites for old-fashioned American steaks and traditional Italian fare. The meatballs, usually an accurate barometer of Italian cuisine, are outstanding at Twin Oaks.

INSIDE SCOOP

CHEF	WILLIAM SMITH	SMOKING	PERMITTED IN
OWNER	THE DEANGELUS FAMILY		DESIGNATED AREAS
OPEN SINCE	1933	SERVICES	BANQUET FACILITES
CUISINE	ITALIAN FOOD AND		SENIOR CITIZENS, EARLY BIRD,
	ALL-AMERICAN STEAKS AND CHOPS		LUNCHEON, AND CHILDREN'S
SPECIALTY	BAKED STUFFED SHRIMP,		MENUS
	OPEN STEAK TENDERLOIN		HEALTHY/LOW-FAT MENU ITEMS
PRICE RANGE	APPETIZERS $2 TO $7		VEGETARIAN MENU ITEMS
	ENTREES $6 TO $21		HANDICAPPED ACCESSIBLE
CREDIT CARDS	MAJOR CREDIT CARDS ACCEPTED		TAKE-OUT ORDERS AVAILABLE
RESERVATIONS	RECOMMENDED FOR		FIREPLACE
	PARTIES FOR 15 OR MORE	DRESS CODE	BUSINESS/CASUAL
HOURS	TUESDAY THROUGH SUNDAY	PARKING	AVAILABLE ON THE PREMISES
	FOR LUNCH AND DINNER		
LIQUOR	FULL LIQUOR		

APPETIZERS

JALAPENO POPPERS

FRIED CALAMARI WITH HOT PEPPERS

SPCIY FRIED CHICKEN WINGS

FRIED MOZZARELLA STICKS

CLAMS CASINO

SNAIL SALAD

STUFFED CHERRY PEPPERS

ENTREES

VEAL PARMESAN

MACARONI, PEPPERS, MEATBALLS AND HOT SAUSAGE

BROILED EXTRA-THICK LAMB CHOPS

20-OUNCE CHOICE SIRLOIN STEAK

BROILED HAWAIIAN HAM STEAK

BAKED STUFFED SHRIMP WITH DRAWN BUTTER

SAUTÉ LOBSTER IN CASSEROLE WITH TOAST POINTS

BROILED WHOLE CHICKEN

ROAST DUCK WITH ORANGE SAUCE

CHATEAUBRIAND FOR ONE WITH BEARNAISE SAUCE

Tyler Point Grille

32 Barton Avenue, Barrington | 401-247-0017 | www.menusmenusmenus.com

MARINER'S DELIGHT

Contemporary Italian cuisine and fresh seafood are what Tyler Point Grille in Barrington does best. The owners, Mario and Cheryl Micheletti, have turned this waterfront restaurant into a very successful operation. Chef Ian Sullivan plays to a demanding full house almost every night. Together, they pride themselves on their moderate prices, generous portions, and high-quality ingredients. The house specialty is Chicken C.V.M., chicken breasts pan fried until they are golden brown with arugula, radicchio, onions, tomatoes and balsamic vinaigrette. Tyler Point Grille is one of the very few restaurants with a liquor license in this "dry" town.

INSIDE SCOOP

CHEF	IAN SULLIVAN	LIQUOR	FULL LIQUOR
OWNERS	MARIO AND CHERYL MICHELETTI	SMOKING	PERMITTED AT THE BAR
OPEN SINCE	1997	SERVICES	BANQUET FACILITIES
CUISINE	CONTEMPORARY ITALIAN-STYLE		CHILDREN'S MENU
	CUISINE WITH AN EMPHASIS ON		VEGETARIAN MENU ITEMS
	FRESH SEAFOOD		HANDICAPPED ACCESSIBLE
SPECIALTY	CHICKEN C.V.M.		TAKE-OUT ORDERS AVAILABLE
PRICE RANGE	APPETIZERS $4 TO $12		LIMITED CATERING
	ENTREES $8 TO $21		SEMI-PRIVATE DINING ROOM
CREDIT CARDS	MAJOR CREDIT CARDS ACCEPTED	DRESS CODE	CASUAL
RESERVATIONS	RECOMMENDED	PARKING	AVAILABLE ON THE PREMISES
HOURS	OPEN SEVEN NIGHTS A WEEK		
	FOR DINNER		

APPETIZERS

CRAB CAKES WITH SPICY REMOULADE SAUCE
ARUGULA, FENNEL AND ORANGE SALAD
BAKED CLAMS TYLER POINT
ENDIVE, BABY SPINACH, PEAR AND GORGONZOLA
SEAFOOD SALAD WITH LEMON-HERB DRESSING ON BRUSCHETTA

ENTREES

VEAL PAILLARD WITH CRIMINI, PANCETTA AND SAGE CREAM
SHRIMP WITH CRISPY SPINACH, HOT PEPPERS, GARLIC AND TOMATOES
DOUBLE-CUT PORK CHOPS WITH SAGE AND MADEIRA WINE
HALIBUT FILLET WITH A PANKO POTATO CAKE AND A FRESH CITRUS
    DRESSING
SWORDFISH WITH A SWEET GRAPE TOMATO AND BOSC PEAR COMPOTE
SIRLOIN WITH MUSTARD DEMIGLACE, GORGONZOLA CREAM AND
    ONION RINGS
SEA SCALLOPS WITH FENNEL, CITRUS FRUIT AND PORT WINE

The dining room at 22 Bowen's Wharf in Newport

Up River Cafe

SOMETHING OLD, SOMETHING NEW

Whether it's a warm summer evening and you're sitting on the patio watching pleasure boats glide by, or a snowy winter afternoon and you're tucked into a corner table near the fireplace in the pub, Up River Cafe is most appealing. This multi-level restaurant, formerly known as Three Fish, has the feel of an old New England tavern and the menu of a very modern chef, Andrew Nathan. Talk about unusual… how about the Roasted Beet Salad, the Andouille and Corn Hush Puppies, the Crispy Gnocchi, and the Linguine Carbonara? If that doesn't whet your appetite – and your curiosity – we give up. Live music for easy listening is also on tap.

UP RIVER CAFE BLOODY MARY

Serves 1

Celery salt, as needed
1 ounce vodka
3/4 cup tomato juice (Sacramento is recommended)
Juice from 1/4 lemon
2 dashes Tabasco sauce
2 dashes Worcestershire sauce
Pinch of horseradish
1 dash Pick a Peppa sauce
Salt and pepper, to taste

Rim a large glass with celery salt. In another glass, combine the vodka with remaining ingredients. Pour into celery salt-rimmed glass. Garnish with a celery stalk, if desired.

INSIDE SCOOP

CHEF	ANDREW NATHAN	LIQUOR	FULL LIQUOR
OWNERS	DANIEL AND JENNIFER KING	SMOKING	PERMITTED AT THE BAR
OPEN SINCE	2001	SERVICES	BANQUET FACILITIES
CUISINE	AMERICAN BISTRO		CHILDREN'S MENU
SPECIALTY	PAN-SEARED SEA SCALLOPS		HEALTHY/LOW-FAT MENU ITEMS
	WITH LOBSTER HOMEFRIES		VEGETARIAN MENU ITEMS
	AND LEMON SAFFRON SAUCE		HANDICAPPED ACCESSIBLE
PRICE RANGE	APPETIZERS $8 TO $12		TAKE-OUT ORDERS AVAILABLE
	ENTREES $10 TO $28		CATERING
CREDIT CARDS	MAJOR CREDIT CARDS ACCEPTED		PRIVATE DINING ROOM
RESERVATIONS	RECOMMENDED		FIREPLACE
HOURS	MONDAY THROUGH SATURDAY	DRESS CODE	CASUAL
	FOR LUNCH AND DINNER	PARKING	AVAILABLE ON THE PREMISES
	DINNER ONLY ON SUNDAY DURING		
	SHOULDER AND SUMMER SEASONS		

APPETIZERS

ROASTED BEET SALAD WITH TALEGGIO FONDUE, WALNUTS AND SHERRY
 VINAIGRETTE
WARM HAZELNUT-CRUSTED GOAT CHEESE SALAD WITH ARUGULA,
 TOMATOES AND ONION CONFIT
LOBSTER NACHOS
ANDOUILLE AND CORN HUSH PUPPIES WITH SPICY TOMATO DIPPING
 SAUCE
HOMEMADE GRILLED PIZZA OF THE DAY

ENTREES

SEARED SEA SCALLOPS WITH LOBSTER-SPINACH POTATO CAKE AND
 SAFFRON SAUCE
GRILLED SALMON WITH POTATO AND VEGETABLE TART WITH A
 ROASTED TOMATO AND OLIVE VINAIGRETTE
SEAFOOD CIOPPINO WITH LOBSTER, SHRIMP, SCALLOPS, CLAMS AND
 MUSSELS IN A SPICY TOMATO AND SAFFRON BROTH
ROASTED RACK OF LAMB WITH GRILLED VEGETABLES, GARLIC MASHED
 POTATOES AND BASIL-LAMB JUS
PAN-ROASTED WILD BASS WITH ALLUMETTE POTATOES, ORGANIC
 TOMATOES, BASIL, LEMON AND OLIVE OIL

NOW THAT'S ITALIAN

You can shop here and there in Providence, but if you want the real thing when it comes to Italian products, at very reasonable prices, there's only one place to go – Venda Ravioli. This gourmet shop is simply dazzling, from the gourmet-to-go section to the deli to the fabulous selection of imported olives and cheeses. And then there are the refrigerator cases filled with every kind of fresh pasta and various sauces. Stop for a few minutes and enjoy a savory lunch or a leisurely cappuccino, maybe with a bit of authentic gelato. Make sure you get some bread before it sells out. Ah, Venda Ravioli – a little bit of Italy right here in Providence, Rhode Island.

GRAPEVINE GEM: Venda Ravioli also offers an incredible line of gourmet gadgets and beautiful Italian ceramics, everything you will ever need to entertain graciously, as they do in Italy.

INSIDE SCOOP

CHEF	SALVATORE CEFALIELLO	LIQUOR	FULL LIQUOR
OWNER	ALAN COSTANTINO	SMOKING	NO
OPEN SINCE	2000	SERVICES	OUTDOOR DINING (WEATHER
CUISINE	ITALIAN		PERMITTING)
SPECIALTY	FRESH PASTA		HEALTHY/LOW-FAT MENU ITEMS
PRICE RANGE	APPETIZERS $7 TO $8		VEGETARIAN MENU ITEMS
	ENTREES $7 TO $13		HANDICAPPED ACCESSIBLE
CREDIT CARDS	MAJOR CREDIT CARDS ACCEPTED		TAKE-OUT ORDERS AVAILABLE
RESERVATIONS	RECOMMENDED FOR	DRESS CODE	CASUAL
	LARGE GROUPS	PARKING	AVAILABLE ON THE STREET
HOURS	LUNCH ONLY, MONDAY THROUGH		AND IN A NEARBY LOT
	SATURDAY, 11:30 A.M. TO 3:30 P.M.		

APPETIZERS

VENDA ANTIPASTO — SWEET AND HOT SOPRESSATA, CRACKED SICILIAN OLIVES, PROVOLONE AND PARMIGIANO-REGGIANO WITH MARINATED PEPPERS

GRILLED MARINATED PORTABELLO MUSHROOM SERVED OVER SAUTÉED RABE TOPPED WITH SMOKED MOZZARELLA

ASPARAGUS WRAPPED WITH PROSCIUTTO, GRILLED AND TOPPED WITH SHAVED PARMIGIANO

DRY CURED BEEF, THINLY SLICED, OVER ARUGULA WITH A LEMON VINAIGRETTE AND PARMIGIANO

FRESH OVEN-BAKED OYSTERS WITH FRESH HERBS, BUTTER, BREAD CRUMBS AND FRESH LEMON JUICE

ENTREES

FRESH CLAMS SAUTÉED IN OLIVE OIL, GARLIC, HERBS AND WHITE WINE AND TOSSED WITH HOMEMADE LINGUINE

PAPPARDELLE SAUTÉED WITH OLIVE OIL, GARLIC, IMPORTED ITALIAN WILD MUSHROOMS, WHITE WINE AND DICED TOMATOES

GRILLED POUNDED VEAL CUTLET WITH FRESH HERBS AND OLIVE OIL WITH A LIGHTLY DRESSED SALAD

RAINBOW TROUT SAUTÉED WITH OLIVE OIL, ONIONS, TOMATO, BLACK OLIVES AND WHITE WINE, SERVED WITH SALAD

FRESH CALAMARI STUFFED WITH EGGS, BREAD CRUMBS, CHEESE AND HERBS, SERVED WITH SALAD

BALSAMIC RICE SALAD

Serves 10

3 cups arborio rice
6 cups water
2 portabello mushroom caps
1 cup sliced roasted red peppers
12 ounces fresh baby spinach
1/2 cup balsamic vinegar
1 3/4 tablespoons salt
1 tablespoon granulated garlic
1 tablespoon black pepper
2 cups olive oil and corn oil, mixed
1/8 cup chopped garlic

Add rice to boiling water (two parts water to one part rice) and cook for about 30 minutes, or until three-quarters done. (It will finish cooking in the dressing.) Drain rice under cold water in strainer to cool. Put rice in bowl.

Slice portabello mushroom caps and add to rice. Add roasted red peppers and spinach to bowl. Add vinegar. Add spices.

Heat oil; when very hot, add garlic. Stir garlic; brown lightly. Do not let burn. Pour hot oil and garlic over spinach. Let stand 2 to 5 minutes. Mix well. Serve warm or at room temperature. Keeps up to 1 week in the refrigerator.

Walter's

286 Atwells Avenue (Federal Hill), Providence | 401-273-2652 | www.chefwalter.com

HISTORICAL FINE DINING

No one in Rhode Island serves the kind of food you will find at Walter's. Chef-owner Walter Potenza is an expert on Italian history, so you won't see any tomato-based dishes on his menu which does offer unusual savory dishes that date as far back as the 4th century. Each appetizer and entree are prepared to order. All this in a beautiful Italian Victorian setting on the second floor of the Italian Center for Culture and Gastronomy, where cooking classes are taught and where Aquaviva Ristorante & Tapas Bar can be found on the first floor. This is Italian dining at the finest level.

BONELESS FILET OF VENISON IN WILD BERRY SAUCE
Serves 4

12 venison medallions from the filet (1 and 1/2 pounds)	1 tablespoon unsalted butter
Salt and pepper, to taste	1 cup wild berries*
12 fresh bay leaves	1 tablespoon sugar
	2 tablespoons Grappa

Place the venison medallions on a cutting board and season both sides with salt and pepper. Place a bay leaf on each medallion.

In a large skillet, melt the butter until it foams. Add the medallions and cook until browned on both sides but still pink inside, turning once (about 4 minutes). Season with salt and pepper. Remove the medallions from the skillet and set aside.

In the butter remaining in the skillet, place the wild berries and sprinkle them with sugar. Cook over high heat for 2 minutes, then add the Grappa and light a match to the pan (keeping your hair and clothes away from the pan). As soon as the flames have died down, return the medallions to the pan and turn them in the sauce to warm the meat and to incorporate flavors.

Serving suggestions: Serve over a galette of sweet potatoes and Yukon Gold potatoes blended with Gorgonzola cheese.

* Wild berries are available in the gourmet shop at Walter's and in Middle Eastern or Mediterranean markets.

INSIDE SCOOP

CHEF-OWNER	WALTER POTENZA	SERVICES	BANQUET FACILITIES
OPEN SINCE	2002		HEALTHY/LOW-FAT MENU ITEMS
CUISINE	AUTHENTIC ITALIAN		VEGETARIAN MENU ITEMS
SPECIALTY	VENISON IN WILD BERRY SAUCE		HANDICAPPED ACCESSIBLE
PRICE RANGE	APPETIZERS $8 TO $$12		TAKE-OUT ORDERS AVAILABLE
	ENTREES $17 TO $29		CATERING
CREDIT CARDS	MAJOR CREDIT CARDS ACCEPTED		PRIVATE DINING ROOM
RESERVATIONS	RECOMMENDED	DRESS CODE	CASUAL
HOURS	THURSDAY THROUGH SATURDAY	PARKING	AVAILABLE ON THE STREET,
	FOR DINNER		IN A PARKING LOT IN THE
LIQUOR	FULL LIQUOR		REAR, AND THROUGH THE
SMOKING	NO		VALET SERVICE

APPETIZERS

FRESH STUFFED ARTICHOKES WITH MATZO, DUCK, OLIVES, GARLIC AND MINT

SMOKED BEEF TONGUE MARINATED IN SUGAR, CORIANDER AND BAY LEAVES

FRESH ORGANIC SPINACH SAUTÉED IN OLIVE OIL AND GARLIC, TOSSED WITH TOASTED PINE NUTS, LEMON AND GOLDEN RAISINS

VENETIAN-STYLE PASTA AND BEAN SOUP, WITH VEAL SAUSAGE AND WHITE CHARD

SAVORY TART MADE WITH PUMPKIN FILLED TORTELLINE, PAIRED WITH BECHAMEL, PARMIGIANO AND CINNAMON

ENTREES

FRESH TUNA STEAK SEARED WITH BLACK PEPPER AND OLIVE OIL

FRESH SNAPPER COOKED IN WINE AND HERBS

RACK OF LAMB

PORK FILET SEARED WITH ROSEMARY AND WALNUTS

MOSCOVY DUCK ROASTED WITH CINNAMON, DATES AND NUTMEG

LOBSTER WRAPPED IN CREPES WITH A LOBSTER-GINGER CREAM SAUCE

West Deck

One Waites Wharf, Newport | 401-847-3610 | www.eatri.com

IN THE ROUGH

When you finally find the West Deck, off the far end of Thames Street in Newport, don't let its ramshackle exterior scare you off. Within this waterfront restaurant, wildly popular in the summer, is a chef, Robert Biela, who really knows how to cook. His fusion cuisine is done right, with restraint. We love his Caribbean Cod Cakes, served with a corn and black bean salsa. The bar scene is simply a blast, with some of the best bartenders around. The West Deck might seem a bit rough around the edges, but like many an oyster, it's worth investigating.

INSIDE SCOOP

CHEF	ROBERT BIELA	LIQUOR	FULL LIQUOR
OWNER	MICHAEL CHENEY	SMOKING	NO
OPEN SINCE	1993	SERVICES	BANQUET FACILITIES
CUISINE	FUSION		(UP TO 45 PEOPLE)
SPECIALTY	FILET MIGNON WITH STILTON		VEGETARIAN MENU ITEMS
	BUTTER AND PORT WINE SAUCE		HANDICAPPED ACCESSIBLE
PRICE RANGE	APPETIZERS $6 TO $12		WOOD STOVE IN FALL AND WINTER
	ENTREES $18 TO $27	DRESS CODE	CASUAL
CREDIT CARDS	MAJOR CREDIT CARDS ACCEPTED	PARKING	AVAILABLE ON THE PREMISES
RESERVATIONS	RECOMMENDED		
HOURS	OPEN SEVEN NIGHTS A WEEK FOR		
	DINNER		
	SEASONAL SUNDAY BRUNCH		

APPETIZERS

PASTA CARBONARA WITH PARMESAN CREAM AND PEAS

VIETNAMESE CRAB CAKE WITH MANGO SALSA AND TAMARIND COULIS

SEARED SEA SCALLOPS, BLOOD ORANGE, CAPERS AND CAULIFLOWER PUREE

BAKED OYSTERS AU GRATIN WITH LEEKS, FENNEL SAUCE AND PARMIGIANO

GOAT CHEESE SALAD WITH PARMESAN CRISP, SUN-DRIED TOMATOES AND ROASTED BEETS

ENTREES

PHYLLO-WRAPPED MONKFISH SALTIMBOCCA WITH GREEN PEAS, PROSCIUTTO AND TOMATO-CLAM BROTH

POACHED COD WITH BLACK BEAN-MANGO SALSA AND JAMAICAN JERK SAUCE

PISTACHIO-CRUSTED RACK OF LAMB WITH PEANUT SATAY AND POMEGRANATE DEMIGLACE

GRILLED FILET MIGNON WITH STILTON CHEESE AND PORT WINE SAUCE

PASTA WITH CANNELLINI BEANS, RED AND YELLOW PEPPERS, PARSLEY AND PARMESAN

SPINACH FETTUCCINE WITH VEGETABLES PRIMAVERA IN GARLIC WHITE WINE SAUCE

Twilight at XO Cafe

White Horse Tavern

A THOROUGHBRED

The venerable White Horse Tavern has been offering sustenance since 1673. Chef Chris Ferrell's seasonal menu, however, is anything but old. His creative American cuisine is a mix of French, Asian and Italian influences, served in a meticulously restored historic landmark complete with beamed ceilings, candlelit tables and cavernous fireplaces. The White Horse Tavern is the recipient of numerous awards, including "Best Restaurant in New England" from the *New England Travel Guide*. Chef Ferrell's favorite dish is the Fresh Lobster and Seafood Risotto, served with a truffle, basil and roasted garlic cream. When the chef isn't cooking fish, he's catching it. He goes fishing to relax.

FRANGELICO WHIPPED SWEET POTATOES

Serves 4

3 large sweet potatoes, washed, peeled, cut and cooked
3 tablespoons unsalted butter
1 ounce Frangelico liqueur
1/4 teaspoon mace or nutmeg
Pinch of salt and white pepper
Splash of heavy cream

In a large mixing bowl, combine all ingredients and mix well. Serve immediately.

INSIDE SCOOP

CHEF	CHRIS FERRELL	LIQUOR	FULL LIQUOR
OWNER	O.L. PITTS	SMOKING	PERMITTED AT THE BAR
OPEN SINCE	1957	SERVICES	BANQUET FACILITIES
CUISINE	CREATIVE AMERICAN: A		HEALTHY/LOW-FAT MENU ITEMS
	MIX OF FRENCH, ASIAN AND		VEGETARIAN MENU ITEMS
	ITALIAN INFLUENCES		PRIVATE DINING ROOM
SPECIALTY	FRESH LOBSTER WITH SEAFOOD		FIREPLACE
	AND WILD MUSHROOM RISOTTO,	DRESS CODE	BUSINESS ATTIRE
	SERVED WITH A TRUFFLE, BASIL	PARKING	AVAILABLE ON THE PREMISES
	AND ROASTED GARLIC CREAM		
PRICE RANGE	APPETIZERS APPROXIMATELY $18		
	ENTREES APPROXIMATELY $35		
CREDIT CARDS	MAJOR CREDIT CARDS ACCEPTED		
RESERVATIONS	RECOMMENDED		
HOURS	WEDNESDAY THROUGH SATURDAY		
	FOR LUNCH		
	OPEN SEVEN NIGHTS A WEEK FOR		
	DINNER		
	SUNDAY BRUNCH		

APPETIZERS

SEA SCALLOPS IN A ROSEMARY ALMOND CRUST, PAN-SEARED WITH A
  BLOOD ORANGE BEURRE BLANC
PEACH BARBECUE-GLAZED QUAIL STUFFED WITH ITALIAN SAUSAGE,
  MUSHROOMS, ARUGULA AND WILD RICE
MUSSELS STEAMED WITH WHITE WINE, GARLIC, ONIONS, TOMATO AND
  HERBS WITH A SAFFRON AIOLI
SMOKED SALMON NAPOLEON WITH CRISPY NORI, PICKLED
  WATERMELON, AVOCADO AND CITRUS GINGER VINAIGRETTE

ENTREES

SAUTÉED LOBSTER TOSSED IN A TRUFFLE, BASIL AND ROASTED GARLIC
  CREAM SAUCE WITH MIXED SEAFOOD RISOTTO
CITRUS-PEPPER GRILLED SWORDFISH WITH BROCCOLI RABE TOSSED
  WITH SHALLOTS AND CRISPY PROSCIUTTO
POACHED FILET OF SOLE STUFFED WITH CRABMEAT AND AVOCADO
ORANGE COGNAC-GLAZED DUCK BREAST OVER WILTED MUSTARD
  GREENS, WILD RICE, CHESTNUTS AND SCALLIONS

Windward Grille

WHAT A CATCH

One of the best-kept secrets in Newport is the Windward Grille, the restaurant located in the Hyatt Regency at Goat Island. Chef Robert Daugherty is a force to be reckoned with on the Rhode Island culinary scene. His contemporary American menu is geared toward healthy cooking techniques (most of the time) with the abundant use of fruits and vegetables. For his American seafood grille, Daugherty focuses on finding the best fish available and preparing it in a simple fashion, yet with a twist. For example, the Oysters Rockefeller with its hint of chorizo.

GRAPEVINE GEM: Before your visit to the Windward Grille, stop in at Pineapples on the Bay, located near the hotel's salt water pool, for drinks and a spectacular view, especially at sunset.

INSIDE SCOOP

CHEF	ROBERT L. DAUGHERTY	SMOKING	NOT PERMITTED
OWNER	HYATT HOTELS	SERVICES	BANQUET FACILITIES
OPEN SINCE	MORE THAN 30 YEARS AGO		CHILDREN'S MENU
CUISINE	AMERICAN CONTEMPORARY SEAFOOD		HEALTHY/LOW-FAT MENU ITEMS
SPECIALTY	POACHED WILD SEA BASS AND		VEGETARIAN MENU ITEMS
	PAN-SEARED YELLOWFIN TUNA		HANDICAPPED ACCESSIBLE
PRICE RANGE	APPETIZERS $6 TO $20		TAKE-OUT ORDERS AVAILABLE
	ENTREES $14 TO $28		CATERING
CREDIT CARDS	MAJOR CREDIT CARDS ACCEPTED		PRIVATE DINING ROOM
RESERVATIONS	RECOMMENDED		SATURDAY/SUNDAY BRUNCH
HOURS	SEVEN DAYS A WEEK,	DRESS CODE	CASUAL TO DRESSY
	FROM 6:30 A.M. TO 10 P.M.	PARKING	AVAILABLE ON THE GROUNDS
LIQUOR	FULL LIQUOR		OF THE HOTEL AND THROUGH
			THE VALET SERVICE

APPETIZERS

YELLOWFIN TUNA CARPACCIO WITH SEAWEED SALAD AND SOY VINAIGRETTE

SEAFOOD STACKER — A SAMPLING OF OYSTERS, SHRIMP AND JONAH CRAB

LOBSTER BISQUE

INDONESIAN CHICKEN AND ASIAN BEEF SKEWERS WITH WON TON CHIPS AND
MANGO DIP

STEAMED LOCAL MUSSELS IN A GARLIC, FENNEL AND PANCETTA TOMATO
BROTH

JUMBO LUMP CRAB CAKE WITH AVOCADO SALSA, VINTAGE BALSAMIC AND
CRISPY LEEKS

ENTREES

MEDITERRANEAN VEGETABLE PASTA WITH MARINATED ARTICHOKES,
TOMATOES, OLIVES, CAPERS BERRICA, CHARDONNAY AND ASIAGO

GRILLED PEPPERED HALIBUT WITH SMOKY SCALLION CORN CAKE IN A ROASTED
TOMATO CREAM SAUCE

POACHED WILD SEA BASS WITH GRILLED BASIL POLENTA AND FRICASSEE OF
FOREST MUSHROOMS

ROASTED CHICKEN WITH GARLIC MASHED SCALLION POTATO AND A PANCETTA
AND MUSHROOM RAGOUT

PAN-SEARED YELLOWFIN TUNA WITH MIXED VEGETABLE COUSCOUS

GRILLED LOBSTER WITH DRAWN BUTTER AND FRESH LEMON, SQUASH NOODLES
AND FINGERLING POTATO

GRILLED FILET MIGNON WITH WHITE TRUFFLE OIL, WHIPPED POTATO,
CABERNET REDUCTION AND SUN-DRIED TOMATO AIOLI

APPLE CARAMEL PAN TART
WITH ROASTED PISTACHIOS AND VANILLA BEAN ICE CREAM

Serves 2

1 1/2 Granny Smith apples
2 1/2 tablepoons butter
3 tablespoons sugar
4 ounces puff pastry
1 teaspoon pistachios, shelled, toasted and chopped
1 small bunch mint leaves
Vanilla bean ice cream, as needed

Preheat oven to 375 degrees. Peel and core apples; thinly slice apples crosswise.

Grease an 8-inch omelet pan evenly with butter and sprinkle with sugar, coating the surface evenly.

Arrange and fan apples, round side down, in the pan.

Roll out puff pastry to 1/4-inch thick. Cut out a circle the size of the omelet pan and cover the apples with the pastry.

To cook, place pan over high heat until butter and sugar are bubbling and have turned into caramel.

Bake in 375-degree oven until puff pastry is fully baked, about 10 minutes. Remove pan from oven and turn tart onto serving plate. Be careful not to burn yourself.

Garnish with pistachios and mint leaves. Place a scoop of vanilla bean ice cream in the middle. Garnish with mint leaves.

Woody's

IT'S NOT A '34 WAGON

Woody's will surprise you. It's located near Narragansett Town Beach, but you won't find any surfers hanging ten there. The name doesn't really seem to fit with the concept of this restaurant, which on a warm summer night can seem almost dream-like. Reservations are a must in this small restaurant, done in cool shades of celadon green and a bit of cobalt blue. Billowing full-length white drapes reveal an ultramodern award-winning wine bar. Chef-owner Ted Monahan's cuisine is a combination of Euro bistro and regional New England. His signature dish is Pistachio Encrusted Spring Lamb with Wild Greens and Pomegranates.

INSIDE SCOOP

CHEF-OWNER	TED MONAHAN	LIQUOR	FULL LIQUOR
OPEN SINCE	1996	SMOKING	NO
CUISINE	REGIONAL NEW ENGLAND/NEW AMERICAN	SERVICES	HEALTHY/LOW-FAT MENU ITEMS VEGETARIAN MENU ITEMS
SPECIALTY	PISTACHIO-ENCRUSTED LAMB WITH POMEGRANATE DEMIGLACE		HANDICAPPED ACCESSIBLE TAKE-OUT ORDERS AVAILABLE
PRICE RANGE	APPETIZERS $8 TO $10		CATERING
	ENTREES $15 TO $23		PRIVATE DINING ROOM
CREDIT CARDS	MAJOR CREDIT CARDS ACCEPTED		PRIVATE WINE TASTINGS
RESERVATIONS	RECOMMENDED	DRESS CODE	UPSCALE/CASUAL
HOURS	WEDNESDAY THROUGH SUNDAY FOR DINNER	PARKING	AVAILABLE ON THE PREMISES

APPETIZERS

ROASTED SHRIMP WITH SUN-DRIED TOMATOES AND HERBS

MEZZE WITH WHITE BEAN PUREE, ROASTED RED PEPPERS, OLIVES, HEIRLOOM TOMATOES, PORTABELLO MUSHROOMS, GRILLED EGGPLANT AND GOAT CHEESE WITH GRILLED FLAT BREAD

ROASTED SQUASH, RED PEPPERS, RED ONIONS AND JACK QUESADILLA WITH CHIPOTLE-LIME CREME FRAICHE

WILD ARUGULA AND PORTABELLO MUSHROOM SALAD WITH BALSAMIC VINEGAR AND SHAVED REGGIANO

ENTREES

BRICK-SEARED FREE-RANGE CHICKEN WITH WILD GREENS AND MASHED POTATOES

ROASTED EGGPLANT RAVIOLI WITH FRESH TOMATO AND CREAM

SEARED SEA SCALLOPS WITH CAPPELLINI AND THAI VEGETABLES WITH A SPICY TOMATO BROTH

GRILLED VEAL CHOP WITH BALSAMIC ONION RELISH AND SUMMER RATATOUILLE

PISTACHIO-ENCRUSTED SPRING LAMB WITH WILD GREENS, MASHED POTATOES AND POMEGRANATES

Wright's Farm

SOMETHING TO CROW ABOUT

Since 1972, Wright's Farm has been a landmark in northern Rhode Island, serving falling-off-the-bone chicken dinners family-style – platter upon platter brought to your table until you're about to burst. This is a big place, able to serve 1,600 people at a time in its six dining rooms with 75 ovens producing that famous roasted chicken and accompaniments. The dinner rolls and French fries are simply wonderful. The classic Italian dressing on the iceberg lettuce and the red sauce on the shell macaroni (they don't call it pasta here) are sold by the bottle in the on-premise gift store and at local supermarkets. Unpretentious food at its best.

INSIDE SCOOP

CHEFS	DANIEL JENNESE AND MICHAEL MOULICO	LIQUOR	FULL LIQUOR
OWNER	THE GALLESHAW FAMILY	SMOKING	NO SMOKING IN DINING ROOMS
OPEN SINCE	1972	SERVICES	6 DINING ROOMS (1041 SEATS)
CUISINE	FAMILY-STYLE CHICKEN DINNERS		BANQUET FACILITIES
SPECIALTY	CHICKEN		CHILDREN'S MENU
PRICE RANGE	ADULTS, $8.25 PER PERSON		HANDICAPPED ACCESSIBLE
	CHILDREN, $4.75 PER PERSON		TAKE-OUT ORDERS AVAILABLE
	STEAK SPECIAL, $17 PER PERSON		FIREPLACE
		DRESS CODE	CASUAL
CREDIT CARDS	NOT ACCEPTED, CASH OR PERSONAL CHECK ONLY	PARKING	AVAILABLE ON THE PREMISES AND THROUGH THE VALET SERVICE
RESERVATIONS	RECOMMENDED FOR PARTIES OF 10 OR MORE		
HOURS	SATURDAY AND SUNDAY FOR LUNCH THURSDAY THROUGH SUNDAY FOR DINNER		

MENU

DINNER ROLLS
FAMILY-STYLE SALAD
FAMILY-STYLE BAKED CHICKEN
FAMILY-STYLE FRENCH FRIES
FAMILY-STYLE MACARONI WITH RED SAUCE
16-OUNCE SIRLOIN STEAK ALSO AVAILABLE

XO Cafe

EXTRAORDINARY

XO Cafe burst upon the Providence restaurant scene in 1997 and was applauded for its sexy elegance and artsy decor. Owner John Elkhay's thinking was: "Life is short, so enjoy the best that life has to offer now." It's often said that the food at XO Cafe is ahead of its time. To this day, XO Cafe continues to be one of the city's most successful and popular restaurants, offering contemporary American cuisine with global influences, now under the talented hand of Chef Rachel Klein Gates, most recently from New York. She feels the best item on her seasonal menu is the Oven-Roasted Halibut with Artichokes and Coriander Emulsion, Taylor Bay Scallops and Herb Salad. Now that's a mouthful.

GRAPEVINE GEM: XO Cafe is known for its martinis and the wood-burning oven that produces outstanding gourmet pizzas.

INSIDE SCOOP

CHEF	RACHEL KLEIN GATES	HOURS	OPEN SEVEN DAYS A WEEK
OWNER	JOHN ELKHAY,		FOR DINNER
	RICK AND CHERYL BREADY	LIQUOR	FULL LIQUOR
OPENING	1997	SMOKING	PERMITTED AT THE BAR
CUISINE	CONTEMPORARY AMERICAN	SERVICES	HEALTHY/LOW-FAT MENU ITEMS
	WITH GLOBAL INFLUENCES		VEGETARIAN MENU ITEMS
SPECIALTY	OVEN-ROASTED HALIBUT WITH		HANDICAPPED-ACCESSIBLE
	ARTICHOKES AND CORIANDER		BATHROOM
	EMULSION, TAYLOR BAY		TAKE-OUT ORDERS AVAILABLE
	SCALLOPS AND HERB SALAD		CATERING
PRICE RANGE	APPETIZERS $7 TO $12		PRIVATE DINING ROOM
	ENTREES $19 TO $27	DRESS CODE	UPSCALE CASUAL
CREDIT CARDS	MAJOR CREDIT CARDS ACCEPTED	PARKING	AVAILABLE ON THE STREET AND
RESERVATIONS	RECOMMENDED		THROUGH THE VALET SERVICE

DESSERTS ("LIFE IS SHORT, ORDER DESSERT FIRST!")

TRIO OF CREMES BRULEE

MOLTEN LAVA CAKE WITH KAHLUA CHOCOLATE SAUCE AND COCONUT SORBET

PEACH TARTE TATIN WITH GINGERSNAP ICE CREAM AND GINGER TUILLE

APPETIZERS

CRISP CALAMARI IN RICE FLOUR, SMOKED JALAPENO MAYONNAISE AND
    CHOPPED RED PEPPERS

VIETNAMESE STEAK SALAD WITH ASIAN PEARS, PEANUTS AND LIME
    VINAIGRETTE

LOBSTER WONTON WITH THAI MANGO DIPPING SAUCE

BENTO BOX FOR TWO — CALAMARI, LOBSTER WONTON, BEEF SATAY WITH
    SESAME NOODLES AND TEMPURA VEGETABLES

ENTREES

PAN-SEARED DUCK BREAST WITH GRILLED GEORGIA PEACHES, CANADIAN WILD
    RICE, SUMMER GREENS AND DRIED CHERRY VERJUS

WOOD-FIRED PORK LOIN, CREME FRAICHE POTATO SALAD, WATERCRESS, RED
    CURRANT AND CREOLE MUSTARD SAUCE

SPICE-RUBBED CHICKEN WITH PRESERVED LEMON COUSCOUS, FRISEE AND
    VIDALIA ONION SAUCE

GREAT SOUND ALASKAN HALIBUT WITH LOCAL CLAMS, BRAISED YOUNG FENNEL
    AND CORIANDER EMULSION

BUCCATINI WITH SMOKED CHICKEN, ASPARAGUS, CARAMELIZED GARLIC AND
    MASCARPONE CREAM

ROASTED DUCK
WITH POMEGRANATE AND MANGO MINT RELISH
Serves 2

1 raw duck, with gizzards and neck removed
2 oranges, cut in half
1 bunch fresh thyme

For the marinade:
Juice from 2 pomegranates
2 cups soy sauce
4 tablespoons honey
1 dried chili
Star anise, to taste
Sake, to taste

For the mango relish:
1 ripe mango, chopped
1 bunch scallions, chopped
1 bunch fresh mint, chopped
1 red pepper, diced
1 bottle Pukka (hot) Sauce
Juice from 2 limes
1/4 cup simple syrup

Trim the duck of excess fat. Trim the wings (so they don't burn). Stuff the duck with the oranges and the thyme. Truss the duck (tie the legs to preserve the duck's shape).

Combine the marinade ingredients. Marinate the duck in the refrigerator for 2 to 3 days (for best results) in a large covered casserole dish containing the marinade. If a shorter time period is necessary, remove the sake from the marinade.

Remove the duck from the marinade. Place the duck on a V-shaped rack inside a deep roasting pan. Roast at 400 degrees for 20 minutes. Prick the duck with a fork on its fatty areas to let the fat escape as it cooks. Repeat this step several times during the cooking process.

Reduce the oven heat to 350 degrees and finish roasting for an additional 1 hour and 10 to 20 minutes. The baking time always depends on how large your duck is and how accurate your oven temperature is. (Most household ovens are about 50 degrees off!)

Chill the roasted duck (you must do this because warm skin tears). When cool, cut the duck in half. Remove the backbone and rib bones. Just before serving, place the duck halves on a sheet pan. Place the sheet pan in a 450-degree oven for 10 to 15 minutes, or until crisp. Serve with corn pancakes and mango relish. If you like sweet duck, brush the duck with orange marmalade during the re-heating.

To make the mango relish, simply combine the ingredients in a medium-size bowl.

Yesterday's/The Place

28 Washington Square, Newport | 401-847-0116 | www.yesterdays.com

DOUBLE YOUR PLEASURE

This two-in-one restaurant is rather unusual. For a casual lunch or informal dinner, you bear to the left and enter Yesterday's, a dark and friendly pub with really good grub. If you're more in the mood for upscale dining, then stay to your right and dine at The Place, where fine wines accompany truly inspired dinners. Alex Daglis is the remarkable chef for both restaurants, and his contemporary American food is just wonderful. We are big fans of his Grilled Tuna Sandwich with Wasabi Mayo which showcases his affinity for Asian cuisine. Definitely one of Newport's best places to dine.

YESTERDAY'S

CHEF	ALEX DAGLIS	LIQUOR	FULL LIQUOR
OWNER	RICHARD KORN	SMOKING	PERMITTED AT THE BAR ONLY
OPEN SINCE	1973	SERVICES	CHILDREN'S MENU
CUISINE	CONTEMPORARY AMERICAN		HEALTHY/LOW-FAT ITEMS
SPECIALTY	"THE DIVERSITY OF OUR MENU"		VEGETARIAN MENU ITEMS
PRICE RANGE	APPETIZERS $7 TO $9		HANDICAPPED ACCESSIBLE
	ENTREES $20 TO $27		TAKE-OUT ORDERS AVAILABLE
CREDIT CARDS	MAJOR CREDIT CARDS ACCEPTED	DRESS CODE	CASUAL
RESERVATIONS	RECOMMENDED	PARKING	AVAILABLE ON THE STREET
HOURS	OPEN SEVEN DAYS A WEEK FOR LUNCH AND DINNER		

THE PLACE

CHEF	ALEX DAGLIS	HOURS	WEDNESDAY THROUGH SATURDAY FOR DINNER
OWNER	RICHARD KORN		
OPEN SINCE	1992	LIQUOR	FULL LIQUOR
CUISINE	CONTEMPORARY AMERICAN WITH ASIAN INFLUENCE	SMOKING	NO
		SERVICES	HEALTHY/LOW-FAT MENU ITEMS
SPECIALTY	THAI CURRIED SHRIMP		VEGETARIAN MENU ITEMS
PRICE RANGE	APPETIZERS $7 TO $9		HANDICAPPED ACCESSIBLE
	ENTREES $20 TO $27	DRESS CODE	CASUAL
CREDIT CARDS	MAJOR CREDIT CARDS ACCEPTED	PARKING	AVAILABLE ON THE STREET
RESERVATIONS	RECOMMENDED		

APPETIZERS

THAI NOODLE SOUP WITH MUSSELS, TEMPURA SHRIMP, SCALLOPS, SOBA NOODLES AND COCONUT BROTH

SPICY BEEF CARPACCIO WITH SEARED CORIANDER CRUST, THAI VINAIGRETTE, GINGER, JALAPENO AND CILANTRO

ASIAN LOBSTER POTSTICKERS WITH LEMON GRASS, GINGER, SWEET PEPPERS, LOBSTER ESSENCE AND CRUNCHY WONTONS

ENTREES

HOISIN-GLAZED SIRLOIN WITH JALAPENO PEACH SALSA – GRILLED VIDALIA ONIONS, GARLIC MASHED AND GRILLED ASPARAGUS

GRILLED THAI CHICKEN WITH MANGO SALSA, COCONUT RICE, HARICOTS VERTS AND GRILLED VEGETABLES

JAMAICAN JERK RED SNAPPER WITH SHRIMP, SCALLOPS AND MUSSELS IN COCONUT GINGER BROTH, STICKY RICE AND PINEAPPLE SALSA

Z Bar & Grille

244 Wickenden Street, Providence | 401-831-1566

LAST BUT NOT LEAST

One restaurant you can always count on is Z Bar & Grille, which seems to almost always be open. "Regulars" account for a major part of this neighborhood restaurant's customer base, with some loyal fans eating there four or five times a week. And that's because Chef Giulio Medizza's food is exceptional, the prices are reasonable, and the big bar is friendly. The odd-shaped dining area offers cozy nooks, with oversized pillows that make you want to linger. In warm weather, the flower-filled patio in the rear is the perfect spot for that first date or a reunion with old friends.

GRAPEVINE GEM: You won't find a Fryolator in the kitchen at Z Bar & Grille. All the food is fresh and healthy. The "fries" are oven roasted – and delicious.

INSIDE SCOOP

CHEF	GIULIO MEDIZZA	LIQUOR	FULL LIQUOR
OWNER	KEVIN KILLORAN	SMOKING	PERMITTED IN SMOKING SECTION
OPEN SINCE	1996	SERVICES	BANQUET FACILITIES
CUISINE	SIMPLE FRESH FOOD WITH		OUTSIDE PATIO AVAILABLE
	AN EMPHASIS ON HIGH		SEASONALLY FOR PRIVATE PARTIES
	FLAVOR, LOW FAT		HEALTHY/LOW-FAT MENU ITEMS
SPECIALTY	FRESH FISH		VEGETARIAN MENU ITEMS
PRICE RANGE	APPETIZERS $6 TO $12		HANDICAPPED ACCESSIBLE
	ENTREES $12 TO $24		TAKE-OUT ORDERS AVAILABLE
CREDIT CARDS	MAJOR CREDIT CARDS ACCEPTED		CATERING
RESERVATIONS	RECOMMENDED	DRESS CODE	TASTEFUL
HOURS	OPEN SEVEN DAYS A WEEK	PARKING	AVAILABLE IN LOT ACROSS
	FOR LUNCH AND DINNER		THE STREET
	SUNDAY BRUNCH		

APPETIZERS

MUSHROOM RAVIOLI WITH SHIITAKE ROSEMARY CREAM SAUCE

PAN-SEARED CRABCAKE WITH ROASTED CORN AND TOMATO SALSA,
 JALAPENO AIOLI AND BALSAMIC GREENS

STEAMED MUSSELS IN WHITE WINE WITH GARLIC, SHALLOT, LEMON
 AND FRESH HERBS

ENTREES

LOBSTER RAVIOLI WITH SEARED SEA SCALLOPS IN A TOMATO SHALLOT
 TARRAGON CREAM SAUCE

WOOD-GRILLED SUSHI-GRADE TUNA WITH ORGANIC MIXED GREENS,
 FETA CHEESE AND TOMATOES WITH OVEN-ROASTED FRIES

SALMON WITH ORZO, FRESH CORN AND SWEET PEPPERS, SERVED WITH
 A DILL CHARDONNAY SAUCE

TENDERLOIN BURGER WITH BOURSIN CHEESE, GRILLED BERMUDA
 ONIONS AND FRIES

PORK LOIN WITH GRILLED SWEET POTATOES, SUMMER VEGETABLES
 AND A LIME-CHIPOTLE SAUCE

Recipe Index

About the Authors

Linda Beaulieu and Deborah Moxham, partners in Grapevine: The Food Consultants, are the behind-the-scenes publicists for many of the best restaurants, gourmet shops and special events in Providence.

Linda Beaulieu

A true friend to many chefs and restaurateurs, Linda is the author of the best-selling book, *Divine Providence: An Insider's Guide to the City's Best Restaurants* (Covered Bridge Press, 2000).

Linda received the prestigious James Beard Award for magazine writing in 1994. She now writes about food, chefs and restaurants for The Associated Press, *Chef Magazine, East Side Monthly, and Providence Monthly.* She also has served as the food critic for Ocean State Online (www.oso.com), and she consults on the culinary programs for both the Providence Learning Connection and the Boston Learning Society.

For 10 years, she worked as a publicist for Johnson & Wales University, where she produced the popular "Cooking with Class" television show, and she has taught a course on food writing there.

Linda is an active member of the American Institute of Wine & Food (AIWF), International Foodservice Editorial Council (IFEC), Culinary Guild of New England (CGNE), and Women Chefs & Restaurateurs (WCR).

Deborah Moxham

Deborah Moxham has worked in the culinary world since 1989.

She founded and produced COOKS&BOOKS, a fundraiser that paired cookbook authors and local restaurants. The annual event attracted the best-known names in the business, from Julia Child and Jacques Pepin to Paul Prud-homme and Paula Wolfert.

Deborah established the Culinary Arts program for Rhode Island School of Design's Continuing Education, a program which brought luminaries to RISD and quadrupled the attendance at the school's classes. Deborah also created a line of spice rubs, known as BISTRO!BISTRO!, which she manufactured and sold nationally for several years.

Before working in the culinary world, Deborah worked in television in New York City. She was a producer of NewsCenter 4, the local Emmy-winning two-hour news show that aired on NBC TV. Deborah is a member of American Institute of Wine & Food and the Women Chefs & Restaurateurs.